From Things Lost

Rudolf Schwab, September 1944, Johannesburg. Courtesy of Yad Vashem.

From Things Lost

Forgotten Letters and the Legacy of the Holocaust

SHIRLI GILBERT

Wayne State University Press | Detroit

ISBN 978-0-8143-4265-7 (paperback); ISBN 978-0-8143-4398-2 (hardcover);
ISBN 978-0-8143-4266-4 (ebook)
Library of Congress Cataloging Number: 2017934987

Typeset by Keata Brewer, ET Lowe

Wayne State University Press
Leonard N. Simons Building
4809 Woodward Avenue
Detroit, Michigan 48201-1309

Visit us online at wsupress.wayne.edu

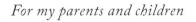

For my parents and children

אין יחיד יכול להבנות בלי שום קשר עם העבר

From things lost you were cast
Paul Celan (1920–1970)

Contents

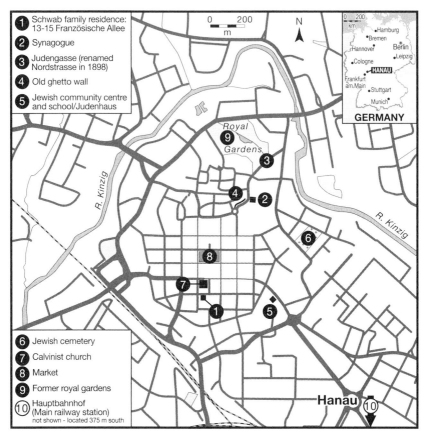

Current map of Hanau showing relevant historical locations, with inset identifying the position of Hanau in Germany in its current borders. Of the Jewish locations, only the Jewish cemetery and the old ghetto wall have survived. A small memorial has been erected opposite the location of the former synagogue. Both the Schwab family residence and the adjacent Calvinist church were destroyed during World War II. One half of the Calvinist church has been restored; the ruin of the other half serves as a memorial. A new tenement block has replaced the house in which the Schwab family lived. (Cath D'Alton)

The Family of Rudolf Schwab

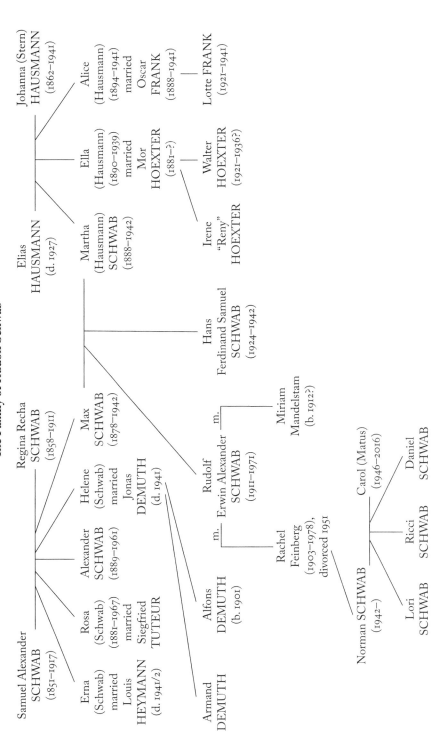

Introduction

> It is the historian's duty to report the facts, not to gloss over anything
> and not to paint too gloomy a picture.
>
> *Max Schwab, writing in Hanau to his son Ralph*
> *in Johannesburg, 16 December 1935*

Norman and Carol Schwab live in a single-story stucco home in the quiet Johannesburg suburb of Glenhazel. Their children have long since married and left home, though their youngest, Daniel, returns frequently on business trips. One warm autumn evening in March 2011 I turn into their driveway past a slatted iron electric gate, that ubiquitous marker of the suburban South African landscape. Plant life is everywhere, sprouting from beds and borders and window boxes, evidence of years of patient and loving attention.

As I walk into the house, Norman stops to show me a large, framed document displayed to the left of the entrance. It has all the unmistakable elements of a family tree: names of individuals, dates of birth and death, marriages, children, the passage of generations assembled in an elegant web. The ornate shield on the top left proclaims this to be the "Genealogical table of the family of Ralph Erwin Alexander Schwab"—Norman's father, and the last of twelve esteemed generations of Schwabs to reside in Hanau, a German town twenty miles east of Frankfurt on the Main River.

The family tree is an artifact with a remarkable past. It was conceived by Norman's grandfather Max, a successful businessman and World War I veteran, who began drafting it shortly after Hitler came to power in January 1933. Uneasy about the new regime's growing assaults against Jews, Max turned to his single greatest source of reassurance: the Schwabs' history as the oldest and most distinguished Jewish family in Hanau. "This is the direct line of the heads of the family," he wrote to his son Ralph in November 1934. At the beginning, he noted, "No records were available and it was extremely difficult to work without any

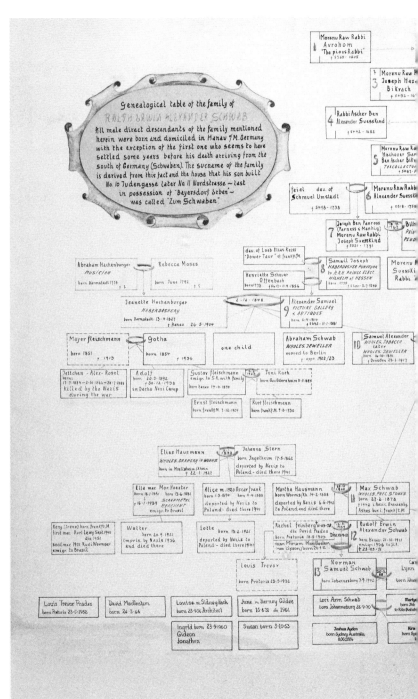

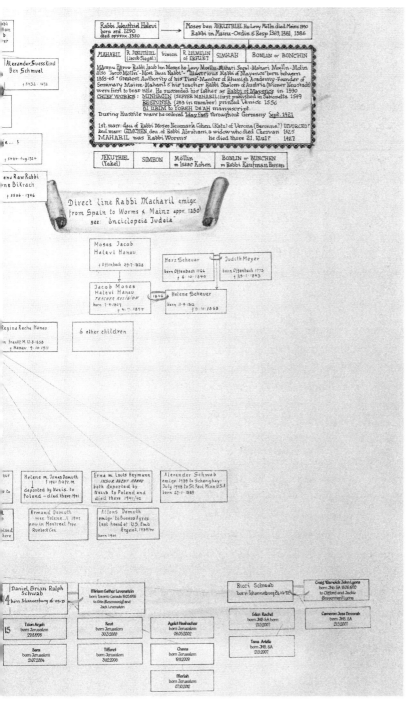

Schwab family tree. Courtesy of the Schwab family.

documentation," but having meticulously scoured local archives and registers he had made considerable headway. "Moreover, I hope my sons will one day continue the tradition that I have cultivated and will not allow the graves of their ancestors, which I have taken such trouble to research, to fall into decay."[1]

Sometime later Max sent a draft of his work to Ralph, then living in South Africa, providing details about relatives and the family's history before its arrival in Hanau in the 1600s. It was only after the end of the Second World War, as the survivors of the Nazi genocide began the task of absorbing the extent of their loss, that Ralph rediscovered his father's family tree. As individuals gradually reemerged, scattered across the globe—an uncle in China, an aunt in France, a cousin in Brazil—Ralph updated the tree, in many cases noting simply, "Deported by Nazis to Poland." In later years, as his own circumstances improved and he began to turn his attention toward the past, Ralph resumed his father's work in earnest, conducting careful research in libraries and archives to fill in the gaps and complete the picture of the family lineage.

When an accidental fire engulfed the Schwab home in 1986, the family tree was one of the few surviving relics.[2] Another object that survived, little noticed at the time, was a large wooden trunk tucked away in a corner of the garage. Inside the trunk, neatly wrapped in paper and string, were thousands of letters—typewritten and handwritten, holiday postcards and New Year's greetings, yellowing Red Cross messages and official documents and aerogrammes, mostly in German but with a sizeable portion in English and a smattering in French. The person who had assembled the trunk's contents obviously placed some value on them: he had not only kept letters from familiar and far-off provenances, but also carbon copies of his own responses, preserving a largely complete correspondence spanning almost four decades and five continents. According to Ralph, the maintenance of the archive was the result of efficient organization rather than a concern for posterity. Writing to a friend in 1959, he claimed that "it's only by chance that I still have all this old junk in my possession; I wanted to burn it all but haven't gotten around to it yet."[3]

Norman put the trunk into storage after his father's death in a hit-and-run accident in 1971. That it was worth keeping was clear, but since Ralph had never spoken German to his son, Norman had little idea of what was buried inside. It was only on a quiet Sunday afternoon in 2009, when Ralph's grandson Daniel began to leaf through the yellowing papers, that the extraordinary story of the long-forgotten letters began to unfold.

Revering the past, denying the past, confronting the past: each of these in varying measure informs the story that this book tells. My curiosity began with the

Ralph's trunk. Courtesy of the Schwab family.

latter: not Ralph or Max or Daniel's desire to confront the past, but my own. The Holocaust was a quiet but constant presence in my childhood Johannesburg home, manifest in the prohibition on throwing away any morsel of food, the ingenious economy with which every part of the chicken was used, and the sporadic Yiddish references to what had happened "over there." My maternal grandparents had managed to make it out alive through a combination of initiative and sheer luck, yet to my childish imagination their story was curiously distant: bombs dropping over Warsaw, illicit border-crossings, Siberian labor camps.

My fierce attachment to my grandmother had somehow to do with the enormity of the burden she bore. The photographs on her wall evoked a vanished world in which I envisioned myself; the child she had lost I reimagined as my own absent sibling, much to my mother's chagrin. In my mind I magically guarded my grandmother against inscrutable forces, acutely aware of a vulnerability that I did not understand. Not a word of this was ever spoken between us, and by the time my flood of questions about "over there" was released, she was no longer around to answer. But this unquantifiable bond was at the root of my energetic pursuit of the subject in the years that followed. Talking with survivors was a voyage into a past that felt strangely comforting and familiar, perhaps because I was finally able to have the conversation I had never had with my grandmother herself.

I first learned about Ralph Schwab during a study I was conducting on Holocaust survivors in South Africa. An email arrived from Ricci Schwab, a friend of a friend with whom I had recently crossed paths. My name had come up in connection with a trunk of letters her brother had found in their parents' garage. Given my research, would I be interested in helping them decide what to do with the material they had discovered? The family, I learned, had already begun to have some letters translated in order to ascertain their content. Ricci and Daniel's Grandpa Ralph had evidently fled Germany in May 1933, just months after Hitler's accession to power, escaping first to Antwerp, then to Brussels, then to Holland. By early 1936 he had decided to head for South Africa, one of the few places still relatively open to Jews. Soon after his arrival at the port of Cape Town he moved to Johannesburg, where he gradually made a life for himself. This part of the story was familiar to the family. But what, they wanted to know, had happened to Ralph's parents, his younger brother Hans, his grandmother Johanna? Had they tried to emigrate? Had he tried to help them?

I am sometimes approached by people who have discovered family archives and are not sure what to do with them. As a historian, I find the encounter with these kinds of original documents to be thrilling, an opportunity to dip into unfamiliar lives and relationships, unknown places and times. In most cases I recommend the most appropriate repository for the materials, and my work ends there.

In this case, however, my interest was piqued. On the one hand, a huge amount of material has already been amassed about the Holocaust, including thousands of witness testimonies. I would need to ascertain whether, beyond the personal story of the Schwab family, these letters had something of wider historical significance to offer. On the other hand, the scope of the source was extraordinary. Consisting of over 2,000 letters and more than 4,000 written pages, it was by far the largest collection of personal correspondence I had encountered, and the fact that both sides of the correspondence were preserved made it unusually rich and substantial. Most publications of Holocaust-era letters draw on much smaller source bases, and even collections a quarter of this size are considered extensive.[4] Not very many victims of Nazism ended up in South Africa, and even fewer recorded their stories, so the letters potentially filled an important gap. There was certainly enough here to warrant further investigation.

Looking through the collection, it appeared that correspondence from Germany had continued to reach Ralph in Johannesburg well into the war years. In their letters, his relatives chronicled their day-to-day lives under the Nazi regime: working, eating, socializing, going to school, even celebrating bar mitzvahs. "Yesterday was the big day and he did very well," wrote Ralph's mother Martha in February 1936. "So life goes on and the children are growing up."[5] In addition to the family's attempts to maintain a semblance of normality, the letters related the creeping effects of Nazi rule: the emigration of beloved friends, the forced sale of Max's business, the loss of the family home, Max's sudden arrest. Much of what was contained in the letters was not surprising to me as a historian, and yet I was struck by their vivid contemporary perspective.

By definition, postwar testimonies are retrospective accounts, describing the experiences of those who survived, when the outcome of the events is already known. The letters, by contrast, conveyed all the uncertainties and ambiguities of life as it was lived at the time, when the future was unclear. How did the family make sense of what was happening as new laws and restrictions were passed, as international opinion ebbed and flowed, as life around them disintegrated? What did they talk and think about as the months and years rolled on? Unlike diaries or chronicles, the letters had survived in the form of a dialogue, since Ralph kept copies of his replies.[6] They offered a glimpse into the questions with which his relatives were preoccupied, the issues about which they sought advice, the dilemmas with which they grappled. Such a rich and detailed contemporary account was, I advised the family, a rarity.

I hastened to discover what else was in the trunk. In addition to the prolific correspondence from Nazi Germany were several other distinct threads. The catastrophe of German Jewish exile was here in microcosm, personified in tales of hardship received from the most unlikely corners of the globe. Ralph's uncle Alex, a decorated German war veteran, had survived the war on UN food rations in Shanghai before playing out the rest of his lonely life as a janitor in the American Midwest. Aunt Rosa had been deported to the Gurs internment camp, and survived the war in extreme poverty in rural France. Similar stories trickled into Ralph's letterbox from Buenos Aires, Stockholm, São Paulo, and Montreal. If those lucky enough to flee had until now seemed less central to the Holocaust than the "real" victims, the stories that unfolded in the letters forced me to question how lucky the tens of thousands of refugees had actually been— and to wonder why history had so quickly forgotten them.

The most striking of the refugees was Ralph himself. In correspondences spanning the years and decades, I watched him transform from an exile into an entrepreneur, a father, a divorcé, and a reclusive communal leader. I was intensely aware that I was reading a confidential, at times painfully exposed, correspondence, one that moreover remained largely unknown to those closest to him. Ralph's son Norman remembered him as an undemonstrative, hard, and aloof man who had sent him to boarding school and about whom he knew little. The man I encountered in the letters was more vulnerable and sympathetic than this portrayal suggested.

Rudolf Schwab, c. 1950s. Courtesy of Yad Vashem.

His name was also not Ralph. The decision to change his name from Rudolf upon arrival in South Africa at age twenty-five portended a shift far more profound than perhaps even he himself could envisage. He took his new identity seriously, learning the local languages, traveling widely, and even involving himself for a time in local politics. But on Sundays, dressed in his suit and tie, he would enter his study and return to Europe. The Rudolf I came to know in the letters aspired to live up to his father Max's legacy: that of a proud Jew, communal leader, and patriot. Rudolf had arrived in South Africa with nothing, and over the course of four decades struggled to shape a new life for himself, remaining devoted to his surviving relatives despite his own extreme difficulties, and placing his deepest hopes and affections—though impossible to express—in his son.

The South African persona that Rudolf shaped was a compelling one. A fierce opponent of the Afrikaner-dominated National Party with its policy of apartheid, he campaigned actively for the opposition United Party. In his letters he often drew comparisons between the "Nats" and the Nazis—a striking analogy, I thought, for a German Jew to choose—and enjoyed ridiculing apartheid policies with a friend back in Hanau. But he also strenuously defended South Africa against international criticism, grumbling that foreigners did not understand the complexity of the country's racial problems. Probed on apartheid by his cousin Reny, he retorted that at least "I don't have to worry that an atom bomb might unexpectedly fall on my head early one morning."[7] Within just a few years of his arrival, Rudolf had freely adopted the values and vocabulary of White South Africa. He was hardly exceptional in his attitudes toward apartheid, and yet for a Jew newly escaped from Hitler's clutches, his casual comfort with local racist mores took me by surprise.

Among the increasingly familiar cast of characters that I got to know in the letters, one name that appeared again and again was Karl Kipfer. He was, as Daniel explained to me matter-of-factly, his grandfather's best friend growing up, a temperamental sort but someone with whom Rudolf clearly got on exceedingly well. The correspondence revealed lots of joking, familiarity, and sentimental reminiscing between them. A Nazi Party member, Karl was the person who encouraged Rudolf to leave Germany in 1933. He also later helped him to recover the family's property. Daniel knew nothing else about him, and there seemed to be little else of interest in this minor sidelight.

Rudolf's correspondence with Karl was unexpectedly comfortable. The two seemed to have lost touch after Rudolf's departure in 1933, but they reconnected in early 1948 and were soon exchanging long, familiar letters every few weeks. Karl undeniably had a hard edge and harbored a lot of anger and mistrust, perhaps predictably given his dire postwar circumstances: a wartime injury had left him partially paralyzed, his home had been destroyed in an Allied bombing raid, and he had been left with little apart from a lonely, uncertain future. But he also had a dry sense of humor and I liked him immediately despite my instinctive reservations. I knew that he had been a Nazi, but what did that actually mean?

Millions had joined the Party in order to safeguard their livelihoods and families. As I got to know him better, I reasoned that even if Karl was a Nazi, someone like him could not have been a *real* perpetrator. He was disarmingly forthright about what he called his "undemocratic past," and he showed genuine concern for his Jewish friend. His offer to take on the Schwab family's restitution and reparations claims, a task that consumed him for the rest of his life, went far beyond the practicalities of a legal process, though that would have been complex and arduous enough in itself. Karl worked on the claims with an energy bordering on fanaticism, determinedly hobbling from office to office and from city to city in the relentless pursuit of acknowledgment and justice. Watching this process unfold in the letters, I felt increasingly that what I was witnessing was a protracted, unspoken penance.

When I reached the end of the correspondence, the question of Karl's wartime activities remained unanswered. The two friends had lost contact for fifteen vital years, and Karl's letters offered only a few clues as to where he had been in the interim. An initial search turned up two stepdaughters still living in Hanau, but they remembered little about him. The "marriage of companionship" with their mother had been short-lived, and they had been infants when he died in 1955. The archives yielded slightly more, including his Nazi Party membership application, scattered army records, and his postwar appeal for denazification. There were also some intriguing documents from Dachau. But what did it all mean? And how exactly should I make sense of this man whose dark-witted cynicism I had quite come to enjoy?

In discussions with my students, I often stress that Nazi perpetrators were ordinary human beings with lives and families. It would be too easy to typecast them as fanatics who intentionally committed monstrous crimes and denied them after the fact. If we wanted to understand how so many people could follow a murderous regime for so long, we would need to ask more nuanced questions. What aspects of the Nazi worldview did individuals adopt, and which did they ignore? To what extent were they driven by antisemitism? How important were factors like career ambition, peer pressure, propaganda, and fear? How did they make sense of what they were doing at the time, and how did they subsequently make sense of what they had done?

Karl's letters offered exemplary insight into these questions. An ideologically committed perpetrator he clearly was not, but the category of "Nazi" was certainly wide enough to contain this "undemocratic" *Wehrmacht* soldier with more ambiguous motivations. He was an unremarkable German man with a small-town childhood and a few Jewish friends in his circle. Whatever his reasons for joining the Nazi Party, his life took a course he probably did not intend or foresee, and in his final years he seemed to make a concerted effort to confront his past and to move beyond it. The eloquent record that Karl left behind offers a glimpse into the mind of an ordinary Nazi trying to make sense of where he has been and what he has become.

Well before I had finished reading all 4,000 pages of the correspondence, it was clear to me that the Schwab story needed to be told. It was the very ordinariness of the protagonists that clarified for me the letters' significance and appeal. On the one hand, the Schwabs were not entirely typical of German Jewry. They were prominent in Hanau's public life, and many family members distinguished themselves as communal leaders. It was also not exactly commonplace for a family to amass such a rich and extensive correspondence. The letters spanned a huge range—the five continents across which the family was scattered, and almost four decades between Rudolf's departure for South Africa in 1936 and his death in 1971—and many of them were unusually substantial, perceptive, and articulate. On the other hand, the family could hardly be counted among the leaders of German Jewry. Hanau was a comparatively tiny community of 477 souls, with limited connection to the larger Jewish centers in Germany. The Schwabs were, in the main, unassuming citizens, devoted Jews and patriots, confronted with the same challenges as German-speaking Jews everywhere. Their letters wouldn't necessarily tell us much about the larger course of events that we didn't already know, but they offered vivid insight into how people experienced the Nazi onslaught in their daily lives, in encounters with neighbors and bank clerks and innkeepers, at home and in the synagogue, in their attempts to maintain normal life, as the noose tightened over the course of weeks and months and years.

I was also struck by the ordinariness of Rudolf and Karl and the relationship between them. As I thought about the attitudes and choices that led Karl along his life's path, it occurred to me that if his story could not be reduced to the category of "perpetrator," neither could Rudolf's be reduced to that of "victim." Perhaps understandably, historians have been reluctant to critically appraise survivors' postwar lives, not wanting to judge the victims or undermine their suffering. But in order to fathom the Holocaust and its legacies we need to move beyond labels that reduce a complicated reality to mere stereotypes. Both Rudolf and Karl were multi-dimensional human beings, and neither conformed to simplistic assumptions about what he ought to have done or become.

If the historical value of the letters was clear to me from early on, it took some time to recognize the full significance that they held for the Schwabs themselves. From the moment that Rudolf fled Germany, his letters took on a powerful importance for his grieving family. "When your letters arrive you're so close to me and it's as if I can live alongside you," wrote his forty-nine-year-old mother, Martha, in December 1937, "but when you don't write, then you're so endlessly, unreachably far away."[8] As relationships were reduced to letters, family members on both sides invested them with immense emotional weight. Rudolf took the task of writing seriously, sending long and detailed descriptions to his family about his life in South Africa. After the war, as he made contact with motley stranded relatives, the postcards and aerogrammes that passed between them acquired a significance transcending their modest content. They became nothing less than a virtual world, an alternative source of identity and belonging, of connection and order.[9]

Rudolf never mentioned the letters to Norman, and he did not include them in his will. Despite his professed intention to burn "all this old junk," however, I would like to believe that there was more than just laziness or happenstance involved in the letters' preservation, and that he imagined they might someday be discovered by someone who would recognize their historical worth. Entire branches had been violently lopped from the Schwab family tree. Of the physical world these people had inhabited, almost nothing remained. To this devastation the letters were a quiet rejoinder—a substitute, even if woefully inadequate, for gravestones that did not exist and funerals that were never held to honor lives and legacies. They were not merely letters, but bearers of memory. By the very fact of their being, they affirmed the family's enduring connections to one another, to Germany, and to the world of the living.

I

A Jewish Family in Nazi Germany

In the well-tended Jewish cemetery of Hanau stands the grave of a certain Bilha Schwab, deceased on 21 October 1796. Bilha's tombstone tells us that she was the wife of Joseph, a communal leader and seventh generation in a distinguished line of Schwabs residing in the town. Hers is one of several dozen Schwab graves in the cemetery, marking the family's enduring presence in Hanau. The oldest headstones are in Hebrew, adorned with a distinctive family icon in the manner unique to Jewish cemeteries in this region. On more recent gravestones the inscriptions are in Hebrew as well as German, reflecting a community increasingly at ease with its surroundings and its German Jewish identity.[1]

The cemetery is the last remaining site of Jewish presence in Hanau, one of the only places to which you can go today to find traces of the more than three hundred years of Jewish life that thrived here. Viewed from the air, it is a lush wooded area extending over an entire street block, crisscrossed by meandering stone pathways and filled to the edges with gravestones large and small, some grand and upright, some leaning at awkward angles. At street level, however, the cemetery lies hidden behind thick stone walls and imposing iron gates, invisible to curious passersby and idle troublemakers, a peaceful marker of how what was—entire lives, families, communities—can remain buried not only beneath the ground but also in broad daylight.

Hanau is a medium-sized town surrounded by dense forest. Its claim to fame is that it was the birthplace of the Brothers Grimm, the renowned collectors of fairy tales. A Brothers Grimm monument stands prominently in the marketplace, and in 2006 it was officially designated the *Brüder-Grimm-Stadt* (Grimm Brothers' Town). The town is also the starting point for the scenic German Fairy-Tale Route: an "enchanting" and "always magical" meander across Germany, the official

Tombstone of Bilha Schwab, Hanau Jewish Cemetery. Courtesy of Martin Hoppe/ Fachbereich Kultur, Stadtidentität und Internationale Beziehungen der Stadt Hanau am Main.

website tells us, "connecting the places and landscapes of [the Grimm brothers'] collected fairy tales into a route of wonders."[2]

Hanau has its charming elements, including historic buildings and museums and some delightful parks. It also has substantial industrial areas, and although not merely a commuter town—many take the short train ride to work in Frankfurt every day—its eyes are firmly cast in the direction of its larger neighbor.

On my first visit, my impression of the new town was that it had become one sprawling shopping mall, with motley nondescript stores and restaurants beneath worn-out apartments. I was also struck by the absence of Jewish life. Where the Jewish community center had once stood on the Nürnberger Strasse were a pharmacy and an apartment block. At 13-15 Französische Allee, the site of the former Schwab residence, was a series of tired 1950s apartment buildings occupied by immigrant families. In part this was the result of the Allied bombings of 19 March 1945, which had devastated most of the town center. But not even a plaque marked where the infamous *Judenhäuser* (Jews' houses) had once stood. I tried to imagine what Jews would have seen on their way to synagogue, what the Jewish school and playground had sounded like, who had come to meet friends at the community center, but it was difficult to make any connection with today's Hanau. In the area of the old town, a memorial had been placed to mark what had been the medieval ghetto wall, and opposite the former synagogue, now also an apartment block, a small memorial honored the Jewish presence in the town and its destruction by the Nazis. By and large, however, the average visitor could be forgiven for failing to realize that Jews had ever lived there at all.

In 1933, there were 477 Jews living in Hanau, making up just over 1 percent of the town's population. They were a small but lively community, with their own Jewish school, *mikveh* (ritual bath), and cemetery, and a network of welfare and educational organizations. Survivors recalled a rich social and communal life. Jews held prominent positions in the town as doctors, academics, lawyers, and businessmen, and played a key role in the gold and precious stones industries that earned Hanau the nickname *Stadt des edlen Schmuckes* (Town of precious jewels). They were patriotic and actively engaged in public life.[3]

Max Schwab, aged fifty-four, was a well-known community member and family man. His wife, Martha, had grown up in an observant Jewish household in Worms, one of Germany's longest-established Jewish communities, and they lived together with their two children: twenty-one-year-old Rudolf and eight-year-old Hans.[4] Their large apartment was the archetype of well-heeled middle-class existence: full of tasteful oak furniture, Persian carpets, oil paintings, a piano, crystal and silverware for entertaining, and two sets of tableware befitting a religious Jewish household.[5] The Schwab family had lived in Hanau for almost 330 years, well respected for its contributions to Jewish and non-Jewish life.

Max was a successful diamond and precious stones dealer, a recognized expert in the jewelry market, and soon-to-be owner of Abraham Schwab & Co., his father Samuel's reputable jewelry business founded in 1875.[6] In his leisure time, he was involved in an array of local societies, from the Hanau historical association to stamp collecting and sports clubs.[7] He was also well known in

Max Schwab. Courtesy of Yad Vashem.

Martha Schwab. Courtesy of the Schwab family.

the Jewish community, having served for many years as chairman of the *chevra kadisha* (burial society) and the local branch of the *Centralverein* (Central Association of German Citizens of Jewish Faith). Martha ran an elegant home with the help of servants, and thanks to her husband's vocation boasted an impressive collection of jewelry.[8] The family bookshelf contained several copies of the *Tanakh* (Hebrew Bible) and three sets of Hebrew prayer books, alongside an extensive collection of German classics. A portrait of Frederick the Great took pride of place on the living room wall.[9]

In the early months of 1933, Max began work on his family tree. He sorted his papers, scoured the archives, and painstakingly located all the family tombstones in the cemetery. Writing to his son Rudolf, he proudly emphasized the Schwabs' religious pedigree and their status as one of the oldest families in Hanau:

> They were also among the first to use a surname in those early times, perhaps even the very first, given that we are the oldest Jewish family in Hanau. The oldest document I've discovered is in the archive of Hanau's Old Town, from 1689, page 24, Appendix: 'Received – Jews – Money for Fire Bucket – Regulations', and it says there: "Samuel Schwab zum Schwaben 1689," who paid 2 florins for a leather fire bucket for the town hall. The only existing letter confirming our family as protected Jews in Hanau . . . is from 1791 and I have it framed in my possession.[10]

Max noted proudly that when Jews first settled in Hanau in the early 1600s, at least one Schwab ancestor—the "pious Rabbi" Avrohom, as he appears on the family tree—was among them. Jews had been invited to the area by Count Philipp Ludwig II in the interests of expanding trade and industry, and, within a few years, twenty-six families were living in the Judengasse (Jews' alley) on the southeastern periphery of the old town. When Rabbi Avrohom's son built a home at 10 Judengasse, he named it *Zum Schwaben*, in honor of the family's origins in the Swabian region of southwestern Germany. Many houses on the street followed suit, and this was ultimately how family surnames were derived. Subsequent generations of Schwabs, Max continued, were "pious, religious, scholarly, and God-fearing," a succession of distinguished leaders, descendants of the rabbi and legal authority Yaakov ben Moshe Levi Moelin (known as the Maharil).[11]

Max was an enthusiastic *Heimatforscher*, or amateur local historian. For him, history was not merely a pastime but a foundation for existence, a necessary mooring point for one's sense of place in the world. It was a point to which he would repeatedly return as the Nazis later threatened his business, his family, and eventually his life. With growing resolve he would intone the same refrain: Had his family not lived in Hanau for over three centuries? Had he and his fellow Jews not given their all on the battlefield in spirited defense of their homeland? Had they not shown themselves to be trustworthy and valuable citizens?

Local historical research became especially popular among German Jews after the newly unified Empire was established in 1871, the event that finally confirmed their full civil and political rights. Almost a century earlier, Jews across Europe had begun to glimpse the prospect of equality after decades of slow but steady acculturation—adapting their religious observance, acquiring secular education, learning languages. They were awarded legal rights first in France, in the wake of the Revolution, and subsequently in the territories conquered by Napoleon's armies as they advanced eastward. When the Napoleonic legions arrived in Hanau in 1806, it is chronicled that they tore down the ghetto gates, proclaiming the equality of Jews with the Christian inhabitants of the town.[12]

But German Jews' path to formal emancipation was longer and more complicated than it was for their French co-religionists. Whereas in France equality was granted first, followed by a period of adaptation, in Germany the order was reversed. Emancipation hinged on the fulfillment of certain conditions, and as a result the progress was slow and uneven for most of the nineteenth century, complicated by the decentralized nature of the German states. The removal of the last barriers to equality in 1871 at last gave German Jews of Max's ilk the opportunity to prove their loyalty to their homeland. Historical research was just one way in which they could express both their rootedness in local communities and an enduring sense of attachment to Germany.[13]

The Schwabs, like most of their Jewish neighbors, were fully invested in both halves of their identity. They spoke German, went to public schools, and had Jewish as well as non-Jewish friends. Many Jews in smaller communities like Hanau were able to simultaneously maintain Jewish lifestyles while also integrating with their Christian neighbors. Even the son of such a central religious figure as Hanau's cantor recalled that he had good Christian friends among his schoolmates. Germanness and Jewishness were not at odds but complementary elements of life, not so much sources of conflict as compatible layers of an integrated identity.[14]

The theme of Jewish integration was portrayed by one of Hanau's most celebrated sons, the artist Moritz Daniel Oppenheim. In his painting *The Return of the Volunteer from the Wars of Liberation to His Family Still Living in Accordance with Old Customs* (1833–1834), Oppenheim focused on the figure of the Jewish soldier, decorated for patriotic service for his German homeland. Around the table, Oppenheim depicted the soldier's observant Jewish family, adorned in traditional dress and skullcaps, celebrating the Sabbath with a festive meal and wine. His painting hinted at some of German Jewry's most persistent dilemmas. Did the young soldier feel rooted in the Jewish hearth, or was he looking longingly beyond it? Did his family honor his secular achievements, or did they fear the erosion of the "old customs" that they portended? Or was it perhaps all of these simultaneously?

Oppenheim's choice of the soldier for the central figure of his painting was not coincidental. Military service was, for Jews, a highly symbolic act, inextricably linked to their identity as Germans. The Jewish soldier was the ultimate

Moritz Daniel Oppenheim, The Return of the Volunteer (Die Rückkehr des Freiwilligen), c. 1868. Oil on canvas (57.4×70.1 cm). Courtesy of the Jewish Museum New York.

embodiment of commitment to the fatherland, proof that Jews were worthy of membership in the German national community.[15]

When World War I broke out in the autumn of 1914, Jewish men across the German Empire turned up in droves to fight for their country. Among them were the thirty-six-year-old Max Schwab and his youngest brother, Alex, eager to participate in Germany's glorious victory against her enemies.[16] Historians interpret this eagerness as a marker of German Jews' patriotism, of their desire to demonstrate their value to the nation that had only recently granted them equality. Of course, Jewish soldiers did not escape the denunciations of anti-semites, who cast them as shirkers and persuaded the government in 1916 to initiate a "Jew count" (Judenzählung) that, regardless of its results, could ultimately only undermine Jewish efforts. For many this was a moment of profound disillusionment, the beginning of a long process of questioning whether Jews would ever be fully accepted in Germany. For Max and many others, however, military service during the Great War was a mark of pride, one that would be emphasized repeatedly under the Nazis. Their devoted service would, they reasoned, surely silence the claims of their detractors once and for all.

Upon volunteering for the army, Max asked to be placed in a regiment that would be sent to the front line. He quickly rose through the ranks, and eventually earned an Honor Cross for bravery. He was captured by the French in the spring of 1915 and spent five years as a prisoner of war before finally returning to Hanau in 1920, when he was forty-two.[17]

Despite his ordeal, Max remained committed to the ideal of Jewish military service, and upon his return from the war he funneled his energy into historical research on the subject. In the old part of Hanau's Jewish cemetery—the very same cemetery in which his ancestors had lain for over three hundred years, and where he would finally be laid to rest twenty years after his own untimely death—he found the grave of Leon Wertheim, who had distinguished himself in battle against the Napoleonic armies. Max discovered that Wertheim was one of a number of Jewish Hanauers who had participated in the "Wars of Freedom" in the early 1800s, among them a woman so patriotic she disguised herself as a man to join her husband at the front.[18] In a series of articles published by the Hanau historical association in the 1920s and early 1930s, Max carefully documented the contributions of Hanau's Jews to the German military, lauding their bravery in defense of their town and fatherland.[19] Upon discovering that Wertheim had no remaining relatives, Max assumed the responsibility of caring for his grave, symbolically taking upon himself the role of defender of Hanau's Jewish history and memory.

In the first few years of the Nazi onslaught, the most profound impact on German Jews was arguably psychological. Before it became an assault on the body, it was an assault on identity—on Jews' sense of who they were and where they belonged in the world. The threat they faced was more gradual and less easily comprehensible than what would later befall their eastern European brethren, who were thrust headlong into war in 1939. Fully aware of German Jews' deep sense of attachment to their homeland, the Nazis fostered their misperceptions, rejecting their presence in countless ways while making it ever more difficult for them to leave. "Where do I belong?" wrote the diarist Victor Klemperer in Dresden in October 1935. "To the 'Jewish nation' decrees Hitler. And *I* feel . . . nothing but a German or German European." Almost seven years later, at the height of Hitler's genocidal war, he would write: "I am German and am waiting for the Germans to come back; they have gone to ground somewhere."[20]

By the time Hitler became chancellor in January 1933, the Nazi presence in Hanau was firmly established. During the interwar years the political left had a strong presence in the town, even if the center parties combined commanded a modest majority and nationalistic sentiment was widespread. Thanks to the Communist Party's strength, the Nazi Party's share of the vote in Hanau in the late 1920s was still well below the national average.[21] As the Great Depression spread across the globe, however, the Nazis began to attract more voters. Brownshirts became an increasingly common sight in Hanau's streets, and there were frequent and sometimes violent clashes with communists. In the election of March 1933, the National Socialist German Workers' Party took first place in Hanau far ahead of any other party, with seventeen out of thirty-six seats.[22]

The harassment and exclusion of Hanau's Jews began quickly. One Jewish resident, Carl Schwabe (unrelated to Rudolf), recalled that the local newspaper, the *Hanauer Anzeiger*, suddenly became "more National Socialist than the party press," its tone noticeably more antisemitic. On 1 April 1933, local Jewish shops and businesses felt the effects of the nationwide Nazi boycott. Brownshirts stood outside shop fronts and intimidated customers, vandalized property, and goaded Jews to leave Germany. "I will never forget it," recalled Schwabe. "The street was filled with people. Young fellows howling, older people curious, many incensed. In front of each Jewish store the SA men in brown were lined up. The leaders, in snappy new uniforms, checked the guards. I closed up and went home."[23] The Jewish-owned Wronker department store in the center of town was another of the businesses targeted, and its Jewish director was soon replaced by a member of the Nazi Party.[24] Analyzing the effect of such public actions on the ordinary citizens who witnessed them, the historian Michael Wildt insists that even curious passersby and onlookers were "an indispensable component of this operation": "regardless of their internal disposition toward the event, they were active accomplices in anti-Semitic politics."[25]

One of Wronker's employees was Rudolf Schwab. Aged twenty-one, he was dutifully undertaking assorted work placements to prepare him for his ultimate calling, the role of partner in his father's firm. The new regime, however, had different plans. The boycott was followed by a torrent of discriminatory legislation aimed at removing Jews from economic life. Whether as a result of the legislation or simply at the whim of his employer, Rudolf was soon dismissed from his job.[26]

Even if Nazi antisemitism was unambiguous, many German Jews reasoned that antisemitic political regimes had come and gone before. There had been many instances of anti-Jewish discrimination in Hanau's history, in the form of laws as well as everyday social encounters. There had even been cases of physical violence. In 1819, as the Hep!Hep! riots exploded across the German states, Jews in the Judengasse were assaulted and driven from their homes and the synagogue was desecrated; soldiers had to be called in to restore order. Even after emancipation was formally granted, Jews had continued to encounter prejudice.[27] In the 1880s, the success of a Hanau political party on an antisemitic ticket mirrored the rise of political antisemitism both in the region of Hesse and throughout the German states.[28] On balance, however, Hanau's Jews enjoyed a safe and comfortable existence. They had made rapid advances in German society while also preserving a rich communal life. Though later generations would question whether the fêted German Jewish symbiosis had ever actually existed, in the minds of many Jews, among them Max, it remained their incontestable reality.[29]

Less sanguine than his father, Rudolf fled Germany early on, in May 1933. Over twenty years later, explaining to compensation authorities why he decided to leave, he said he had been warned by a close friend and official of the Nazi Party, Karl Kipfer, that he was to be arrested. Rudolf's only position of leadership at the time was in a youth movement, however, and none of his other known activities seem to have warranted arrest. Those who left Germany in 1933 tended to be active on the political left, among them a minority of Jews, but Rudolf certainly did not fit this bill.[30] His hasty departure was perhaps more likely related to a growing rift with his parents caused by his retreat from Jewish observance.[31] Young people like him, unimpeded by careers and families and perhaps more prone to optimism than their parents, also often found the decision to emigrate easier to make.[32]

Rudolf made his way first to Belgium, where he connected with relatives in Antwerp; from there he went to Brussels and later to Holland. Unable to secure a visa or work permit, and increasingly determined not to return to Germany, he decided in early 1936 to make his way to South Africa, one of the few viable alternatives left.[33]

On the eve of his departure, his forty-two-year-old aunt Alice wrote:

Your . . . journey is into the unknown but is still full of hope and expectations of building a new life and of what we hope will be a future full of happiness. I hope and wish with all my heart that all the things we yearn for, just as you do, will come true for you: that this huge step will be a success and that you'll have the strength to make a new life for yourself. Above all: stay healthy, and may you be spared any and all unpleasantness, though of course disappointments in life cannot be avoided; what's needed is courage and perseverance to cope with them and overcome them, and what I hope for you is that you'll approach them with energy and tenaciousness, and that far away from your home here you'll manage to find a second home and do a life's work there that you can be proud of. . . . Who knows, perhaps all of us might be able to join you there. We're discussing every possible option but in the long term I don't think we'll have another chance. Perhaps at some stage you'll have the chance to ask around and find out if there are any possibilities for us over there. I'm sure the days you all spent together were very pleasant and contemplative; you were often in my thoughts. For you the difficulty of the separation will now be washed away by all the new experiences you'll be having. Perhaps your parents and Hans will be able to join you too at some point. Just keep both feet on the ground, be realistic, and "Allen Gewalten zum Trotz sich erhalten, rufet die Arme der Götter herbei" [Defend yourself against all forces, call for help from the arms of the gods]. Some lines from Goethe that have given me much strength and the courage to face life in the last few years; perhaps they will do the same for you too. So for now, keep well. All the very best to you and for your future, faraway life.

Your loving Aunt Alice.

Lotte is already asleep and Uncle Oskar is away; they send their greetings. P.s. Beware of "vipers" and lions, they are dangerous animals.[34]

Alice's parting words revealed a perception of remotest Africa shared by many of the Schwab relatives, and probably also by Rudolf himself.

Close to a quarter of Hanau's Jews left within a few months of the Nazi takeover. Jews in smaller communities were often the first to flee: compared to the large cities, there was limited scope for avoiding the authorities or carving out sheltered spaces. Most did not leave the country, however, but moved to cities where they felt safer from persecution, in this case to nearby Frankfurt, where the Jewish community of 26,158 made up close to 5 percent of the population.[35] Some, like Rudolf, traveled to the Low Countries or France, planning to return once the Nazi threat had abated. Many others—attached to homes and businesses, to friends and family and community, inclined more to the known than the unknown, perhaps convinced they could endure what was surely only a temporary threat—chose to stay.

For Max Schwab, leaving Germany was unconscionable. His sense of security stemmed in large part from his belief, shared by many other German Jews, that his status as a war veteran set him apart, that he would not be significantly affected by the new regime and its antisemitic policies. After all, hardly a month went by under the Nazis without an event to commemorate the Great War, and its soldiers were fêted as national heroes.

Max was a particularly dedicated veteran, leader of the Hanau branch of the *Reichsbund jüdischer Frontsoldaten*, the German Jewish war veterans' association. Staunchly nationalist, the *Reichsbund* was one of the most vocal champions of the message of Jewish loyalty. Jewish military service in World War I was portrayed as only the most recent manifestation of a phenomenon dating back at least to the Franco-Prussian war of the 1870s.[36] The *Reichsbund* saw itself not only as a Jewish organization but as an integral part of the German veteran community. It rejected the Zionist vision of a political-national Jewish community, emphasizing instead its ties to the German homeland. Its members were proud to march through the streets wearing their medals and decorations. Max wholeheartedly embraced its values, as did thousands of his fellow Jews: the *Reichsbund* grew to become the second largest Jewish organization in interwar Germany, with up to 40,000 members organized into 360 local branches.[37]

In the early years of Nazi rule, Jewish war veterans like Max and his brother Alex were largely unaffected by discriminatory measures. When the euphemistically named Law for the Restoration of the Civil Service was passed in April 1933, for example, dismissing thousands of Jews from their jobs, war veterans were exempted. While "ordinary" Jews were increasingly excluded from society, veterans received additional welfare rights, and were even honored for their contributions in World War I. They interpreted these concessions as a sign that Jewish veterans would continue to be protected under the Third Reich, and that Jewish soldiers, at the very least, would have a place in the new Germany.[38]

As Nazi rule grew increasingly repressive, Max spoke often about his experiences during the First World War. He was hardly alone. Diarist and fellow veteran Victor Klemperer noted caustically: "Altogether: the Jews' favorite topic, immediately after Gestapo and the current situation: their participation in the 1914–1918 World War."[39] Providing information to support his brother Alex's later application for an emigration visa, Max emphasized that Alex had "completed two years of active service in a field artillery regiment in Darmstadt and in Mainz, and fulfilled his patriotic duties and obligations in the World War from start to finish."[40] Max also took care to preserve numerous documents testifying to his and his relatives' military service.

One of the most extraordinary of the documents preserved by Max was a certificate awarding Alex "The Honor Cross for Veterans of the Front Line." Such certificates were awarded to decorated Jewish war veterans across the country in recognition of their military service in 1914–1918. More remarkable than the honor the certificate conferred, however, was its date: 21 February 1936. More than three years into Nazi rule—years during which Germany's Jews endured increasing assaults, repression, and the loss of their citizenship—Jewish war veterans were being acknowledged for their patriotic service. The document bore the stamp of the director of the Hanau police, replete with Nazi eagle and swastika, and was signed "in the name of the Führer and the Chancellor of the Reich." It was not hard to see why some Jewish veterans, desperate for signs of reassurance, were persuaded by these mixed messages.

For those who remained in Germany during the early years of the Nazi regime, the departure of family members was especially painful. Rudolf's mother, Martha, begged him to write as often as possible. On the eve of his departure for South Africa in April 1936, she wrote: "We lived together for such a short time and spoke so little. Don't you think? Have a fine voyage and good luck."[41] A few days later, she wrote:

Certificate awarding Alex Schwab the "Honour Cross" (21 February 1936). Courtesy of Yad Vashem.

All day long I've been thinking about the big box that's carrying you minute by minute a bit further away from us. You've been travelling for 10 days now and hopefully you've had a good voyage and been spared any sea sickness. You must have already seen and experienced many fine and interesting things.

Perhaps, wrote his seventy-three-year-old grandmother Johanna, the parting was easier for you?

Thank God, we've managed to recover a little from your leaving and we hope you have too. Perhaps it was a little easier for you, you're young and you look at the world with open eyes, seeing it as new, beautiful and interesting.[42]

Writing to his uncle Alex in Shanghai, Rudolf reflected: "Even in the most difficult of circumstances, you must never lose your head; you must always think about how hard things are for those you've left behind."[43]

In September 1935, Jews in Hanau and across Germany were stripped of their citizenship with the passing of the Nuremberg Laws. Some held out hope that the clarification of Jews' legal status would signal the end of indiscriminate harassment, but their optimism was misplaced. Signs prohibiting Jews from public places multiplied. The Nazi propaganda newspaper *Der Stürmer* was prominently displayed on the streets. On 25 October, the Hanau Gestapo triumphantly reported that people were buying less from Jewish stores. More and more Jewish enterprises in Hanau were forcibly scaled down or "Aryanized," among them Max's jewelry business. On 29 November, the *Hanauer Anzeiger* published an article about "racial education in schools," affirming the impossibility of mixing students of "Aryan" and "Jewish blood" and stressing the responsibility of educators to help students fulfill their racial duties.[44]

Hanau's Jews attempted to maintain a sort of normality amid this growing barrage of harassments and restrictions. Rudolf's eleven-year-old brother Hans attended school and played football in the park. Max busied himself with his work and historical research, and Martha maintained a warm social circle. In February 1936, she gave Rudolf a typical account of recent goings-on:

Yesterday I also sent 2 parcels, one with vegetables and meat and the other with meat, so hopefully you won't be so famished the next time you have visitors.... Otherwise we're doing really well and I was very glad to hear from both your letters that the same goes for you. If I do go to Frankfurt this week I'll inquire about the books you mentioned. I probably won't be able to get them second-hand. I'm finding managing the household along with work very challenging and there's very little time for many other things, even the important ones. But it's like that everywhere now. Of course anyone who has a grown-up daughter who's willing to work has it a little easier.[45]

Max and Martha spent a lot of time worrying about Rudolf's welfare in far-off Johannesburg. They connected him with German Jews who might be able to offer him support, and Max solicited the help of Jewish veterans' organizations abroad:

A long time ago I sent you a letter by ordinary post to Cape Town or Johannesburg (for collection from the central post office!) with, among other things, an identity card for you confirming that you're the son of the Chairman of the *Reichsbund* in Hanau, and a request from the head office in Berlin to the South African Jewish Ex Service League [*sic*] in Johannesburg requesting that you be given advice and support. (Stamped by the German and English governments!) Why haven't you mentioned this in your letters? We don't even know where you're living or what you're living on! This can't be the point of emigration, surely— breaking off with and tearing up a perfectly good citizenship and then ending up with nothing? Don't you agree? Finding a new existence for yourself cannot be done easily or quickly, that's obvious, but with your knowledge and adaptability it will all soon work out, don't worry![46]

Max's reprimanding tone, tempered with words of encouragement and reassurance, revealed his frustration at the weakening of his fatherly authority. His advice was sincere but aggrieved, the despair of a father whose son had taken an unadvised path and was moving further and further from parental reach. He and Martha nonetheless went to great lengths to help Rudolf materially. As late as June 1939, Martha requested permission to send Rudolf clothing, tablecloths, and bed linen, explaining that he did not have the means to buy these himself. The German Exchange Control Office duly agreed.[47]

Excluded from German social life, many Jews turned to religion and community. Only a small proportion were strict observers of Jewish law, but most cities and towns retained an *Einheitsgemeinde* (united community) made up of synagogues ranging from liberal to Orthodox. Many continued to engage in communal life, and rituals such as *brit milah* (circumcision), bar mitzvahs, weddings, and funerals continued to be widely practiced.[48]

The Schwabs had always observed *kashrut* (the Jewish dietary laws), *Shabbat* (the Sabbath), and the holy festivals to a greater extent than many German Jews. On the whole, Jewish life tended to be better preserved in smaller communities like Hanau than it was in the large cities, even if the spectrum of observance was quite broad.[49] Max was active in Jewish community affairs, and by his late teens Rudolf was following enthusiastically in his footsteps, taking on the local leadership of the *Kameraden*, a nationalistic and anti-Zionist youth movement.[50]

The family's Jewish observance remained strong under Nazi rule. In Max's letters to Rudolf, the passing of seasons and years was marked by the Jewish festivals: greetings and prayers were regularly shared at *Rosh Hashanah* (the Jewish New Year) in the autumn, *Chanukah* in the winter, and *Pesach* (Passover) in the spring. When Rudolf sent money from South Africa, scrounging together pennies to help alleviate his family's hardship, Max prioritized the purchase of kosher food, even though it was difficult to come by and the costs were exorbitant.[51] In one letter, Max wrote to Rudolf of their attempt at a Passover celebration:

> Soon it will be Pesach again with the Holy Seder evenings—will we have the usual guests this time? With so little kosher meat and money so scarce, I just don't know. The busy housewife certainly has plenty to say about it. First and foremost, though: thank you very much indeed for the pound of meat you paid for, we'll use it sparingly. We fell very far behind with our finances and have a lot of catching up to do.[52]

Max regularly talked to Rudolf about the importance of living by "decent" religious values. He also encouraged his wayward son to embrace the Jewish community in Johannesburg, which would act as a source of support and comfort.

> Now, listen to your father once and for all and make a positive commitment to religious Judaism, otherwise you'll lose contact with precisely those members of the faith who can support you and be useful to you, those who can act in your interest. If not, you'll very much regret it one day, I just hope by then it won't be too late. No one is exactly falling over themselves to embrace us at the moment and there will be dozens of disappointments along the way, that's why our faith in G-d will help us and give us the courage to persevere in all our work and at all times.[53]

In November 1937, almost five years after Hitler had come to power, the Schwab family celebrated Hans's bar mitzvah. As was the typical practice, his rite of passage was marked with a synagogue service on *Shabbat* and a party the following day. Though many of Hans's friends had done the same, it was a notable public affirmation of Jewishness.[54] With the inimitable light-heartedness of a thirteen-year-old, Hans's letters to Rudolf described making silly speeches and preparing food for the festivities:

> Dear Rudi,
>
> Today we bottled the Laubenheim wine for the bar mitzvah. Your "old sweetheart" helped us out and worked very hard. Mama and I pushed in the corks and Papa had a job too: he had to sample it immediately. I picked and shelled the borlotti beans in the garden. Here it's already becoming quite cold, so I think there the seasons must have changed and the sun is now facing in your direction. The day of the bar mitzvah is getting closer and closer. My voice is getting stronger after singing the whole thing a hundred times over for Mr. Wgn. Just a few moments ago Mama and I were thinking about what I should do with the boys we're inviting over.[55]

After the event he wrote:

> My dear brother,
>
> Thank you for your kind letter for my bar mitzvah and for the lovely present. It hasn't arrived yet. The few lines you wrote arrived here on 17 December. My bar mitzvah was on 27 November! How is it that the Jewish date in South Africa and in Hanau is completely different??? Ernst had his turn on the 20th of November. . . . My bar mitzvah went very well even though I was terribly nervous beforehand. Grandma was the only guest from out of town. She arrived on Friday afternoon. The Höxters were in the synagogue the next morning as well as lots of other people. Uncle Mor was so nervous that he couldn't remember the *brocha* [blessing], so at half past three in the morning he wrote it down and learned it off by heart. But he wasn't called up. When my turn finally came, I "mumbled" my way very quickly through the first *parsha* [Torah portion]. The second one was much better and by the time it was nearly over my stage fright was gone and I had found my bearings, and then I was finished. For my bar mitzvah I received the following: a gold watch

and a tie pin, etc. (Papa), a coat, a cap and an umbrella, etc. (Mama), 30 Marks and a bar mitzvah suit (Grandma), a football and 5 Marks (from the Franks), table tennis bats, 18 books, 8 mechanical pencils, 3 mosquito nets (really?), a set of portable eating utensils, a lamp and a dynamo, a travel blanket, a suitcase, a cigarette case, a travel pharmacy kit, tools, a wallet, business cards, etc.[56]

Hans's letter reflected the quiet persistence of ordinary life: the dutiful but slightly cheeky thank-you letter (why had his brother been late with his greetings?), the adolescent's predictable nerves before a public performance, the communal celebrations of rites of passage, the meticulous lists of gifts received. It only hinted at something more insidious: the preponderance of travel items among the gifts (travel blanket, mosquito nets, travel pharmacy, suitcase), and the attendance of only one out-of-town guest.[57]

But Max and Martha's letters to Rudolf exposed a deeper anxiety. Why had Rudolf not sent anything for the bar mitzvah, his mother chided?

My dear Rudi,

I've just arrived home and found a card from your dear Grandmother to let me know quickly that she's just received a letter from you dated 29 November. This is the first sign of life you've given us in three weeks. Your last card was on 8 November & you can well imagine how we've been feeling. And what's doubly incomprehensible about it is that two weeks ago today (on 27 November) it was Hans's bar mitzvah, so of course we expected to receive a letter from you then. Did something get lost in the post? ... When your letters arrive you're so close to me and it's as if I can live alongside you, but when you don't write, then you're so endlessly, unreachably far away. And so I'm asking you, again, not to leave such long gaps between letters; I'm so anxious & life is difficult enough and full of worry and upset without this as well.[58]

By 1937, even the most patriotic Jewish organizations in Germany were talking about emigration. Thousands of Jews were making reluctant provision to leave, or at least coming up with contingency plans. The decision to emigrate was not an easy one, particularly before it was clear that lives depended on it. Prospective emigrants were faced with a barrage of travel restrictions, extortionate taxes, and legal impediments, not to mention the emotional trials of leaving homes

Hans Schwab, c. 1937.
Courtesy of the Schwab family.

and livelihoods, often with insufficient skills or resources to support new lives in unfamiliar destinations.[59]

The spring and summer of 1938 were months of escalating anti-Jewish actions across Germany, spurred by the *Anschluss* (annexation) of Austria and the Sudeten crisis. The tension was felt in Hanau as well.[60] On 15 May 1938, the Nazi SD (Security Service) District Office reported that the previous week, local Nazis had initiated a renewed boycott of Jewish shops. Guards were posted outside, and those who insisted on entering despite warnings were photographed and led through the town by Hitler Youth members carrying signs reading, "I bought from the kike," "Whoever shops at a Jewish store is a traitor to the people," or "I'm a Jew's lackey." Hanau resident Carl Schwabe recalled the eager participation of young people in the assaults:

> One morning all Jewish stores found on their display windows signs with the inscription "Jew Store." Naturally, we removed them, but the next morning they were there again, now with a small inscription at the bottom: "Whoever tears this off is a betrayer of the people." . . . Every adult was assigned a few schoolboys, who naturally enjoyed the whole thing tremendously. To be able to behave insolently toward adults with

official sanction, that was something altogether new. If someone stopped in front of the display window of a Jewish store, the little heroes were right on the spot. Signs for "betrayers of the people," who might dare to enter the stores, were readied. Cameras were to immortalize the image of such an "*untermensch*" for the *Stürmer*. In short, it was a great time for young people. Sometimes they threw fireworks and stink bombs into the stores, all that under the supervision and with the approval of the teachers and dignitaries.[61]

The Security Service report confirmed that the boycott "was enthusiastically received by the population, and the hope is that the remainder of the Jewish firms will soon disappear. The operation was carried out with a high degree of discipline, and there were no excesses of any kind." Similar boycotts were held in the subsequent weeks, and two of the remaining Jewish stores in Hanau began sale negotiations.[62]

The synagogue on Hanau's Nordstrasse (as the Judengasse had been renamed) also became a frequent target of attack. On the eve of the Jewish New Year in 1937, a black chamber pot was placed inside bearing the message "dangerous explosive."[63] On 13–14 May 1938, the Jewish sabbath, the entrances to the synagogue were barricaded shut and the word "verkäuflich" (for sale) scrawled on the building's front wall. The Security Service report noted that the bricks used to block the doors had been removed from nearby construction sites, but that "the construction firms affected have not filed a formal complaint regarding missing materials." The communal Jewish leader Josef Strauss, who arranged for the barricades to be removed, was taken into so-called "protective custody." "There is a sense of great outrage here over this Jew," the report stated, "and this measure had to be taken in order to prevent violent excesses." The graffiti on the synagogue was not removed, and local glaziers refused to replace the glass in the windows. "After these events," the report concluded, "probably hardly a craftsman could be found who would undertake a job for the Jews."[64]

There is evidence of some opposition in Hanau to the Nazis' actions. In May 1938, the Security Service report observed that some of the so-called bessere Leute—a term generally used for the liberal bourgeoisie—continued to insist on shopping in Jewish stores despite the boycott.[65] Carl Schwabe, too, recalled that "with few exceptions," local business people disapproved of boycotts.[66] The report noted an incident when the wife of a former Communist Party informer refused to boycott a certain store, declaring that she always shopped there "and would continue to do so." The report noted that her action triggered a protest action among the persons present. In no time, a large crowd formed around the woman, and she had to be brought to her apartment under the protection of several civilians. Unavoidable was an incident where several individuals threw rotten eggs at her.[67]

It is difficult to extrapolate political attitudes accurately from such sources, but they indicate that some opposition did exist, even if most voices were ultimately silenced into submission.[68]

For many German Jews, the turning point—the moment at which any lingering hopefulness about the Nazis' intentions crumbled—was the pogroms of 9–10 November 1938, euphemistically labeled *Kristallnacht* (Night of Broken Glass) in reference to the windows of Jewish shops and homes and synagogues that were shattered across Nazi-occupied Germany and Austria.[69]

Hanau's synagogue did not escape that night's violence. Several hundred people attacked the building, desecrating Torah scrolls and throwing furniture into the street before setting it alight. Apart from ensuring that the blaze did not threaten neighboring buildings, the local police did nothing.[70] The Jewish community center a few streets away was also targeted. A crowd burst into the building, plundering property and attacking resident teacher Josef Sulzbacher, who died of his wounds several days later. They also attacked the cemetery, desecrating gravestones and burning down the mortuary. As dawn broke, the crowd split into smaller groups. Shops and businesses all over the town were plundered and looted, doors were smashed, tables thrown out of windows, goods scattered in the streets.

On the evening of 10 November, the marauding crowds turned to private homes. Almost a decade later, Rudolf learned for the first time from a non-Jewish neighbor and friend, Sepp Weigelt, of his family's fate during that night:

> Your father was in Worms at your grandmother's house. I had only been home for half an hour when I heard noises coming from your apartment. I ran over there right away, on the street in front of your building was a car. Just at that moment four or five men came out of the building and jumped into the car and drove off. (Who opened the front door to them??) I immediately went up to your apartment, but, oh my God, by the time I got to the stairs I already knew something had happened. Believe me dear Rudi, my heart was heavy. Everything in the front hall had been completely destroyed, the windows had been shattered and the doors broken to pieces. I climbed over the debris and went into the other rooms, everything had been destroyed. The door to your parents'

Hanau's synagogue on 10 November 1938. The "verkäuflich" (for sale) graffiti from the May 1938 attack is clearly visible. Courtesy of Yad Vashem.

room was lying open. All I could see was shards of glass and splintered wood. Even the feathers from the bedding had been scattered all over the place. Even the water pipes in the bathroom had been smashed up and the water was running out of them. First I shut off the water at the mains (with an axe I found in the bedroom). Your mother and Hans were nowhere to be seen. On the ground floor a family, from Poland, walked past, they didn't even flinch (according to your father he, the Pole, was a member of the S.A. and was the only person who could have opened the front door). Then I saw that the door to your garden was open and I went outside and called for Hans. He and your mother were sitting in your old shed under some branches, arms around each other, barely dressed, on top of an old wooden box in the corner. Your mother was unconscious. I carried her back into the house, then she woke up. Hans went upstairs and took some clothes and coats. I boarded up the front hall and door as best I could using nails and pieces of wood that were lying around, and took your mother and Hans to my home until the next morning. I didn't go to work the next day and instead drove to Worms to collect your father. In Worms the scene at your grandmother's house was exactly the same. We drove back to Hanau right away. During those few days all the Jewish shops and synagogues were attacked and set on fire. Furniture was thrown onto the streets, anything that wasn't nailed down was smashed to smithereens. It was shameful.[71]

At reparations hearings in the 1950s, other witnesses confirmed the devastation of the Schwab home that night. In his statement Sepp Weigelt also emphasized, more ominously than he had in his letter, that the fifty-year-old Martha Schwab had been "severely ill-treated," suggesting sexual assault.[72]

All over Hanau, local residents had watched the pogrom unfold before their eyes. Some attempted to help; most were horrified but largely silent. Hardly a Jewish business or home in Hanau had remained untouched. Most Jews made hurried plans to find safe havens abroad, or at least to retreat into the safety of numbers in the larger cities. Among them was Hanau's Rabbi Dr. Hirsch Gradenwitz, who moved to Frankfurt and from there fled to Holland.[73]

Forty Jewish men from Hanau, among them forty-nine-year-old Alex and sixty-year-old Max, were deported to Buchenwald. Many years later, legal documents confirmed that Max was released on 26 November 1938, two weeks after his imprisonment, and Alex a few weeks later.[74] For thousands of Jewish men deported to camps after *Kristallnacht*, valid emigration papers were the only means of securing freedom. Whether or not Martha actually provided these, emigration was—for Max, at least—not yet seriously on the agenda. According to Weigelt, his efforts after his return went into putting the family's home back in order, replacing key items of furniture. Within a few weeks he had arranged for several items of Biedermeier furniture to be repaired by a local carpenter, and also purchased some new items: two cupboards, some beds, a mirror, and a sofa.[75]

After the pogrom, the Jewish war veterans' association under Max's leadership was disbanded. A new deluge of anti-Jewish restrictions followed. "Aryanization" was aggressively intensified, and the *Hanauer Anzeiger* launched a renewed antisemitic campaign, claiming that local Jews were engaged in smuggling and black marketeering. As harassment increased, Jews scrambled for visas and permits and pleaded for money from distant relatives and friends. In August 1939, Max's brother Alex departed for Shanghai. All Jewish organizations apart from those organizing emigration were disbanded.[76]

By the summer of 1939, only eighty-two Jews remained in Hanau, less than a fifth of the community that lived there just six years earlier. The vast majority of those remaining expressed their desire to emigrate.[77] A few days after the outbreak of war, on the night of 5–6 September, they experienced yet another violent attack. Weigelt recalled to Rudolf that his family was once again one of those targeted:

> When I got there I could see on their faces that something wasn't right; what had happened? Your father told me the following: at about two o'clock in the morning, four men (two in SS uniforms) had knocked on your door. (How did they get into the building? The front door should have been locked?) Your father got up and asked them what they wanted. All they said was "Gestapo, open up!" He opened the door and right away a very tall chap in uniform smacked him in the face. First they wanted to go into the bedroom but your father told them your mother was still in bed. In the meantime Hans fled to your parents' room. They shoved your father in the chest, pushing him over, and forced their way into your parents' room, and there are no words to describe what happened in there. Your parents told me all this with tears in their eyes. I could write it all down for you, but my heart still bleeds when I think about it. Perhaps I can tell you in person some time when you come to Hanau. When the business in the bedroom was over, your father was forced to go to his office, open the safe and hand over all the valuables, they took them and said they were confiscating everything. The next morning when your father went to the Gestapo they told him not to get worked up about it and that everything was in good order, but despite several attempts he never received even a single receipt.[78]

Once again, Sepp strongly implied that Martha had been raped.[79] Similar scenes played themselves out in other Jewish homes in Hanau, including those of the synagogue chairman Nathan Sichel and the teacher Julius Weingarten.[80]

In his reparations claims after the war, Rudolf dispassionately chronicled everything that had befallen his family: the gradual loss of freedom and livelihood, the concentration camp after *Kristallnacht*, the forced sale of the family business and home, harassment, plundering, robbery, and physical assault.[81]

And yet in all their prolific correspondence at the time, Rudolf's family told him almost nothing of what they were experiencing. "If everything had been completely destroyed," Rudolf later rationalized, "I'm absolutely certain my parents would have at least hinted at it in their letters."[82] In early 1939, Max wrote to Rudolf that Hans was happy, had lots of friends, and enjoyed playing football. He assured him that their clothes were old but perfectly usable, and that they had enough to eat.[83] In a letter written sometime in 1941, Hans assured his brother:

> As regards food, you can rest assured that strict measures are being taken to ensure that everyone gets the same with no preference given to the capitalist classes. No hoarding like there was, sadly, during the World War. We're able to get every type of food here. We eat our fill, just like everyone else.[84]

Jews in Germany had been receiving reduced food rations since the beginning of the war, but this and many other details never found their way into the family's letters. The question of what to include in correspondence to family abroad was a delicate one, and many Jews chose to skip over their most frightening experiences. Part of the reason for their silence was undoubtedly censorship, which would have been virulent in a small community like Hanau's. By 1938 it was Nazi policy to punish criticism of the government by imprisonment or even the death penalty. Letters were read randomly by censors and thousands of people were prosecuted. Even if censorship could not be all-pervasive, Jews especially were selective about what they wrote for fear of retribution.[85]

Rudolf's family seems also to have wanted to spare him the anxiety, to offer him some reassurance that they were all right. Or were they partly refusing to acknowledge the reality of what was unfolding around them? On one level, the family's troubles were not absent from the letters. Martha wrote frequently of her loneliness and uncertainty, her anxiety and growing hopelessness. "The things that keep us busy and preoccupied these days can barely be put on paper," she confessed in one undated letter; and, with a nod to the censor, "if they were, they would travel too far."[86] In March 1940 she wrote:

> Today is our dear Alice's birthday; it's safe to assume this is the last one we'll celebrate here, and no matter what we do or what we think about, we're consumed by sorrow and worries for the future.[87]

Max, too, grieved the loss of his livelihood and the gradual death of his community. He was not blind to the violence against Jews and the growing flood of emigrants around him. "There would be no point in telling you that we're doing well when that simply isn't true," he wrote in May 1939. "And we have very few friends who are good to us."[88]

Nonetheless, Max remained devoted to Jewish life in Hanau. In October 1939, as Europe was going up in flames, he lamented that only forty Jews remained in town. Synagogue services could no longer be held daily but only on Mondays, Thursdays, and Saturdays. He complained that the rabbi and other communal leaders had long since abandoned their responsibilities and moved to Frankfurt. He disapproved, he wrote to Rudolf, of the decision to send the community's possessions to larger communities for safekeeping:

> It's just a shame that a community once so noble and wealthy is disin-
> tegrating bit by bit, silently, without so much as a whimper, and that its
> "men at the top" are treating the community's property the way they are,
> sending everything to Berlin and leaving nothing here for us.[89]

Max took it upon himself to preserve the community's religious artifacts, and soon assumed responsibility for the community itself. In June 1940 he submitted the following report to the local Nazi authorities:

> The small Jewish cultural association of Hanau consists of approxi-
> mately 15 families or 45 people. The community is the religious center
> for Jews in the town and the surrounding countryside. Langenselbold
> has its own center. Our members meet for religious services, usually on
> Friday evenings or Saturday mornings, but sometimes during the week
> too. Approximately 15 men and women generally attend; this figure
> includes those who travel in from the surrounding area. The commu-
> nity's senior representatives are Salli Hirschman and Isi Levi; how-
> ever, both men moved to Frankfurt am Main months ago and rarely
> attend. . . . Most members of the community are receiving welfare sup-
> port and very few can still afford to pay their contributions. For the sake
> of good order and tradition (my family has lived in Hanau since 1603),
> and because I am sufficiently knowledgeable to do so, I have taken over
> the religious leadership of the community under the supervision of the
> Secret State Police in Hanau. I am at your disposal should you require
> any further information, or wish to inspect the former Jewish commu-
> nity building.[90]

As the war raged on, Max wrote repeatedly of God as his "best friend" and called on God to "give us strength to bear the reality of today as well as the future." He

Max Israel S c h w a b ,
Französische Allee 15.

Hanau den 19. Juni 1940
Telefon 4113

An den

Herrn Schulrat E u r i c h

H a n a u a/M.
======---------------------=====

Betr. Unterrichtswesen
der Jüdischen Kultusgemeinde .

Unter Bezugnahme auf die , mit Ihnen geführte Unterhaltung ,
beauftragte ich den Lehrer Julius Weingarten einen eingehenden
Bericht über diejenigen Fragen auszuarbeiten , welche Sie mir
vorlegten und überreiche Ihnen denselben mit der Bitte um gefl
Kentnisnahme .
Ich ergänze diesen Bericht folgendermassen :
Der Kleine Jüdische Kultusverein Hanau besteht nosh aus etwa
15 Familien mit etwa 45 Seelen , er bildet das Religiöse Centr
der Juden des Stadt u. Landkreises , - Langenselbold bildet
sein Centrum für sich . - Die gottesdienstlichen Zusammen -
Künfte finden meistens Freitag Abend und Samstag Morgen statt
ab und zu auch innerhalb der Woche . Sie werden besucht von
durchschnittlich je 15 Männer und Frauen , eine Zahl in der au
die Besucher der Umgegend einbegriffen sind .
Die Gemeindeältesten heissen : Salli Hirschmann u.Isi Levi ,
Beide wohnen seit Monaten in Frankfurt a/M. und treten kaum no
in Erscheinung .- Der Lehrer , Vorbeter und Prediger heiss
Julius Weingarten , Sterngasse 21 , der Gemeindesekretär ist
Karl Löbenstein , Hammergasse 6 (Rechnungswesen u. Wohlfahr
Die meisten Mitglieder sind Wohlfahrtsempfänger , nur ganz wen
ge können noch Steuern zahlen .
Aus Gründen der Ordnung und Tradition (meine Familie wohnt se
1603 in Hanau) und weil ich darin bewandert bin , habe ich d
Religiöse Führung übernommen , unter der Kontrolle der Geheime
Staatspolizei Hanau .
Mit weiteren Aufklärungen , sowie Mitbesichtigung des ehemalig
Jüdischen Gemeindehauses stehe ich gerne, jederzeit, zur Verfügu

ergebenst

Max Israel Schwab

Kennkarte A 00161

Letter from Max Schwab to the Nazi authorities in Hanau, 19 June 1940.

maintained his Jewish observance, and in late 1941 he was arrested for illegally purchasing wine for *Shabbat*.[91]

Right up until his death, Max seemed unable to accept or even fathom his betrayal by his country. Convinced that his military service and esteemed standing in Hanau would protect him from the Nazis, he refused to seriously contemplate leaving even as life around him disintegrated. Explaining to Rudolf in July 1939 that he was one of the few Jews to have been given permission to operate his business until the end of October, he wrote:

> Thank G–d! Where would your father be today if the authorities hadn't intervened on his behalf time and time again?[92]

While other Jews made increasingly desperate plans to leave, Max angrily rebuked Rudolf for filling his younger brother's head with ideas about emigration. Hans still needed his parents during his early teenage years, Max wrote, and he was a good distraction for them in these difficult times:

> You're still saying things in your letters that upset me greatly and I want to make something very clear once and for all: your continuing to write to your mother as you do, despite my repeated requests for you not to do so, saying that you hope she'll soon be able to perfect her English in Springs, or that Hans-Ferdinand could go to an English school there, has had the most pernicious consequences for me: I've had bronchitis and sinus pain for the last four weeks and have had to stay in bed almost the entire time. . . . Now, do one thing for me, please, and stop writing to your mother and Hans about emigration and the like; things are bad enough for me—and those things you said about me and the sacrifice of Isaac, they were a poor comparison.[93]

Max's letters revealed his gradual isolation and descent into paranoia. Everyone was ganging up on him, he ranted. Martha's family did not appreciate his suffering during World War I, made fun of him, and ruthlessly swindled him out of money. The stress was making him sick and he was physically and emotionally finished. Later he wrote:

> Emigrating from Germany these days is not as easy as you imagine. First I have to sell both my houses and then pay off my debts. Only then can I begin thinking about finding a temporary place where we could live for

a while, such as Stuttgart or some other large town. Enclosed you'll find the family tree that I've now managed to complete from 1603 through to the present day. Our forefathers, who came from Württemberg, settled in Hanau around 330 years ago, only for us now to begin emigrating after living in Germany for 1,800 years. . . . If you had any idea what we've been going through then you wouldn't write to me this way. The business isn't functioning at all anymore. We can only hope that G-d will keep us in good health and that we won't lose our nerve when we leave our old home behind. If this is really how things have to be then it's important we don't lose our composure. We must rely on our faith in G–d and leave together with the few possessions we can manage to take with us. . . . My concerns about emigrating are not based on egotism or self-interest, they're perfectly understandable. I don't care about the honorary positions I'll be leaving behind, in any case they'll all be liquidated along with everything else. You're intelligent enough to read between the lines and see how heavily this weighs on my heart—me, a front-line veteran and a patriot, just like my father and grandfather before me, may their memories be a blessing. . . . When you're young like you and your cousin Reni these things don't affect you much, but for old people who are set in their ways it's much harder to adapt to living like a nomad. . . . I'm not doing any more literary work; it's very unlikely I'll ever be able to publish it so I've gradually lost interest. But I'd still like to make a good copy of the family's history so it'll be preserved for you boys, and for those who come after you. At least I still take some pleasure in my furniture, my pictures, the cacti, my stamps, my coins, the house, the yard and the garden. I even still have a telephone, but the *Reichsbund* has been paying the bill for several months now—the only concession that's been made for me on account of everything I've done for victims of the war.[94]

Max recognized that the family business was lost, that his research would never be published, and that he would probably eventually be forced to leave Germany. He nonetheless continued to insist on doing things "properly" out of respect for his family's reputation, his own dignity, and the welfare of his town and country. Many years later, a local architect named Jakob Hack recalled that even after Max's assets had been confiscated, he had insisted on paying his outstanding balance by instalments.[95]

 Martha's attempts to challenge her husband were in vain. By 1937 their marriage was under intense strain, partly because she was pursuing options for emigration without Max's approval. Women were often the first to recognize the severity of the Nazi threat, because their everyday contact with neighbors, teachers, and shopkeepers made them more keenly aware than their husbands of the extent to which ordinary citizens were willing to participate in the "social death" of the Jews. Largely ensconced in domestic life, and with less investment in professional careers, they perhaps also felt that less was at stake in encouraging their families to emigrate.[96]

Since 1936, Martha had wanted to join Rudolf in South Africa. She was unable to convince Max, however, and for a few years resigned herself to her circumstances. Probably the ferocity of the attack on *Kristallnacht*, however, and what was almost certainly a sexual assault witnessed by her husband and son, convinced her that leaving was now urgent. Immediately following the pogrom, on 29 November 1938, her personal tax records indicate that she received a bank transfer of 10,000 Reichsmarks from her mother in Worms for the explicit purpose of emigration. She may have expedited the transfer in order to secure Max's release from Buchenwald; she may also have intended to leave whether he joined her or not.[97]

We still know very little about the incidence of sexual assaults against Jewish women during the 1930s, before the unprecedented brutality of war and internment.[98] It is difficult to imagine the level of strain the rapes placed on Martha and Max's marriage, not to mention Max's continuing refusal to countenance emigration afterward. While popular perception may have idealized the loving Jewish family as a bulwark in the face of persecution, stories like this one remind us how easily the institution was ripped apart by the ferocity of the Nazi onslaught.[99] The last surviving photograph of Martha, one of only two that Rudolf was able to preserve of his mother, shows her looking resigned and far beyond her fifty-some years.

How can we make sense of Max's refusal or inability to see the writing on the wall? Historians often remind us to beware the dangers of hindsight, to remember that what we call History was once someone's lived reality, full of uncertainties and multiple possible outcomes. It would be naïve to assume that Jews were simply too blinded by their loyalty to Germany to recognize the Nazi threat. Nazi policy progressed incrementally and ambiguously, emphasizes the historian Marion Kaplan, and it is too simplistic to suggest that Jews should have known better: "Hindsight that condemns them for not having left in time fails to acknowledge how unimaginable Nazism was to most contemporary observers or how earnestly Jews tried to emigrate once the danger was apparent."[100] The historian Mark Roseman similarly defends German Jews from the charge of complacency. Even though many Jews recognized there was no collective future

Martha Schwab, c. 1940. Courtesy of Yad Vashem.

in Germany, they had complex reasons for deciding not to emigrate, and in the interim they contacted relatives, applied for visas, acquired languages and skills, and migrated to the big cities. "Whatever the calculations and obstacles were that kept many in Germany until it was too late," he concludes, "complacency and blindness seems to have played little part."[101]

In his letters to Rudolf, Max emphasized that there were serious practical impediments to their emigration. They could take very little with them and could not even afford the cost of the journey. In any event, it was nearly impossible to get a visa to go anywhere. Going to Palestine was out of the question for Max, who remained a committed anti-Zionist long after most Jewish organizations, including even the conservative *Reichsbund*, had changed their stance.[102] "About 75% of the people you used to know are now Zionists," he wrote to Rudolf, "and despite everything they're all crazy about Palestine. They say the weapon of the mind is all that's needed to bring about an agreement between the Jews and the Arabs, and they really believe it too. I doubt it very much."[103]

The decision to remain in Germany went to the heart of who Max was and his place in the world. He reluctantly researched emigration options, made some applications, and offered generous help to family members, but he chose to remain in the only place where his life, his history, his self, made sense. His loyalty was not only to Germany but specifically to Hanau, and when the town's Jews were ordered to move to Frankfurt in the summer of 1939, he was devastated:

> Even just the thought of leaving my old home for an unknown destination and an unsure future, never mind everything else that that entails, makes me feel very homesick. The very thought of moving from the house where I've lived, come rain or shine, for 47 years, makes me shudder.[104]

Upon the outbreak of war he wrote to Rudolf:

> My dear Rudi,
>
> So war is here after all. Nevertheless, as I've told you many times, I've been praying to G-d day and night that all mankind will know peace; the chances of it really were so good. I don't know if you'll get this letter or if there's any chance we'll be able to write to each other, which upsets us greatly. We'd like to try via neutral foreign countries if that's allowed, but of course in wartime all letters are censored. But for the time being, please accept my sincere good wishes for the New Year and for your birthday; above all, may you remain in good health and be successful in your work, in your new life, and have a little luck in financial matters too! Whether we'll ever meet again or we can arrange for us to emigrate, that all lies in the hands of various governments and in the destiny G-d has chosen for us. . . . Needless to say, not being allowed to fight for Germany in the war is extremely difficult for us, and I'm not just saying that because as a veteran company commander from the Champagne Front I'm obviously going to find it incomprehensible; I mean it in a more general sense; should you think that this somehow works to our advantage then you're gravely mistaken. I still remember the motto of the sons of England on the banner they carried in the war: "Right or wrong, my country!" This

is how I still feel and no one can hold it against me. For almost 2,000 years we've lived in Germany, 336 of those in Hanau. This is no matter of mere arithmetic; the bones of our forefathers rest in peace in this earth and G-d willing will continue to do so. This earth is sacred to me, which is why I'll pray for an honorable peace that leaves no hatred in its wake. The fact that our family was counted among the most respected citizens of this town, that I did everything to make myself their equal, and reached similar levels of success, what does it all matter? These are sacred memories for me and I'll take them with me to the very last place I live. They are my only war trophy. And so, my dear son, be well, think of me from time to time. I've always tried to do what's right by all men as long as they were upright, honest and G-d fearing. My future is veiled in darkness, but whatever the Almighty decides, that will be good enough for me. . . . Take care, farewell, warmest wishes,

Your father[105]

Max's outpouring of rage and incredulity, of grief and despair, seems to have been directed not so much at Rudolf as at Germany, the Nazis, the censor, anyone who might have been listening. His desire for an "honorable peace"—even more, the opportunity to fight for his country's honor—seems, on the face of it, unfathomable. Such sentiments were pervasive in the autumn of 1939, however, not only among the Nazi Party's supporters but also many of its opponents. As the historian Nicholas Stargardt explains, "Support for the Nazi regime and for the war were not the same thing."[106] Most Germans at the time, including those who did not back Hitler, understood themselves to be fighting a defensive war, one that was "forced upon them by Allied machinations and Polish aggression." More than simply Nazi propaganda, it was the memory of the First World War that fundamentally shaped their attitudes.[107]

The sentiments of a nationalist Jew at this historical moment are nonetheless striking. Max's loyalty outlasted that of his most patriotic Jewish countrymen, even after the unambiguous onslaught of *Kristallnacht*, the vicious attack on his family, the rape of his wife, his imprisonment in Buchenwald, and the growing tide of violence that followed in the pogrom's wake. Only now, after the outbreak of war, did his letters acknowledge the necessity of emigrating, and only grudgingly:

We're still living in Hanau but we're thinking about where to go. Frankfurt, Stuttgart or Hamburg are the only options. It'll be easier to emigrate from there as soon as we get approval. We can't stay in Hanau any longer. The most utterly grotesque things happen in a small town like this in comparison to the city, because even if you are discrete about your presence you are always exposed. Our community has shrunk down to nothing from around 1,200 people, so it has had to be disbanded. Now, I want to emphasize that so far, the local authorities have always behaved decently toward me and I hope our relationship will remain that way until we emigrate in the very near future. But first of all we really must get out of Hanau, which will happen very soon indeed. I've heard that despite the war Jews are getting approval for various emigration routes and that the German authorities have no objections as long as it's done via a neutral foreign country. Have you heard that too?[108]

By the time war broke out, however, emigration had become virtually impossible. Two earlier requests submitted by Rudolf to the South African Ministry of the Interior had been denied, a setback that Max blamed on Martha's incompetent paperwork. America was not an option as their only local relative and guarantor declared himself unable to cover the cost of their passage. Max's brother Alex seemed to have secured the family permits to join him in Shanghai, but Max and Martha had read negative newspaper reports and decided that this was not a good alternative. "We're becoming more and more willing to emigrate," they wrote in November 1939, "but where to?"[109]

Focus turned particularly to finding a destination for Hans. Australia had fallen through and the Scandinavian countries were a possibility, but the most viable option seemed to be Palestine. Max still had reservations about whether it was ideologically the right option, but in the meantime they would send Hans to prepare at a *hachsharah*, an agricultural training camp for prospective immigrants. Hans had also been taking English lessons and asked Rudolf curious questions about South African life.[110]

In October 1939, Rudolf sent his family the news that he was engaged to be married. "You can't imagine how difficult it is for me to take this important step in my life without you," he wrote. His fiancée, thirty-six-year-old Rachel Feinberg, was eight years his senior and had a seven-year-old son, Louis, from a previous marriage.

My fiancée is a very amiable and intelligent person and is even blessed with earthly goods. She comes from one of the best families in Pretoria and her father was highly respected and valued in the city. A very kind and unconventional character, with whom I expect to be very happy. As these are difficult times, we've decided to keep the wedding very quiet indeed and invite only a few of our closest relatives. . . . Last Sunday I met my future mother-in-law, a very refined elderly lady who went to school in Geneva and later studied at a music conservatory, and so she speaks perfect French. We get along very well.[111]

In a subsequent letter, Rudolf noted that Rachel's father was a military man, who even after his death remained greatly esteemed in Pretoria.[112]

War made correspondence more difficult. Worried letters from both sides trickled through every few months, and halting attempts were made to communicate via neutral countries such as Luxembourg and Sweden.[113] Rudolf became his parents' only promise of salvation, and as war spread across Europe, the letters he received were increasingly desperate. In December 1939, Max pleaded:

I hope you can understand my dear Rudi—because we're thinking of you and we love you so much—why we're hoping that through your connections with an established Pretorian family of good reputation it will be easier for you to arrange for us to emigrate and to come there, and for a speedy reunion with you and your loved ones. But this too is in G-d's hands, and those of the South African government in Pretoria! People are in fact still emigrating even now that the war has started; it's just a little more uncomfortable. For the last few months I've been longing to move far away.[114]

The family's pleas for help grew more desperate as the prospects grew bleaker. Panicky appeals were sent to all possible leads. Max begged for financial help from relatives abroad and from Rudolf himself.[115] In December 1940 Martha confessed:

For now I'll try to follow your recipe of waiting and hoping. It's not easy because the situation is so hopeless. Lately I've been re-reading your old letters; you preached to us and pushed us more than enough, but we just didn't understand. I'm especially sorry now for your little brother.[116]

The Jewish community in Hanau had by this point all but collapsed. In July 1940 the Jewish school was closed, and in September 1941 the community was banned from functioning altogether. A nightly curfew was imposed, and it became compulsory to wear a yellow star. The stubborn few Jews who remained in Hanau—by 1941, they numbered just twenty-eight—were forced violently into *Judenhäuser* (Jews' houses) in the center of town. In the winter of 1941–1942, Jewish men were put to forced labor, clearing the roads of ice and performing other strenuous work.[117]

Communication between the family members was now reduced to short messages delivered via the Red Cross. On 19 June 1940, Max sent Rudolf a typewritten note:

> We were very happy to hear your good news but ask with urgency that you work as hard as possible to secure an emigration permit for us. Things must move—now![118]

Almost a year later, he wrote:

> Entry permit extremely urgent. Alternatively American safe passage guarantee. We have no foreign currency.[119]

On 21 September 1941, a scrawled message revealed that the family had been forced into one of the "Jews' houses":

> Dear Rudi, we hope you are well. We are too. New address: 3 Nürnbergerstrasse [*sic*]. What about our entry permits? It's high time. Greetings for the New Year. Kisses, Max, Martha, Hans-Ferdinand.[120]

Nine days later, increasingly desperate, Max wrote:

> Dear Rudi, Nathan in New York turned us down after all. Will our eldest son continue to neglect his filial duty? Is Johannesburg possible? New address. Greetings.[121]

Rudolf, himself a newly arrived refugee struggling to find his feet on a new continent, was doing all in his power to help. He wrote persistently to immigration authorities in the United States and South Africa, to no avail.[122] In May 1940, the South African Red Cross Society noted cordially: "We do not ourselves feel that there is any likelihood of obtaining a permit under present conditions."[123] Attempts were made to get the family to Brazil, where Martha's brother-in-law Mor and niece Reny had found refuge.[124] In a letter to the UK immigration authorities, endorsed by an acquaintance in London, Rudolf even sought assistance for Hans in England:

I must beg your indulgence, if I ask you a big favour to-day. My only brother, a boy of 14, is still in Germany with my parents. I have been trying very hard to get him here, together with my parents. But as the opposition in this country has very strong feelings against the Jews, the South African government's hand is forced, and they can't allow as many refugees in, as they would perhaps like to. So, when I did not succeed in this endeavour, I tried to get permission for my brother to complete his education in England, sending over a garanty [*sic*] to pay £75 a year for this purpose.[125]

The fact that Hans was now an "enemy alien," however, made England a remote possibility.

With a growing sense of resignation, Rudolf expressed his frustration at his parents' earlier refusal to heed his warnings. In December 1939, he wrote:

If only you'd made a decision sooner when it was still possible!!! Now because of the war all emigration has been suspended except for those who got their permits before the war.[126]

A letter written in August 1940 was the closest that Rudolf ever came to holding Max responsible for the family's predicament:

My dear father, for years I have been predicting that the last train to leave Germany would be extremely full, so much so that getting a seat would be impossible. Now we're going to have to see if there's any way we can find another option for you.[127]

As war spread to the remote reaches of the Soviet Union in the winter of 1941–1942, the family's Red Cross postcards stopped mentioning emigration. In brief scribbled messages, they conveyed bland pleasantries suffused with grief. On 11 May 1942, Martha wrote:

Dear Rudi, we hope you're all well, we are too. We've heard nothing from you or from anyone abroad. We write every month. Always take care of your brother.[128]

Rudolf had not seen Hans for nine long years. Martha's message was a veiled cry of despair, a dying wish that even if she did not survive to look after her younger son, someone else would.

Deutsches Rotes Kreuz

Präsidium / Auslandsdienst

Berlin SW 61, Blücherplatz 2

20. MAI 1942 336727

ANTRAG

an die *Agence Centrale des Prisonniers de Guerre, Genf*
— Internationales Komitee vom Roten Kreuz —
auf Nachrichtenvermittlung

REQUÊTE

*de la Croix-Rouge Allemande, Présidence, Service Etranger
à l'Agence Centrale des Prisonniers de Guerre, Genève
— Comité International de la Croix-Rouge
concernant la correspondance*

1. Absender   *Martha Sara Schwab*
   Expéditeur   *Hanau, Nürnbergerstr. 3*

bittet, an

prie de bien vouloir faire parvenir à

2. Empfänger   *Rudolf Schwab*
   Destinataire   *Johannesburg S. A. U.*
   P. O. Box 740.

folgendes zu übermitteln / *ce qui suit:*

(Höchstzahl 25 Worte!)

(*mots au plus!*)

Lieber Rudi, hoffe Euch gesund, wir desgleichen, hören weder von Dir noch von den Anderen draußen. Schreiben jeden Monat. Kümmere Dich stets um Deinen Bruder.

(Datum / *date*)   *11. Mai 1942*

3. Empfänger antwortet umseitig
   Destinataire répond au verso

Red Cross message from Martha to Rudolf, 11 May 1942. Courtesy of Yad Vashem.

It was the last postcard Rudolf ever received from his family. To a friend in Sweden he lamented:

Ever since I have been here [in South Africa], I have begged my parents to try and come out, while there was still a reasonable chance, but my father held too optimistic a view about the whole situation and so missed the famous last boat. I still have not given up hope that a chance might turn up soon. In the meantime, we can only wait and hope for the best.[129]

2

Dispersal

It's very sad that we, all those who are still alive, are dispersed across the entire world, isn't it? But better that than the alternative.

Rosa Schwab in France to her nephew
Rudolf in Johannesburg, March 1953

By the war's end, only a handful of members of the extended Schwab family remained alive. Dispersed across five continents, they typified the fates of countless Jewish refugees who ended up in the most unlikely places. History would come to regard these refugees as the lucky ones, the prescient ones, the ones who saw the writing on the wall and escaped with their lives. (Their stories would also often cease to hold interest at the point where they escaped mortal danger.) But many of these refugees also felt a deep ambivalence about their choices, which were both bold and by no means the obvious ones to make. Unlike their family and friends they were not subjected to camps, cattle cars, or forced labor, but the effects of their victimhood did not disappear when they arrived at safe destinations. In most cases, they were only just beginning.[1]

The German Jewish refugees' fates diverged widely. They wound up in far-flung places with vastly differing prospects and means of support, thanks mostly to chance rather than design. Some were able to establish successful careers and families, and a few—well-known scientists, intellectuals, musicians, writers— became visible symbols of the cultural devastation inflicted upon Germany by the Nazis.[2] But many refugees did not prosper in exile. Some languished in poverty and illness; some committed suicide. Most hoped simply to get by. Vast numbers continued to suffer the burdens of hardship, loss, and displacement long after the war had ended.

Refugees faced physical as well as spiritual exile. On the practical level, they faced the challenge of reforging an entire existence: finding a country that would take them, a safe place to live there, enough money to keep themselves and their families alive. They also faced the infinitely more prolonged process of creating a new identity in a new language, in unfamiliar places, among unknown people and cultures. How many adapted successfully? How can this even be measured? Surely not simply according to the figures of refugee agencies, who compiled data about jobs attained and permanent addresses secured. Far more interesting, and yet far more difficult to quantify and to square with our desires for happy endings, are the refugees' ongoing struggles to rebuild their sense of self, belonging, and history.

In the years following the war, the letters of the surviving Schwab relatives criss-crossed the globe, from Europe to China, Latin America to Canada, South Africa to the United States. Rudolf arrived in South Africa in late 1936 after being expelled first from Belgium and then Holland. His uncle Alex, Max's brother, a decorated war veteran and businessman, endured ten destitute years in Shanghai before ending up in a studio apartment in St. Paul, Minnesota, where he earned a living as a janitor. Max's sister Rosa wound up in France, where despite support from the local Protestant community she deteriorated into decrepitude and insanity. Beloved cousin Reny made it to São Paulo, but not before the collapse of her health and her marriage. Cousin Armand eventually surfaced in Montreal, where he had been unexpectedly deported following several months in a British transit camp. Most of the relatives never saw one another in person again.

The conversations that unfolded in the family's letters were made up mostly of unremarkable details about work and home and the humdrum of daily life. And yet for all that their stories have been eclipsed by those of the well-known exiles, with their high-profile accomplishments, their rich philosophical reflections, and their influence on culture and politics, the lives of such ordinary refugees have a different and no less significant story to tell. It is they, after all, who constituted the vast majority of exiles from Germany. It is also their experiences that echo those of countless millions who since 1945 have faced similar challenges.

When I began reading the family's letters, I was already acquainted with the research on German Jewish refugees in the United States, Britain, Latin America, and other more and less exotic locations. Some of what I knew was confirmed in the descriptions I now read by Rudolf's relatives: the struggle to adapt to new cultures and climates, to make ends meet, to learn new languages, to find jobs and friends. To this familiar story Rudolf's family members added colorful details and nuances of their own.

But beyond the concrete challenges of daily existence lay something more profound. As I worked my way through the letters, following the slow progress of years and decades in exile, I realized that the transnational web of connections they traced also offered unexpected insight into the process through which uprooted people make sense of and reconstruct their identities.[3] The bonds that developed between the surviving Schwabs were intangible, defined by the ebb and flow of letters, postcards, gifts, holiday greetings, and only very occasionally people themselves. A humble letter would begin its life in Cannes and have several pages added in Shanghai before being shared among relatives in Montreal. Multiple drafts of reparations claims zoomed back and forth between New York, Johannesburg, and São Paulo, acquiring snippets of family news and commentary along the way. Across continents, younger cousins argued about how to support their parents' surviving siblings abroad. Privately, the relatives implored one another to help this or that struggling family member, and reminisced about happier times spent together in the *Heimat*.

Where do these ordinary refugees' stories fit into our understanding of the Holocaust? On the face of it, at least, they have little new to tell us about the events themselves. By the time I finished reading the letters, however, it became clear to me that they hold a multi-layered significance. The victims of the Holocaust included not only those who were killed, or even those who survived camps or ghettos or life in hiding, but also those who made it out of Nazi Europe physically intact. Well-meaning interviewers might applaud their efforts to start anew, to build families, to remake their lives, but in doing so they unintentionally overlook their ongoing suffering. The letters are proof that victimhood is a broad category, and that though it might be tempting, survival should never be romanticized.

The successful and high-flying exiles so prominent in our history books represent only a tiny minority of Jewish exiles from Nazi Germany. The refugees were a diverse group, even if their new host countries tarred them with the same brush. And even if their lives were for the most part unglamorous, or precisely because they were unglamorous, their voices and experiences need to be restored to the historical account, in part as a way of countering the Nazis' attempts to dehumanize them.[4] This is a critically important task, not least because the refugees represent—alongside the millions of murdered victims themselves—one of the Holocaust's most enduring legacies.

Rudolf fled Germany in May 1933 to what he hoped was temporary exile in Antwerp, in neighboring Belgium. Like many other Jews he had not strayed far, so that he could easily return to Germany once the regime had been toppled.[5] Despite his concerted efforts and the help of family friends he was unable to secure a work permit, and a move to Brussels in September yielded similarly disappointing results.[6] Many years later he confessed to a friend:

> How grateful I am to the Belgian government for kicking me out in good time. Back then I thought it was the end of the world, but it turned out to be an enormous stroke of good fortune.[7]

Rudolf next found refuge in Werkdorp Nieuwesluis, an agricultural and vocational training farm that had been founded in early 1934 in the Zuiderzee district of Holland for the purpose of equipping German Jews for re-emigration.[8] Here Rudolf learned to dig foundations, mix concrete and mortar, and lay bricks. Ignoring his family's gibes about his lowly vocational pursuits, he also spent his evenings and weekends studying building engineering so as to increase his chances of finding employment wherever fate abandoned him next.[9] In the spring of 1936, as Berlin began its preparations to host the summer Olympics, Rudolf was forced to leave Holland. He was among tens of thousands of refugees confronting stony-faced and unyielding immigration officers everywhere.

Unlike Rudolf, most Jews did not leave Germany in the months following Hitler's rise to power. The immediate flurry into exile was limited mostly to political opponents of the regime (some Jewish but mostly not), and the pace of emigration slowed in 1934 and 1935, apart from a temporary upsurge after the passing of the Nuremberg Laws. Despite growing restrictions on Jewish lives and livelihoods, it was only after the *Anschluss* of Austria and *Kristallnacht* in 1938 that numbers of emigrants began to increase substantially, by which time much of the world was no longer willing to take them.[10]

After weighing up his options in 1936, twenty-four-year-old Rudolf decided that South Africa offered the most viable prospects. He knew almost nothing about the country, and his family joked about arranging marriages with the daughters of local chieftains in order to secure immigration permits. In later years Rudolf would assure them that Africa was quite civilized and its inhabitants just as industrious and successful as anywhere else. Now, however, he ventured into the unknown for lack of other practicable alternatives.[11]

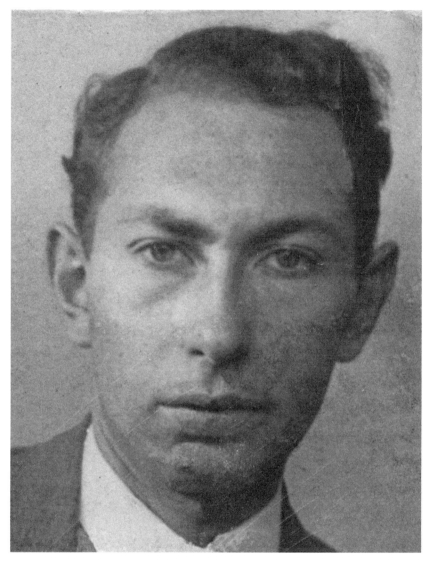

Rudolf Schwab, c. 1936. Courtesy of Yad Vashem.

Rudolf set sail for Cape Town from Southampton aboard a ship called the Balmoral Castle in the spring of 1936. His fellow "alien passengers" (as they were designated by the shipping line) were mostly, like him, single men in their twenties and thirties who had no intention of returning to Europe. Not all were Jews, but among them were several Sznajders, a Rubenstein, and two dozen others listing their last address as 63 Mansell Street E1, home of the Jews' Temporary

Balmoral Castle passenger list showing Rudolf Schwab, April 1936. Courtesy of The National Archives, BT 27/1461.

Shelter in London.[12] The Shelter had over the previous half-century provided refuge to tens of thousands of Jews making their way from the Old World to the New. Now, it was deluged by the exodus from Nazi Germany. Writing from his first station of exile in 1937, the Austrian Jewish writer Stefan Zweig extolled the "House that gives to wandering Jews—and how many must wander—rest for their wearied bodies and solace for their souls, a House that provides them with respite for a few days, and then assists them further on their road from strange land to strange land."[13] During his brief stay in London, Rudolf was helped by a sympathetic young woman named Iris Braby, with whom he continued to correspond for many years after his arrival in South Africa.

From London, Rudolf made his way to the port of Southampton, home of the Union-Castle line. For young bachelors like him the ship journey was an adventure, despite the uncertain future to which it was leading. Rudolf's first letters, written during his long voyage south, showed him to be in "good spirits."[14] Shortly after the ship docked he described to his parents his enchantment upon first viewing the shore of his new homeland:

> It was like a tale from 1001 Nights when, after two weeks at sea during which we hadn't seen even a tiny scrap of land, the lights of Cape Town finally appeared in front of us early one morning. A little while later when the sunlight began to shine across that incredibly beautiful landscape, it was a truly awesome sight.[15]

By lucky chance, Rudolf had arrived on one of the last ships to bring Jewish refugees to South Africa. The country he entered was in the throes of its own political and racial wars, not least of which was a virulent antisemitism directed at the refugees themselves. Within just a few months the ruling United Party, bowing to pressure from the Afrikaner nationalist right, would tighten its immigration laws. Jewish organizations scrambled to bring in as many people as possible before the 1 November 1936 deadline, a move that served only to intensify opposition. After the passage of the Aliens Act in February 1937, immigration permits were generally granted only to relatives of refugees who had become lawful residents (a status that Rudolf was not to achieve until a decade later).[16]

New arrivals like Rudolf were immediately confronted with the dual challenge of navigating South Africa's precarious political waters while also working to build a stable existence. Like other refugees dispersed across the globe, they began with little. Despite their educated, middle-class backgrounds they lived in overcrowded districts, scraping together a living doing menial work. Those lucky few who had rescued possessions from Europe crammed their tiny flats with Biedermeier furniture and grand pianos, which they were often forced to sell for subsistence. In time they moved to better neighborhoods and acquired skilled jobs or started small businesses. In the words of one contemporary observer, "They exhibited qualities which made for good citizenship: they were hardworking, conscientious, reliable." They also gradually founded welfare organizations that offered support to fellow refugees, from employment advice and housing to financial aid. They established their own German Jewish religious congregations and ran cultural forums where they enjoyed German literature and music. Most learned to speak English fluently but socialized among themselves, shopped at German shops, and ate *Sauerkraut* and *Leberwurst* at home.[17]

Soon after his arrival in Cape Town, almost penniless, Rudolf moved to the larger economic center of Johannesburg to look for work. He struggled to find a job despite his earlier efforts to acquire training, and only after several months was he employed as an assistant construction worker, his first paid job in almost three and a half years. When he found himself unemployed again in 1938, with little to fall back on apart from entrepreneurial spirit, he started his own construction business. Whatever he managed to scrape together during those years, it was not enough to warrant an income tax return until 1943.[18] In 1945, his ability to secure regular business was again hampered by the reintegration into the economy of workers who had been involved in the war effort.

Despite his cheerful assurances to family and friends back in Germany, it was almost two decades before Rudolf was earning a regular income.[19] Twelve years after his arrival he wrote to a friend:

> The cost of living here is incredibly high. Here are a few examples: for more than a year I've needed new underwear, suits and bed linen but have been unable to afford them because I simply don't have the money. . . . Furthermore, I was totally unfamiliar with the language, the climate and the general living conditions, and I've had to train myself in a new profession of which I hadn't the slightest notion when I was back in Germany. It hasn't been easy and has cost me a lot in terms of my nerves and health.

"Naturally," Rudolf hastened to add,

> I'm very happy now that things have worked out this way, as even if I weren't a Jew the last ten years in Europe (and not just in Germany) wouldn't exactly have been a bed of roses for me.[20]

As he struggled to re-find the footholds of his own existence, Rudolf was acutely aware of how much worse things were for those left behind. In the autumn of 1941 he learned that his parents and brother had been forced to move into one of the Hanau *Judenhäuser* (Jews' houses) on Nürnberger Strasse 3, the building that had formerly housed the Jewish community center. In late 1941 Max was arrested for the second time along with his "Aryan" neighbor and innkeeper Mr. Valentin Schilling, from whom he had regularly been purchasing wine for *Shabbat* and Jewish festivals. In January 1942, after five weeks in prison, Schilling was released and Max was taken by the local Gestapo to Breitenau, south of Kassel, where a so-called "educational labor camp" had been established in summer 1940.[21]

Max was held at Breitenau for a month, and from there was taken on 2 February 1942 to the Sachsenhausen concentration camp near Berlin, one of the largest in the Nazi camp system. Jewish prisoners were housed in a cordoned-off section of Sachsenhausen known in euphemistic Nazi terms as the *Sonderlager* (special camp), where they were subjected to a harsh daily work routine and brutal treatment. On 19 February, barely three weeks after his arrival, at just after three o'clock in the afternoon, Max Schwab, prisoner number 041042, died of "a weak heart," two days before his sixty-fourth birthday.[22]

Rudolf first learned of his father's fate in a message from his mother sent via the Red Cross in March 1942. Summing up within her allotted twenty-five words the disintegration of her life, Martha wrote to him:

> Long time without message from you. Hope everyone well. Same for me, Hans. Granny also, in Cologne, alone, old-age home. Father taken from us, died of weak heart 19.II. Warmest greetings.[23]

According to a neighbor, the note informing Martha of Max's death did not even mention the name of the camp where he had died.[24] Despite the difficulties of wartime communication the news traveled quickly, and, in the weeks following, anguished responses reached Rudolf from Stockholm, France, and Shanghai.

Martha sent three more short cards to Rudolf in April and May 1942. Then, everything fell silent. Rudolf could do little more than monitor the progress of Hitler's armies in the East and brace himself for the worst. For six months, he heard nothing. Then, on 16 November 1942, he received a letter from Sal Fürth, a family friend in neutral Sweden, handwritten on a single sheet of delicate airmail paper:

> The terrible plight of the Jews in Germany has touched your family too. As an old friend of your father's I feel obliged to write to let you know what has happened. Having not heard from your father for a long time I wrote to a lady in Frankfurt, who used to see and speak to him quite often, to inquire about his well-being. I received her reply on 16 April saying that he was very ill but with no further details. Then I sent a letter to him in Hanau but that went unanswered. Then on 5 June

Nr. 350.

Oranienburg, den 21. Februar 194[

D er Kaufmann Max, Israel S c h w a b - - - - -

- - - - - - - - - - - - - - -, mosaisch - - - - - - - -,

wohnhaft in Hanau am Main, Nürnberger Straße 3 - - - - -,

ist am 19. Februar 1942 - - - - um 15 - - Uhr 10 - - Minuten

in Oranienburg im Lager Sachsenhausen - - - - - verstorben.

D er Verstorbene war geboren am 21. Februar 1878 - - - - -

in Hanau am Main. - - - - - - - - - - - - - - - - - - -

(Standesamt - - - - - - - - - - - - - - - - Nr. - - - - - -)

Vater: Samuel Schwab, letzter Wohnort unbekannt. - --

- -

Mutter: Ricla Schwab, Geburtsname unbekannt, letzter --

Wohnort unbekannt. - - - - - - - - - - - - - - - - - - -

D er Verstorbene war — war — verheiratet mit Martha, Sara - --

Schwab geborenen Hausmann, wohnhaft in Hanau am Main. -

- -

Eingetragen auf mündliche — schriftliche — Anzeige des Lagerkomman-

danten des Lagers Sachsenhausen in Oranienburg. - - - -

D   Anzeigende - - - - - - - - - - - - - - - - - - -

- -

- -

Vorgelesen, genehmigt und - - - unterschrie[

- -

- -

Die Übereinstimmung mit dem
Erstbuch wird beglaubigt.

Oranienburg, den 21.2. 19 42.

Der Standesbeamte
In Vertretung:

Kempfer

Der Standesbeamte
In Vertretung: Kempfer

Todesursache: Herzschwäche.
Grundleiden: Chronische Enteritis und Gastritis.

Eheschließung de Verstorbenen am in

(Standesamt Nr.).

Max Schwab's death certificate from Sachsenhausen. Courtesy of Stadtarchiv Hanau.

Deutsches Rotes Kreuz
Präsidium / Auslandsdienst
Berlin SW 61, Blücherplatz 2

12 MRZ 1942 ★ 277870

(734)

ANTRAG
an die *Agence Centrale des Prisonniers de Guerre, Genf*
— Internationales Komitee vom Roten Kreuz —
auf Nachrichtenvermittlung

REQUÊTE
de la *Croix-Rouge Allemande, Présidence, Service Etranger*
à *l'Agence Centrale des Prisonniers de Guerre, Genève*
— Comité International de la Croix-Rouge
concernant la correspondance

1. **Absender** *Martha Sara Schwab*
   Expéditeur *Hanau a/M. Nürnbergerstr. 3*

   bittet, an
   prie de bien vouloir faire parvenir à

2. **Empfänger** *Rudolf Schwab*
   Destinataire *Johannesburg S.A.U.*
   P. O. Bose 740

folgendes zu übermitteln / *ce qui suit:*

(Höchstzahl 25 Worte!)
(...ts au plus!)

Lieber Rudi! Lange ohne Deine Nachricht hoffe Alle gesund. Desgleichen Hans, ich auch Oma, Köln allein Altersheim. Vater fern von uns an Herzschwäche 19.II. verschieden. Herzlichste Grüsse

10 AVR 1942

(Datum / date) *9. März 1942.*

Martha Sara Schwab
(Unterschrift / Signature)

3. **Empfänger antwortet umseitig**
   Destinataire répond au verso

Red Cross message from Martha to Rudolf, 9 March 1942. Courtesy of Yad Vashem.

1942, I received a postcard from your mother that contained the following tragic news: "News of our great misfortune must have reached you via your acquaintance in Frankfurt and I can't tell you how much I've missed your letters, especially now. A new era is beginning for us. We travel tomorrow! We've been living at 3 Nürnbergerstrasse [*sic*] since October 1941. My husband, may his memory be a blessing, whom you have always been willing to help, wanted to be buried in the cemetery here but unfortunately we were unable to fulfill his wishes. His urn was buried in Frankfurt."[25]

Three loaded words, *Wir reisen morgen!*, underlined in Martha's letter to Sal, were now the only clue Rudolf had as to his mother's and brother's fate. They had been deported in late May 1942 to an unknown destination. As the war continued to rage deeper into the Soviet Union, he also lost touch with his relatives in exile and could do little more than wait.[26]

In the meantime, Rudolf continued the work of rebuilding his life, navigating immense loss on the one hand and tentative new beginnings on the other. In September 1942, just a few weeks before the arrival of Sal's letter, his wife Rachel gave birth to their son, Norman.

In early 1945, as the war neared its end, Rudolf embarked upon the search for surviving relatives. He sent letters to their last known addresses to local Jewish organizations, to the Tracing Bureau, and to the Red Cross. The first sign of life arrived in April 1946 from his first cousin Armand Demuth, son of Max's sister Helene. In eight pages crammed with tiny script, Armand recounted what had happened to him and the little he knew about his relatives' fates.

> I don't want to recall offhand all the sufferings of our fallen back home. I haven't heard anything from them since 1941 or 1942.... However, as I learned from uncle Alex, whose address is: 66 AN KWO LV (formerly Alex Road) SHANGHAI and who wrote me the other day (by the way that touched me very much indeed) says [*sic*]: "Auntie Rosa and Uncle Siegfried have been found living in Southern France." About our other folks, your mother, Hans Ferdinand etc. I am sorry to say he does not mention anything. I am, however, anxious to know who you know about over there, no matter who it is, please let me know immediately!

Armand then turned to his own circuitous story. After *Kristallnacht* he had been interned in Dachau, "the notorious Camp of the Nazi-Bastards." Upon his release he was taken directly to England, to a transit camp that the British Council of German Jewry was able to establish in the atmosphere of increased public sympathy following the pogroms. The Kitchener camp was located on the edge of the medieval town of Sandwich, and during 1939 it received around 4,000 Jewish refugees from Germany and Austria, most of them young, single men. Armand had been living at Kitchener for several months when war broke out in September 1939.[27]

> We were in the war zone and more than once we had to take shelter during the air raids. We saw, generally speaking, a lot of the war, and if I recall those times, I start shivering! Time passed quickly and as we were regarded by "Tribunal" as "friendly enemy aliens," we were at liberty until the general round up of all aliens in Great Britain. This was so far alright. However as you will have read in the papers at that time, the danger of invasion became so acute, that the Home Office, by some mistake as we were later told, gave the order to close our camp and we were interned with all the personal hardships you can get.

The sudden fall of France in the early summer of 1940 caused panic about foreigners in Britain, particularly Germans, and the Kitchener camp was hastily shut down. Some of the Jewish refugees were moved to makeshift army camps a distance away, while others were taken to the Isle of Man, where internment camps were prepared in requisitioned hotels and houses.[28] The men felt "like birds in a cage," reported Armand. In July his group was placed on board the Polish troopship *Sobieski*, where they spent several days at sea heading toward an unknown destination.

When the refugees eventually reached the shores of Canada, they were transported to an internment camp at Île-aux-Noix. Here they were detained for three years, although in Armand's estimation "it was not bad at all." The group was eventually deemed "harmless" and released, initially on strict parole, and later under the looser supervision of the immigration authorities. Extraordinarily, after almost five years of imprisonment and surveillance, the German Jewish deportees became eligible for Canadian citizenship. "Isn't that something?" Armand enthused. "A couple of boys already have their papers and are Canadians! Many served with the armed forces. In other words everything was mixed up and now it turned out alright!" Armand settled in Montreal, where he worked variously in a hospital, a grocery store, and a shipyard. He was content with his lot and composed his letters to Rudolf in his newly acquired English.[29]

A few months later, Rudolf heard from his uncle Alex in Shanghai. Alex wrote:

> Although I haven't yet heard anything from you I assume you and your family are doing well; I too am in good health. We suffered a lot here during the Japanese occupation; we were locked in a ghetto and had other serious difficulties over and above that. . . . I haven't heard anything from our loved ones except for Rosa, Siegfried and Armand, and I've no idea what became of the others. I received a message from Max Heymann, he told me Louis and Erna died in Theresienstadt. It's awful what that Hitler and his gang have done and we should be glad we got out of that hell. . . . We receive food parcels every now and then from UNRRA [United Nations Relief and Rehabilitation Administration] and I'm now working in a small cleaning job for two hours a day. The pay is of course very low and the cost of living very high; making ends meet is extremely difficult.[30]

The youngest of the five Schwab siblings, Alex had fled to China after his experience of four weeks' internment in Buchenwald after *Kristallnacht*.[31] Shanghai was no paradise, he wrote, but how many other options were left?

Alex was not alone. Around seventeen thousand German and Austrian Jews fled to Shanghai out of desperation between 1938 and 1941, drawn solely by the fact that one did not require a visa to enter. (In fact, this was not strictly true: the practice of passport control in the port city had simply been allowed to lapse in the face of internal political tensions, and refugees were able to take advantage of the arbitrary enforcement of visa requirements.)[32]

The historian Walter Laqueur has described Shanghai not so much as a shelter as "a dubious waiting room with few facilities."[33] By 1938 the city was a derelict crime capital. The eruption of the Sino-Japanese war the previous year had brought heavy fighting to parts of the city as well as a flood of homeless Chinese refugees, and local businesses were debilitated by soaring inflation. When thousands of European Jews began to arrive in 1938, the Shanghai Municipal Council refused to support them, and urged Jewish organizations to prevent them from coming. The newly established Committee for the Assistance of European Jewish Refugees in Shanghai, financed by the American Jewish Joint Distribution Committee, established soup kitchens and basic dormitory facilities, the so-called *Heime* (homes), mostly in the overcrowded Hongkou district of the city.[34]

German Jewish refugees observe a Chinese wedding procession in Shanghai. United States Holocaust Memorial Museum (25770), courtesy of Walter Jacobsberg.

Enterprising younger refugees found ways of earning money, but the vast majority, including Alex Schwab, were unable to find even menial work and depended on help from relatives or aid agencies. Little could be done to alleviate the chronic food shortages. The sheer foreignness of Shanghai, from the subtropical climate to the raucous street life, food vendors, and rickshaw drivers, made the smallest aspects of daily life a challenge. The harsh conditions quickly depleted the European refugees' unaccustomed bodies and eroded their self-esteem.

Along with his "comrades" in the Jewish Home on Kinchow Road, Alex lived in miserable conditions for the duration of the war. His bank accounts and luggage had been confiscated by the Gestapo in Bremen before he had even reached China's shores. He repeatedly and ashamedly begged his nephew

Rudolf in South Africa for help. His already dire circumstances deteriorated in the spring of 1943 when the Japanese restricted "stateless refugees"—a clear reference to Jews—to the ghetto at Hongkou. Overcrowding worsened and permission was required to leave and enter the ghetto, imperiling livelihoods even further. For two years, until the armistice, Alex was able to send Rudolf only one brief message: a Red Cross telegram notifying him of Max's death.[35]

The end of the war brought little relief. Possibilities for leaving were virtually non-existent, and most Jewish refugees continued to live in shelters and rely on aid. Living now in the Jewish Home on Alcock Road, Alex worked as a house cleaner, subsisted on UN food rations, and was hospitalized three times for malnutrition. His far-flung relatives, themselves struggling to make ends meet, could do little to ease his poverty-stricken existence. The following year he obtained a job as a *shammes* (overseer) at a local synagogue and began learning English in the hope of immigrating to the United States.[36] In October 1947 he wrote to Rudolf:

> The Holidays will soon be over so I've lots to do in my role as shammes; absolutely everything requires my involvement. I wish you and your family every imaginable good fortune for the New Year. The summer is fading now and it's raining again every day. I received your parcel a few days ago, a shirt and an overcoat, they're very handsome and I'm extremely pleased with them. My sincere thanks to you and Gustav. I have a decent life here now; one can get used to anything. We've planted vegetables, beans, etc., around our barracks. We go to bed early in the evenings and rise early in the mornings with the chickens. I cook most of my food myself on a gas stove and there's always work to do. I've been in Shanghai for eight years now and don't know what's left in Germany or how things are there; of course we read all sorts of things in the newspapers. The Chinese have more or less become used to us and they do business with the immigrants, a country just like any other.[37]

In July 1948, now aged fifty-nine, Alex was finally able to immigrate to the United States, the destination of the majority of Shanghai refugees.[38] His unlikely final haven was St. Paul, Minnesota, where he found rented accommodation in a Jewish neighborhood. Eighteen months after his arrival he wrote to Rudolf in his cautious English:

> I am going to tell you how I spend my day. In the morning I have my breakfast at 7 o'clock, then I catch the streetcar and then go to work. I

have to work very hard as janitor and I don't get very much money for that kind of work, I am getting only enough to pay for my meals and room. Perhaps I would appreciate when you could help me out to meet my expenses. In Saint Paul we still have much snow cold and slippery streets. We are longing for the glorious spring, when the sun will shine, but the winter still asserts his power. I am going twice a week to the international School to learn English. We have an excellent teacher.[39]

Alex endured growing hardships and ill health. He continued to struggle with English and to rely financially on relatives. He nonetheless proudly informed Rudolf when he was granted US citizenship in January 1954, and Rudolf praised his uncle's strength in building a life for himself in a foreign land. But Rudolf's encouraging words belied his pity for the fate of this once robust, accomplished individual, son of an esteemed Hanau family, frontline soldier and recipient of the Honour Cross. Alex died in March 1961 at the age of seventy-two, with few to attend his funeral.[40]

The fate of Alex and Max's sister, Rosa, was even unhappier. Rosa and her husband, Siegfried Tuteur, were deported in October 1940 from Mannheim to the internment camp Gurs, located in the foothills of the Pyrenees in southwest France. Originally established to hold political refugees fleeing the Spanish Civil War, Gurs came under the control of the collaborationist Vichy regime in June 1940, after the French armistice with Germany.[41]

Sizeable numbers of the German Jewish deportees who arrived at the camp that winter were released shortly after internment, or allowed to emigrate. But life outside the camp was not without its perils. The Tuteurs landed in the village of Clairac 130 miles inland from Gurs, where they survived the war years in extreme poverty and isolation. Unable to speak French, homesick for Germany, and cut off from family, Rosa retreated into depression. The Tuteurs received assistance from a certain Pastor Loup of the local Free Evangelical Church, who occasionally provided them with food and clothing.[42]

By the time Rosa established contact with Rudolf in May 1946, their situation was desperate:

Five years ago I received a Red Cross letter from you, which I answered, but then nothing more. Got your address from your late father (may his memory be a blessing) and from our nephew Edgar Tuteur (from the United States) and already wrote to you three times, unfortunately

Alex Schwab, St Paul (1949). Courtesy of Yad Vashem.

you haven't replied yet. He is such a good person and takes good care
of us. . . . But he can't do everything on his own and you, my dear Rudi,
must do something to help me too. I might be your only aunt and relative who's still alive. Have you heard anything from your dear mother
and your brother Hans? I don't know where they all ended up. The last
I heard from Erna was from Theresienstadt on 8 March 1942. . . . So,
dear Rudi, I need clothes, underwear and shoes, size 38, slippers. I'm
now 64 and Ticka turns 81 in July. . . . You used to like your Aunt Rosa

Rosa (right) and Siegfried Tuteur. Courtesy of Yad Vashem.

a lot when I came to visit Hanau, didn't you, and I liked you too my dear Rudi. Now that I'm in need you have to help me. We don't have any dollars. We can't go back to Germany, because, as you'll have read, everything there has been destroyed in Mannheim there's not a single house standing anymore, we don't have a home anymore. I'm not as familiar with the French language as German, which I love, my home. I heard from our dear Alex in Shanghai, he's also doing reasonably well, he doesn't have a dollar to his name and he never received his clothes, underwear, suitcases and boxes.... The Nazi dogs stole everything, took everything from us, our gold, clothes and money. If you can, collect some things together for your relatives we are deportees.... Your mother wanted to go to Johannesburg for such a long time, maybe she's there with you and your brother Hans, I would be very glad if that were so. So, my dear Rudi, answer the letter from Edgar Tuteur and prove that you really are my nephew. We don't get butter or margarine here and very little bread. Send food parcels.[43]

In letter after letter, in jumbled and illegible prose, Rosa described their struggles: hunger, cold, illness, lack of clothes. Her teeth were falling out and her hair had turned white from stress.[44] She declared to Rudolf:

> Despite all this I want to go back to Germany, I don't feel very happy here, I didn't grow up with French. . . . At night we have lots of fleas in our bed and that's very unpleasant and we sleep poorly. . . . For the last 5 years I've had only 1 bed sheet and cushion, completely worn out from frequent washing.[45]

Within a few years, as it became clear that salvation was nowhere in sight, Rosa began to direct her anger at those around her. She bombarded Rudolf with complaints that he was selfish and lazy, didn't write often enough, and neglected his stricken relatives.[46]

Rosa and Siegfried followed Pastor Loup to a small village near Cannes when he relocated there in 1946, but they found themselves even more isolated than they had been in Clairac. Rosa's emotional deterioration was swift. Her writing became incoherent, and she was unable to comprehend even simple questions. She accused neighbors and caregivers of trying to swindle or poison her. Siegfried attached short messages to her letters apologizing for her overwrought state. His presence was clearly the only point of stability in her fragile existence, but his health was also deteriorating.[47] After visiting the Tuteurs in June 1956, the German consul in France reported to Pastor Loup that they were

> in an utterly pitiful state. Mr. Siegfried Tuteur has reached the age of 89 years, he's deaf, and—I have to say—has regressed to infancy. His wife is also completely deaf and gives the impression of being not quite normal.[48]

Siegfried's death in December 1957, on Rosa's birthday no less, was the final blow. Edgar Tuteur, Siegfried's New York–based nephew who had for many years been assisting them, arranged to have her transferred to an old-age home back in Germany.[49] In advance of what must have seemed an unthinkable move for her, he insisted:

> You say you want to bring any of Uncle Dicker's clothing that's still good or new with you. Please do not do that. Throw it all away, or sell it and ask Aunt Rol to help you. Please, do not dare to take old clothes with you. They'll put you in an insane asylum instead of a respectable

home for the elderly because they'll think you're not in your right mind. What do you need all those things for? You also want to take your old torn bed clothes with you. You're not allowed to do that. They must all be in tatters by now if they came with you from Mannheim . . . you left Mannheim 17 years ago! Even if they aren't in tatters, throw them all away. You can buy everything new in Germany; there are no shortages. The world has gone back to normal, just as it was 30 years ago. Perhaps you can't understand that because you've been cut off from the world for so long.[50]

After lengthy discussion with the Jewish community in Mannheim, and despite Rosa's loud remonstrations, Edgar arranged for her to be accommodated at a home in Heidelberg. She moved in on 1 July 1958.[51]

Rosa returned to her homeland physically and emotionally broken. She soon barely recognized her relatives, and she lashed out at the Jewish community workers who tried to help her. No one escaped her suspicion. She died in Heidelberg in March 1967, aged eighty-five.[52]

Rudolf reconnected with various other relatives in the postwar years. In Antwerp, his elderly distant uncle Phillippe Marx was haunted by the death of his daughter Berthe and her young family in Auschwitz, and the obliteration of virtually all of Antwerp's Jewish community. He had recently become a widower, and he described to Rudi his struggles with illness and malnutrition due to shortages of food, coal, and medical supplies.[53] Rudolf also quickly established a warm correspondence with his cousin Reny, who had escaped to São Paulo, where she divorced her first husband and married a fellow German Jewish refugee she had known in Frankfurt. They lived a comfortable life in Brazil, despite Reny's debilitating rheumatism.[54]

By the late 1940s, Rudolf had still not ascertained his mother's and brother's fates following their deportation in the spring of 1942. Even before the war had ended he was fairly certain that they had not survived. In February 1945 he wrote to Armand in English:

I have given up all hope of ever hearing from any of them again. I know this all sounds very callous, but if you think too much about it, it will only lead to the mental home.[55]

Through 1945 and 1946 he informed various relatives and friends about his family's fate, repeating that they had been deported to Poland and that he did not expect they would come back. By early 1947 he had learned that his aunt Alice, her husband Oskar, and their daughter, his cousin Lotte, had been deported sometime in 1941 or 1942 to Litzmannstadt, the Nazi ghetto in Łódź, Poland. They had not been heard from again. Later, Rudolf discovered that his grandmother, Martha's seventy-nine-year-old mother, Johanna, had been deported along with 20,000 German and Austrian Jews to the Latvian city of Riga in December 1941. Almost half the deportees were never admitted to the ghetto that had been established there just a few months before; the sick and elderly, among them presumably Johanna, were taken directly from the railway station and shot. Max's sister Erna and her husband, Louis, were deported to Poland on 24 September 1942.[56]

Rudolf continued to seek information about his family via the International Tracing Service (ITS) and other channels, and placed advertisements in local Hanau and Frankfurt newspapers in January 1948 asking anyone who knew anything to come forward.[57] The information he received was patchy and often unreliable. In late 1949 and 1950, correspondence from the ITS informed him that his mother had been deported to Auschwitz-Birkenau via the ghetto in Częstochowa, and that his brother had been deported on a different transport to an unknown destination. Both points would later be proven incorrect. In September 1948, Rudolf received a letter from Dr. O. Eisenberg, a Hanau lawyer whom Martha had visited three days before her deportation. Afraid that she would not return, Martha had come to deposit some family papers: Max's prized eighteenth-century document confirming the family's status in Hanau, his historical research, and his work on the family tree. The papers had been destroyed in an air raid, and Dr. Eisenberg had never heard from Martha again. The only consistent information Rudolf had was that the family's last known address was Nürnberger Strasse 3, Hanau, the site of the former Jewish community center turned *Judenhaus* (Jews' house), and that Martha and Hans were deported to Poland on 30 May 1942. No further information was available.[58]

It is not clear when Rudolf discovered the details of what happened to his fifty-three-year-old mother and seventeen-year-old brother when they were deported. It is possible that he never did. Rudolf's further inquiries to the ITS in the late 1950s yielded the same frustratingly inconclusive results he had earlier received.[59]

Decades later, historians researching the fate of Hanau Jewry confirmed that two transports had taken Jews from the region in the spring and early autumn of 1942. On 30 May, a sunny Saturday, eighty-four Jews boarded a train at Platform 9 of Hanau's *Hauptbahnhof*. Despite the weather, they brought with them overcoats, furs, and other warm clothing that they might need in the "East."

Deportation from Hanau's central train station, 30 May 1942. Courtesy of Yad Vashem.

Their remaining personal possessions, which they had been asked to itemize on forms in the preceding days, were left behind to be auctioned. Local townspeople watched the proceedings calmly from the station entrance, and the town photographer Franz Weber documented the events with his camera.[60] After a brief stopover at the Kassel *Hauptbahnhof,* the train traveled for seventeen hours before it arrived at the concentration camp and killing center Majdanek, where twenty-six working-age men were separated from their relatives and registered for slave labor. Hans may well have been among them, given his age, but if he was, he did not live long enough to be registered by the camp authorities. The train's final stop was at the killing center Sobibór, where on 3 June the remaining Jews, including Martha, were sent to the gas chamber.[61]

How did the refugees build new lives on the basis of such loss? How did they make sense of what they had become? Who were they in these new, unfamiliar places? Did they think of themselves as refugees, as exiles, as immigrants? Where was home?

   In a profound meditation on exile published in 1943, the German Jewish philosopher Hannah Arendt recounted a joke making the rounds among the refugees. "A forlorn émigré dachshund," went the story, "in his grief, begins to speak: 'Once, when I was a St. Bernard . . .'" Arendt explained that in their desire to build a new life and identity, refugees learned that "one has first to improve on the old one." She depicted a group that was plagued, despite its façade of strength and optimism, by fear, uncertainty, humiliation, an "insane optimism which is next door to despair," a "proclaimed cheerfulness" that is "based on a dangerous readiness for death." Rejected wherever they went, denied dignity and legal protection, her fellow refugees wandered about in "desperate confusion," transforming themselves to the world around them in an attempt to preserve integrity and a sense of belonging. "The less we are free to decide who we are or to live as we like," Arendt wrote, "the more we try to put up a front, to hide the facts, and to play roles." "Our identity is changed so frequently that nobody can find out who we actually are."[62]

Too preoccupied with the daily battle to survive for philosophical reflection, Rudolf and his relatives nonetheless faced precisely the challenge that Arendt so articulately described. As letters traveled back and forth between them, they began to construct new stories about their lives and to reestablish the foundations of their existence. "It is rather strange," Rudolf wrote to Alex in English in February 1951,

> how we, the same as so many people, have been scattered over the whole face of the Earth. You in U.S.A., Armand in Canada, Reny in Brasil, Rosa & Siegfried in France and I in S.A. Actually the strange part about it is, that we accept this as something so perfectly natural, and (at least I) hardly ever think about it. I presume it is the same with you. It is only when now and again, you write in one of your letters about the weather, that I stop and think about it, being in the Southern Hemisphere it is the middle of summer here, when you are in the depth of winter.[63]

The family's physical dispersal was "so perfectly natural" that Rudolf had stopped being aware of it. Instead, the very process of corresponding with his relatives took on for him the form of a virtual parallel existence, a world of letters in which he preserved a semblance of continuity. From a distance, Rudolf's young son Norman observed the Sunday morning ritual in which his father withdrew to his writing table, meticulously dressed in jacket and bow tie and grey flannels, no longer Ralph but once again Rudolf, to undertake the important work of composing his letters.[64] Rudolf continued to write late at night when his wife and son were asleep, approaching the job with an earnestness recalling his own father Max's devotion to the conventions of the German middle class. The "correct way" was to answer letters "the day after receipt, at the latest."[65] Apologies should be given for delays, and the tone should always be gracious and refined. Humor was welcome as long as it was not offensive. Great effort was made to address correspondents in their own languages, and letters were often carefully drafted in handwriting before being typed.[66] Rudolf kept carbon copies of his own letters, primarily to keep track of multiple conversations as they meandered across months and years. Preserving for posterity was, at least by his own account, not his concern; the significance of the letters was what they provided in the here and now.

Letters were a medium for maintaining family ties in the most literal sense. They were the means for conveying news and keeping up to date about mutual acquaintances, for discussing practicalities and legal questions, for reminiscing about old times. By their very existence, the letters also affirmed the refugees' survival and their ongoing attempts to create new lives. Crammed into Rudolf's enormous trunk were four decades of conversations, revealing the gradual rebuilding of selves and connections to a larger whole.

Part of the fabric that bound the surviving relatives together in their correspondence was their Jewishness, even though, paradoxically, most no longer lived as practicing Jews. Following his arrival in South Africa Rudolf did not engage with organized religion, and it was only much later that he turned to Jewish communal activity as a source of identity and support. In Brazil, Reny's family took the High Holidays as an opportunity to go to the seaside.[67] In France, Rosa and Siegfried converted to Protestantism. Siegfried wrote with disdain about observant Jews:

> Those stupid, brazen Jews in Palestine don't know the Lord God, they pray from morning to evening and from evening to morning with their lips but not with their hearts. They think all their gruesome deeds are forgotten and forgiven on Yom Kippur and they can start over again with their murdering and robbing. Unfortunately I've always had bad experiences with Jews, mainly the religious ones. Even Jews who show love for their neighbor and conduct themselves seriously and correctly are condemned if they smoke on *Shabbat*, eat pork and wash themselves regularly. One shouldn't differentiate between people, regardless of whether someone was bar mitzvahed as a Jew or a Christian. The Chief Rabbi of Rome became a Catholic because it was Christian brotherly

love that helped him and the Jews out of trouble. We too have had experience of sincere Christian brotherly love (although there is also the insincere variety).[68]

Rudolf found it "unbelievable" that Rosa and Siegfried would have converted, but a representative of the Joint in Paris confirmed that "they are unknown to the Jewish community in Cannes and Marseilles," suggesting that they had "turned away from the Jewish faith."[69] Only Alex maintained consistent contact with Jewish communities in Shanghai and later in Minnesota, in part out of religious commitment, but in part also because they provided a lifeline of support. He died while at prayer in his local synagogue, and a member of his community was given the task of saying the mourner's *kaddish* for him for a year.[70]

Jewishness was nonetheless a persistent thread in the connections that developed between them. Like many other families in the refugee diaspora, they renewed their correspondence and marked the passing of the years according to the rhythms of the festivals. Fulfilling the Jewish ritual of reciting a daily prayer following a family member's death, Rudolf undertook the task of saying *kaddish* for both his uncle Alex and for Reny's father, Mor. Most of them, including even Rosa and Siegfried, continued to observe the festive rituals in some form or another, and they often embellished their good wishes in the letters with memories of festive celebrations together back in Germany. In these unexceptional acts they affirmed common identities and common origins, reenacting who they had been, where they had come from, and what they had always done.[71]

The relatives were also bound together by absence and loss, and their tireless reminiscing revolved around a dwindling stock of shared memories. In response to Rudolf's first letter in the autumn of 1946, his cousin Reny wrote:

> You wouldn't believe how happy I was to hear from you again after such a long time. On the other hand your letter made me sad too as it made me think back on the wonderful teenage years we spent together; they were so vastly different from the family picture now.[72]

For the first few months after the war, the relatives shared and re-shared the same scraps of information: who had escaped, who had survived, who hadn't been heard from again. They did not lose hope entirely, but as time went on they despaired of ever seeing parents or grandparents or siblings again. They did this together, linked by mutual grief and affection and longing. Reflecting on the responses he received to his requests for information about his family, Rudolf wrote:

> It wasn't just what was written there that shocked me but rather the things I could read between the lines: the fear, disappointment, torment, suffering, pain, and human greed and avarice. Of course I was already very well aware of the torture and suffering my coreligionists and relatives in Germany must have gone through before the "solution" arrived, and I've been reading in the newspapers for years about how things are in Germany and how it's going there. But it's only in the last few days that even I have understood what it all meant in terms of human misery, what it truly meant in terms of despair and pain. Don't you think that poison, the noose and the bullet were too good for those mass murderers, thieves, loot handlers and bandits from Munich, Nuremberg and Berlin? Even if one thinks only of the harm they've done to the German people and nation? And that's only if we completely forget the six million Jews and who knows how many millions of other people they murdered, whipped with devilish enjoyment and tortured to death with the most gruesome and vicious methods ever to be thought up by a sadistic mind; they could never atone for their crimes against their own "people," even by dying a thousand of the worst deaths imaginable.[73]

The relatives agreed that no punishment could compensate for what had been lost. "Whatever steps the Allies take to exact a certain amount of retribution," Rudolf wrote in April 1946, "it will certainly not help our dear ones."[74] He also could not fathom why any Jew would return to Germany, and rebuked Alex and Rosa for even contemplating the idea:

> I think it's very sensible that you're not going back to Germany. I simply cannot imagine how you could ever again live in a country with people who tortured and murdered our closest relatives and friends, never mind Europe's six million other Jews who suffered the same fate. Don't try telling me that the German people themselves aren't responsible. They were always antisemitic and whatever the authorities may say, anyone who goes back will be seen as a scapegoat "guilty of causing all the suffering of the German people during the war." Anyone who

can simply look on passively while mass murder is committed to such an extent, without lifting a finger to prevent it, is just as guilty as the murderers themselves.[75]

But alongside the Germany of the perpetrators, the relatives' conversations were also grounded in the Germany of their family, their culture, and their past. For Rudolf, the linchpin was Max. "Just as meshugge/crazy as my blessed father," he would frequently quip as he described his leadership of motley "comical organizations" in South Africa, his activities and honorary offices in the Jewish community, his involvement in local political life, his scrupulous honesty in business.[76] Until his death, Rudolf's attitudes, priorities, and approach to life were infused with the spirit of Max, active citizen and communal leader, patriotic German and Jew. It was a bond that Max's siblings often recognized. "You are a true gentleman and of course chieftain of the Schwab clan," gushed Aunt Rosa, "just like your father and grandfather, may their memories be blessed."[77]

Rudolf's unwavering support for Rosa, Alex, and other elderly relatives was rooted in his commitment, as *de facto* patriarch, to maintaining his dispersed family. Despite the fact that South Africa experienced its own food shortages and rationing, he sent generous packages of coffee, sugar, pasta, canned fruit, sardines, soap, and clothing. He coordinated reparations claims, arranged loans, drafted letters, and interceded on their behalf with miscellaneous organizations and authorities. He also sent money he could barely afford to spare.[78]

His relatives complained from time to time about his lack of concern, though in so doing they also conceded their growing dependence upon him. "I fail to understand why you didn't respond to my letter of Nov. 15th 1951," wrote Alex in April 1952. "Meanwhile, I've been in hospital for four weeks and had a major operation, if I hadn't had more help from strangers than from my own family, I might not be alive now." Rosa grew increasingly aggressive and paranoid toward her nephew, who she claimed was living a life of wealth and comfort in South Africa while abandoning his relatives in need. In August 1948 Rudolf told a friend that he regularly sent parcels to his relatives "to keep them more or less above water," even though it was not always easy for him to do so: "After all," he grumbled, "I can't shit gold."[79] But he generally maintained a cheerful demeanor and graciously ignored complaints.

Perhaps the most significant, if unlikely, point of connection for the relatives was the prolonged process of seeking reparations.[80] For over twenty years Rudolf fought a protracted legal battle, first with the postwar Allied powers in occupied

Germany, and subsequently with the West German state. Prosaic details of compensation claims filled the family's correspondence: debates about whether and where to claim, the value of a mahogany sideboard or a Persian rug or *Shabbat* candlesticks, the frustration of dealing with obstructive bureaucrats, the reliability of this or that former acquaintance or neighbor as a witness.

When I began working on the Schwab family's story, I expected that the reparations claims would be dry documents, full of tedious legalisms and not particularly relevant to my research. As I read them, however, their symbolism became gradually clearer. They were not only legal claims but also a medium for memory work, for the relatives to begin expressing what they had lost, and to begin mourning it.[81]

Rudolf's first application to the Control Office for Germany and Austria in London was sent as early as 25 November 1946, and the family's subsequent claims dragged on through the 1950s and 1960s with little sign of resolution. One of Rudolf's first claims was for restitution of his father's property at 13-15 Französische Allee, site of the family home and Max's business. The property had been sold under duress in December 1938 to a certain Mr. and Mrs. Bien, who in turn sold it to the local Red Cross in June 1941. The claim was complicated by the fact that the buildings had been destroyed in the 1945 Allied bombings, but the plot was eventually registered to Rudolf in late 1949 and later purchased by the town of Hanau for a modest sum, as was part of an adjoining garden property. Detailed inventories produced for the claims revealed his family's comfortable middle-class existence: his parents' dining and reception room suites ("Louis XV Period style, gold lacquered"), Blüthner piano, two complete dinner services "each of superior, excellent quality," silverware, table linen, bed linen, and a grandfather clock that matched the furniture.[82] Rudolf also submitted compensation claims in the name of his parents and brother, and coordinated claims on the property of his maternal grandmother and grandfather, Johanna and Elias Hausmann, in Worms, his uncle Oskar Frank in Cologne, and his paternal uncle and aunt Louis and Erna Heymann.[83]

No one, least of all Rudolf, ever believed that much would come of these claims. "It is a fight which may possibly carry on for another decade or two," he wrote to Alex in February 1950. "Perhaps my grandchildren will one day receive some compensation or other. I have given up hope, to ever see a penny of it myself."[84] He and his agent in Hanau joked repeatedly about the futile "paper war" in which they were engaged, and the mass amnesia that was now gripping the German nation, making it almost impossible for victims to provide sufficient proof for their claims.[85]

It really is unreasonably harsh to demand that we—who had to leave Germany against our will because of these events despite having done nothing wrong—produce such evidence, when the circumstances in Germany at that time are precisely what now prevent us from doing so. After all, if the situation in Germany back then hadn't been what it was, we wouldn't have had to a) emigrate, b) our loved ones, at least the younger generation, would still be alive, c) we would still have the documentation, and, in particular d) there would be no grounds for us to make a restitution claim in the first place.[86]

Nazi censorship and surveillance had prevented people from writing much about the persecution at the time, and now that the war was over, every office in the country was claiming that its records had been lost or destroyed in the Allied air raids.[87]

But despite the victims' acknowledgment that they were unlikely to receive much compensation, despite their lack of confidence in the legal process, despite unsympathetic responses from reparations courts and ludicrous demands for evidence and endlessly dragging claims, they continued to fight for their rights with remarkable zeal and tenacity. Rudolf spent countless Sunday mornings before his typewriter parsing legal minutiae, dealing with agents in Hanau and Worms and Cologne, drafting and redrafting claims, compiling inventories, and reporting progress to relatives.[88]

While a little extra income wouldn't have hurt, money was a far less significant motivating factor for pursuing the claims than the symbolic issues of morality and justice that they were used to articulate. "I don't see why we should leave those pigs a penny more than is absolutely necessary," Rudolf wrote in August 1946. These "bastards" should not "get away with their loot." For him the German authorities' delays were not just "an injustice" but an "empty con trick," especially "after all the promises of the last few years." Even though the state was evading responsibility, he insisted repeatedly, and even though little was likely to change for the victims, "we must, from the very outset, put up a hard fight."[89]

Rather than communicate with reparations authorities in sober bureaucratic language, Rudolf became angry and confrontational in his correspondence. The issues he raised lay well beyond the courts' ability to address. Even though certain decisions regarding his father's property were legally understandable, as he wrote to the Hanau municipality, they

cannot possibly, in my opinion, be defended on moral grounds. Haven't the rightful owners suffered enough at the hands of the former German

government? How could any right-thinking person reconcile his conscience with hurting them even more?[90]

In response to an appeal submitted by Mr. Bien, the opportunistic "buyer" of the
Schwab home, he wrote:

> It is extremely odd that one so rarely meets anyone in Germany these
> days who supported National Socialism. If you were actually to believe
> what most people claim, then between the years 1933–1945, 98% of the
> German population were active members of underground organizations
> dedicated to toppling the government. I put it to you that under these
> circumstances the government wouldn't have lasted five minutes.[91]

Hundreds of compensation letters in Rudolf's trunk were suffused with similarly
intense emotions. In July 1950, he wrote to the reparations authorities in Hesse:

> I have to say that at this stage, five years after the war, these endless
> excuses for postponement from Germany's compensation authorities
> are beginning to sound extremely monotonous. First and foremost I
> want to draw your attention to the fact that since 23rd Aug. 1946, my
> claims have been submitted for processing to somewhere between six
> and eight different departments and offices, etc.; and that is before Mr.
> [Karl] Kipfer managed to send them to you after your department was
> established. They are therefore incorrect to make the point that by deal-
> ing with my claims within such a short period of time they are in fact
> giving my claims preference over others given that mine arrived late.
> It is a regrettable fact that of my entire family, roughly 25 people in
> Germany at the outbreak of the war, none are still alive because they
> were all killed in the camps of the then German government. This is
> why the explanation that my loved ones were only a tiny fraction of the
> millions of people in the territories occupied by Germany during that
> period who suffered the same fate in unspeakable conditions brings me
> no comfort, nor does the fact that many millions more lost their lives
> or were injured in military combat. All their assets were confiscated in
> a manner that can only be described as theft and robbery. I know that
> today the regional governments in Germany regret this injustice just as
> much as the rest of the world, and that they would move heaven and
> earth if it were possible to bring all these people back to life. Since this

is not possible, their intention is to treat material damages as a debt of honor and to provide swift restitution. Under these circumstances you can perhaps imagine the disappointment I feel when I receive letters such as yours of the 6th of last month. As a former German citizen from a respectable family that resided in Hanau am Main—and nowhere else according to the historical evidence—for approximately 1,600 years, I did not demand from my old friends in Germany, when the war was over, that they provide me with documentary evidence demonstrating beyond all shadow of a doubt that they did not participate in the excesses of the former German government and the organizations associated with it. I did not brush them off with talk of doing something to help them at some point in the distant future; instead, as soon as I was able to, I gave them support by sending food parcels. So, is it now so unreasonable that five years after the war, I expect to have my claims processed somewhat faster than has hitherto been the case? After all, I am not a beggar asking for alms, I am merely making a lawful claim for restitution for an injustice I have suffered.[92]

What is so striking about these submissions is how far they went beyond the remit of legal claims. The process of compiling and submitting claims was a forum for victims to vent their rage at Germany for what it had done, and for its continued refusal to recognize their suffering—yet another "atrocious injustice" after the fact.[93] How else can we explain the family's inclusion in their claims of information that was entirely superfluous to the bureaucratic requirements, and that had little power to influence the legal process—the Schwabs' history in Hanau, their esteemed standing, the irredeemable loss that their deaths had caused?[94] Only many years later did the West German authorities acknowledge that the purpose of reparations was not only to allocate benefits but also to recognize formally the victims' suffering.[95] Rudolf himself did not expect that his protests would elicit much reaction, and when the Hanau municipality eventually made an offer in the interests of redressing the injustice done to his family, he remained unconvinced of its sincerity. In February 1952 he wrote to Alex:

I can now report with great joy that we've succeeded, finally, in forcing the municipality to act on its promise to transfer the ownership of the garden to us. They said a few things in their letter, one of which was this: "Even though we have now succeeded, despite the odds, in making the required sum of money available, we can assure you that it cost us a great deal of effort and we have done so only because we want to help make amends for some of the injustice you have suffered." You can probably figure out for yourself what I think of such acts of Christian brotherly love; nevertheless I thanked them very nicely on behalf of the family, so they can't complain about any rudeness on our part.[96]

In the end, the Schwab family received only a small proportion of the amounts claimed from compensation authorities. Rudolf's initial claims were rejected outright in 1951, and later resubmissions yielded only slightly more success: a combined award of just under DM 37,000 for Max's internment and murder, DM 6,000 for Martha's "loss of freedom," and DM 6,358 for the cost of Rudolf's own emigration and "damage to profession." Claims for Hans were rejected outright. Personal possessions for which Rudolf also submitted claims (household goods, furniture, jewelry) were minimally compensated. The awards were, by the administrators' own admission, very low.[97]

The struggle for compensation was nonetheless a struggle for symbolic recognition of the victims' suffering, and a means for them to confront their betrayal by their beloved homeland.[98] It was also, paradoxically, one of the most important vehicles through which they reforged a connection with their German identities and past.

On a purely practical level, one of the main reasons for the Schwab relatives continuing to correspond so frequently in the first place was to keep updated on the progress of their claims. Well over half of the letters in Rudolf's trunk were, at least on the face of it, concerned with reparations. On a deeper personal level, the claims became a forum for talking about their family's contributions to communal life, for reflecting on their feelings about Germany and their identities as Jews, and for remembering the relationships they had nurtured and the homes they had lived in. As they prepared a compensation claim for their grandmother Johanna Hausmann's home in Worms, Reny and Rudolf reminisced that it was elegant and beautifully furnished, in keeping with the family's wealth and established status in the city.[99] In a submission to the compensation authority at Wiesbaden in June 1960, Rudolf included a 1933 letter from the local rabbinate confirming that his parents "were highly respected and that the Schwab family, which had already lived there for the past three centuries, had always played an important role in the community." He emphasized his father's patriotism, his military service, and his involvement in civic life:

He was not only the head of the Jewish community in Hanau, but also the head of the Central Association for German Citizens of Jewish Faith. Furthermore, he was on the board of Hanau's Athletic Association and of the Wetterau Society, and he was a member of the Veterans' Association and of the Association of Former Hanau Infantry Regiment Soldiers. I know that he also belonged to a number of charitable organizations, both on the board and as an ordinary member.[100]

Such "evidence" was unlikely to influence a compensation panel's deliberations, but that was beside the point. In their debates about how to represent their claims and in the submissions themselves, the victims remembered and mourned what they had lost, from their physical possessions to their sense of rootedness and belonging, and simultaneously constructed a basis from which they could begin to build their identities anew.

Many of the relatives' letters never touched German soil. Even so, Germany was unmistakably at their heart. German was their language and point of reference. Their words resurrected Germany as it had been felt and lived, expressed anger at Germany, sought out ways of continuing to be German. Sometimes this was in the form of conscious conversation. What does Germany mean to us after all that has happened? Would we consider going back? More often, it revealed itself in enduring connections to identities, people, and places that had once constituted the basis of existence, and that were not as easily vacated as homes and furniture. In these conversations arose a Germany of the mind, a Germany defined not by bricks and concrete, but rather by what it had been, and what it no longer was.

3

A Nazi and a Jew

If only there were evil people somewhere insidiously committing evil deeds, and it were necessary only to separate them from the rest of us and destroy them. But the line dividing good and evil cuts through the heart of every human being. And who is willing to destroy a piece of his own heart?

Aleksandr Solzhenitsyn

In January 1948, Rudolf placed a short advertisement in the *Hanauer Anzeiger*.

Are there any former close friends and acquaintances of the JEWELER, MAX SCHWAB, who lived at 15 Französische Allee, who can provide his son Rudi with information about the fate of his father and family and his estate? Reply to R. S., P.O. Box 740, Johannesburg, South Africa.[1]

In late 1947 Rudolf was still searching in vain for details of what had happened to his family. Since Max had been "very well respected and much loved before the Nazis came to power," Rudolf reasoned that former neighbors and acquaintances might be willing to offer some information.[2] One of the first responses he received, which he admitted shook him "to the core," was from Karl Kipfer, whom he described as his "best friend, a former fencing and drinking pal."[3]

Dear Rudi,

    I'm sure you'll be astonished to receive a letter from me, but I saw Helmut Schilling yesterday and he told me about your newspaper advertisement, and suggested I write to you. So that's what I'm doing, and I'll share with you the little that I know. If I know people around these parts, you won't get many replies to your advertisement other than this one. First of all, however, allow me to make a personal remark: I'm writing to you because I'm absolutely sure that if I were in your situation you would help me too. I am not writing—and I want to make this absolutely clear—to obtain any personal benefit for myself. But if you're not convinced or you perhaps think otherwise, then please, simply stop reading this letter and destroy it immediately.

The dire conditions in postwar Germany had led many opportunistic "witnesses" to offer information about former Jewish residents in the hope of receiving food parcels. But Karl's response to his advertisement, Rudolf later confided, was the only one he could fully trust. Contrary to Karl's prediction, he had received twenty letters recounting the devastation of Hanau and the Schwabs' fate. It was difficult to believe, he wrote, that a few small envelopes could contain so much human suffering.[4]

Karl began his letter by recalling what he could of Rudolf's family. About Martha and Hans's fate he knew nothing, but upon his discharge from the army in mid-April 1942 and his subsequent return to Hanau, he had learned of Max's arrest and his death in Sachsenhausen. Karl's own wartime experiences, however, had largely kept him away from Hanau and the suffering of its Jews.

> I've been a cripple since 1940. *We fly against England!*[5] As a souvenir I have my spinal injury, which has caused complete paralysis in my left arm and partial paralysis of the right arm and of both legs. I wear a prosthesis on my left arm and a brace on my right leg. I can move around only with the help of walking sticks. Unfortunately under these circumstances I can't work anymore. On 6 January 1945, I was completely bombed out and so I have no possessions whatsoever. The fact that I lost my voice for 8 days as a result of my injury was a blessing for everyone else but a punishment for me. . . . I probably don't need to point out that life hasn't been a bed of roses for me since 1945. You are, of course, very well aware of my undemocratic past and I have nothing to hide from you, nor do I have anything to add. All my life I've never minced my words and I'm not about to start now.

What Rudolf knew about Karl's "undemocratic past" was not clear. The two lost touch when Rudolf fled Germany in May 1933, and the silence was broken only with Karl's letter of January 1948. Rudolf knew nothing of what Karl had done in the intervening years—Karl did not offer, and Rudolf did not ask.

Karl was born in the town of Giessen on 5 July 1910 and moved to Hanau with his mother, Franziska, and sister, Anna, following the death of his father Joseph, a veteran of the First World War.[6] He and Rudolf probably met at a local fencing society (Karl was a year older), perhaps as students. Fencing was an important site for the building of male identity in interwar Germany, particularly in the context of student fraternities, where it was strongly informed by *Völkisch* ideals about the health of the German race and defense of the Fatherland. More than just a hobby for Karl and Rudolf—as well as for Max, from whom Rudolf probably inherited his interest—fencing signified a rootedness in shared nationalistic and militaristic values, expressed in a resolutely masculine form.[7]

In his 1948 letter, Karl filled Rudolf in on the dire state of their hometown after the war. Large parts of Hanau had been destroyed in the Allied bombings. Unemployment was widespread. Food rations were inadequate, and coal shortages made the winters almost unbearable. Unable to afford heating, Karl was susceptible to frequent ailments, and his injury caused him a lot of pain. His war pension did not cover his basic needs and he could barely afford a place to live. Karl also told Rudolf about the bitter fates of their fencing friends—after all, he wrote, "it was you who made a fencer out of me, and I'm happy to admit that this sport has become my favorite pastime." One friend had been killed in combat; another had committed suicide; others had returned from army service or imprisonment as "living corpses," and most were now "completely bombed out."

But Karl had not only written to tell Rudolf about mutual friends or to describe his own suffering. In the last part of his letter, he explained that the Restitution Law for the American Zone had recently been passed, according to which Jewish assets were being restored to their previous owners or legal successors. Although little more than rubble remained of the Schwab family houses, Karl insisted that his old friend seek restitution, and he offered to act as his local representative. "The old noggin is still in peak condition," he wrote, "as some people have discovered to their sorrow." The extraordinary nature of this offer was not yet clear to either of them.[8]

Rudolf did not respond to Karl's first letter, though he revealed to family members that he was deeply affected by the news of his friend's injury. Several weeks later, Karl sent a second letter offering even more determinedly to assist Rudolf with compensation claims:

This announcement has given me cause to do a lot of thinking over the last few days about you and me, and I've come to the conclusion that we're both to some extent in the soup. You live in Africa, thousands of kilometers from Hanau, and are at an extreme disadvantage when it comes to defending your interests here because of the distance and the poor postal connections. On the other hand, I'm sitting here with nothing to do and looking for a way to relieve the sorrows of my existence. Don't you think that by coordinating our interests we might come to a satisfactory result for both parties? I think so, and what I envisage is that you entrust me with the management of your interests here in Germany. I would then take over the investigations into your parents and would compile, safeguard and submit your legal claims, as well as manage your assets. This way you can be certain that all matters in which you have an interest will be handled as quickly as possible and you won't miss any important deadlines because of the poor postal connections. I don't wish to sing my own praises, but as you know from earlier times, I've always had a knack for legal matters, and when I sink my teeth into something even the devil himself can't turn me off course. You're familiar with my way of doing business, so you can be sure that your affairs will be dealt with in real time and with the same consistency as my own.[9]

Karl had already written up a plan for pursuing the claims, and he listed the documents he would need in order to begin his work. For remuneration, he asked that Rudolf send him coffee, which he could sell on the black market.

When Rudolf finally responded to Karl on 14 April 1948, he did so with great warmth and affection:

You can imagine how pleased I was to receive your letter of 19.1; after all I didn't have very many close friends like you. And particularly because I know I can completely depend on the 100% sincerity and honesty of your letter. With two laudable exceptions, on reading every other letter among the 20 that have arrived so far in response to my advertisement, I've had the uncomfortable feeling that I don't know to what extent I can believe the information they contain. After all, it has now been 15 years since I was last in Germany, and since then a considerable amount of water has passed under the various bridges on the River Main. . . . Of all the things I've heard from old friends and acquaintances and about what has become of them, the news of your injury has upset me most.

But of course that's no reason to make this a speech about my condolences and cause you more upset by assuring you of my sympathies. I hope we still understand each other well enough to make such things unnecessary, even if we are still on opposite sides of the fence as far as our views on life are concerned. Or perhaps your opinions have changed in the last few years? You might well be crippled and even partly paralyzed!! But helpless, worthless and incapable of work? Nowhere near it. . . . I think back happily and often on the great times we spent in the fencing hall and with the sports club at our usual table in the pub, and indeed about other times in the pub that were just as good; and as I also recall, we were often the only ones still able to make our way home respectably and in a straight line on our bicycles or on foot even though we'd had the most to drink.[10]

Rudolf gladly took Karl up on his offer to help with the Schwab family's restitution as well as reparations claims. He foresaw only one potential problem: wouldn't the authorities object to Karl as a representative given his "undemocratic past"?

In the months that followed Rudolf and Karl corresponded regularly, catching up on fifteen missed years of friendship. The sense of mutual affection was palpable. In addition to piecing together the fates of Rudolf's family members and compiling complex legal claims, the two spent hours reminiscing about fencing, old friends, and drunken adventures. Rudolf enthused in his second letter:

I'm delighted to hear that the fencing club still gets together from time to time. Next time you meet up please give everyone my best regards. I'll drink you all under the table again in spirit!!! Or is there no decent beer in Germany anymore? What about cider? When I've built up enough credit perhaps you can send me a crate.[11]

Karl riposted that Rudolf could drink most of them under the table: in the spartan postwar conditions few had retained a tolerance for alcohol. Rudolf admitted that in his early immigrant years he could also not afford to drink, and that in any case "I no longer had the good company required to make drinking a pleasure."[12] Current deprivations did not stop them from toasting one another virtually in their letters and sharing recipes for home-brewed liquors.[13] As Christmas 1948 approached, Karl assured Rudolf that he wasn't going to sit at home while everyone around him feasted and got drunk:

Meekness isn't suited to a cripple who's been completely bombed out and has to fight to save his skin all year round, even just to get what's rightfully his. That's why I've organized a few tasty morsels for myself, within the realms of what's possible for me, and about 4 weeks ago I went down into the cellar and saw a bottle of blackberry juice from the harvest of what is now your rubble garden. It looks scrumptious. There and then I hobbled my way into the village and organized a ¼ liter of schnapps for myself and mixed it with the same quantity of blackberry juice. Since then the bottle has been sitting untouched in the cellar, although I did just taste a sip from it for the very first time. It was absolutely wonderful I tell you, and I'll be gargling to your health on this magnificent beverage during the holidays.[14]

Karl regularly sent interesting stamps for Rudolf's son, continuing a tradition from their youth.[15] He also took great pleasure in complaining to Rudolf about the village where he lived. Unable to afford housing in Hanau, he was forced to live in the neighboring village of Langendiebach among "the dung heaps." "The biggest punishment of my life," he declared, "is that I have to live here in the countryside with the farmers."[16] In January 1949 he told Rudolf that he was under house arrest,

because not one of those accursed pig farmers thinks of putting down salt. Which, as long as it's those shits who are falling over breaking their own thick skulls and knees, is perfectly alright, but for me it's extremely dangerous as I can't just stay at home all the time because I have to go to treatment on a regular basis. So my every step on the way to the masseuse is accompanied by an appropriate number of curses against farmers. But I can promise you this: if I ever fall and hurt myself, the house owner responsible will pay for it until he's blue in the face.[17]

Karl often turned misfortune into an occasion for humor. He was gleefully irreverent about God and religion, and loved to get back at the farmers with surreptitious pranks. They didn't know what to make of him, he drolly remarked.

Langendiebach has been turned upside down by having me as a resident, because someone like me is simply an impossibility here. Half of the villagers have always been fanatical social democrats and the other half fanatical evangelicals. Then I came along. They might have forgiven me my undemocratic past, but my being an unbeliever was too much for them. One even said to me once that I'd learn to accept Jesus Christ someday; I replied that I'd have to take a course first. But I still haven't signed up for my retraining. And on top of all this, ladies of ill repute get me to translate their love letters, which certainly adds to my admittedly poor moral reputation.[18]

To make ends meet, Karl did a combination of private English tutoring and letter writing. When the trade in love letters waned with the departure of the Americans, Karl discovered he could make money out of divorces. Lawyers would send their clients statements from the other party and ask for responses, and since most people didn't know how to "put their thoughts into the right words and then put them down on paper," they came to Karl. He felt himself fortunate "that in my social circle there are so many failed marriages,"[19] and entertained Rudolf with stories of his clients' ridiculous behavior:

> When someone really starts spilling the beans, giving away little details here and there doesn't matter anymore. That's why I've nicknamed the chair they sit on beside my typewriter the confessional. Needless to say I come across a lot of stupidity too. Recently a marriage ended between two people who were constantly beating each other up and shouting at one another. She even claimed that he had a sharpened axe ready to murder her and that was why they slept in separate bedrooms. The battle continued even after they divorced because neither of them wanted to give up any of the furniture or the house. But that didn't stop them from going to bed together; in fact, the night wasn't even enough for them, they had to do it during the day too. In another case, two people were accused of committing adultery. At the hearing when the judge asked if they had ever so much as kissed or embraced one another, they were both indignant and denied it angrily, perish the thought. If all that was true—and I had no reason to doubt that it was—then they had certainly done well to live in abstinence for even a short period of time. The idiots left the courthouse, went straight to bed, and were at it all night.[20]

But Karl was too tolerant to judge their choices: "'Let he who feels without sin cast the first stone' is what Mr. Jesus said at the stoning of the adulteress."[21]

Harking back to the macho banter of their fencing days, Karl and Rudolf took much pleasure in mocking women and commiserating about their hysteria and ineptitude. In May 1948 Rudolf wrote:

I read your report on what you do for a living with great interest, particularly the bit about the various "ladies."—You're certainly not the only one who has "stayed out of all that"; these days it's exactly the same in every country in the world I've been to since the war. The number of divorces has never been as high as it is now. In every country I've been to so far (Germany, France, Belgium, Switzerland, Holland, England, and South Africa) the percentage of honorable and dishonorable women has been roughly the same, and with most it becomes obvious only during times of need. No people of any particular skin, hair or eye color has a monopoly on fidelity or infidelity. So as far as all that's concerned don't complain too bitterly about German women, the others are just as bad—![22]

They grumbled about their respective secretaries' ineptitude and constant eruptions into tears. "I have been at war with these types of women throughout my entire professional career," wrote Karl. Rudolf replied: "Taming wild animals such as these is particularly difficult here." They bragged about their sexual exploits and regaled one another with elaborate jokes, the naughtier the better.[23]

Underlying their banter was a deep familiarity and closeness. As Rudolf's marriage collapsed, Karl was the one in whom he confided. He wrote openly and in detail about his difficulties with Rachel, and sought Karl's advice on the best solution for their son, Norman. Karl in turn confessed to Rudolf his regret at not having children of his own, and shared his anxieties after the stillbirth of his son in March 1953.[24]

In 1951, Karl had entered into an informal "marriage of companionship" with a war widow, a common practice intended to alleviate financial hardship. But in his letters Karl revealed a genuine affection for his wife, and during a long period of illness he cared for her with touching devotion: "As I've already told you she's a jewel, and with the exemplary care she takes of me, she more than deserves for me to look after her in the same way."[25]

Beneath his sardonic exterior, Karl also expressed his determination to live an honest and principled life, even though he sometimes found this difficult. He wrote to Rudolf:

Your views on the black market and other dodgy business do you credit. In fact there was a time when I held exactly the same opinions, but I've had to throw them overboard amid high waves. Even during the war I would rather have smacked myself in the jaw than buy or sell anything

on the black market. When I came home from the army in 1942, I sold
all the clothes and shoes I couldn't wear anymore because of my war
injury, and my bicycle, for the normal price. Including things that I'd
bought shortly before the war and were as good as new. The people
who came to my house told me to my face that they were astonished I
was selling stuff like that for the normal price and only in exchange for
money. My friends laughed until their stomachs ached at my stupidity.
My principles took the first knock when I was bombed out and they
fell by the wayside completely when the war ended. If I hadn't seized
the opportunities available to me wherever and whenever they've arisen
I would have starved over the last few years. So, you see, despite everything I've remained honest, but I've had to be as tough as nails.[26]

In moments of candor, he confessed to Rudolf that his good humor was one of
the few things he had managed to salvage from the war, and that it was a means
of coping with what life had thrown at him. In September 1948 he wrote:

This is the best way, in my opinion, to prevent mental constipation.
Recently I visited our old fencing pal, Willi Fröhlich, now a master
tailor. While I was there he remarked on how amazed he was that a
physical wreck like me could always be in such good form and full of
sarcasm. He said that in this respect I hadn't changed at all in the last 20
years. This is perhaps my good fortune. I've always had a gift for seeing
the funny side and perhaps that's made some things in life which other
people find difficult to bear easier for me. I only have to think back on
my time in the military hospital. There I saw men who ordinarily had
nerves of steel howling like little children as they made futile attempts
to walk with sticks for the first time. If you allow yourself to think while
you're doing it that it's going to be that way for the rest of your life then
it's easy to lose your composure. All that stuff wasn't easy for me either
but seeing it through my funny lenses made everything a lot easier. As
Mr. Bührmann always said: "Humor is when one laughs despite everything"; this old proverb remains true to this day.[27]

Rudolf, for his part, worried about Karl's financial situation and often sent luxury
items that Karl could enjoy himself rather than simply sell on the black market.
He urged him to prioritize his own needs above the costs of reparations matters,
and when Karl asked Rudolf to guarantee a bank loan, Rudolf responded to his

"cry for help" immediately, assuring him that he was the "first and only person" to whom he would lend money.[28] When Karl suggested the possibility of developing the Schwabs' land in Hanau, Rudolf wrote:

> When I read through your letters, I see that you want to live in Hanau again, and the thought occurs to me that you might be able to find some usable accommodation on the plots of land on Französische Allee. There used to be a very nice shed in the garden (a wooden one) and the house at the rear (one-story) was renovated as living accommodation. But those buildings were probably destroyed just like all the others; it was just an idea I had after a drink or two. You know very well of course how "beer leads to baby making." But still, if there's any way it would be possible for you to live there in satisfactory conditions, I want to assure you "in advance" that I wouldn't just agree to it, I'd welcome it joyfully.[29]

They clearly delighted in one another's company, and relished the opportunity to spend time together again, albeit only in their letters.

In addition to Rudolf's claims, Karl offered to take on those of the extended Schwab family, including Alex in Minnesota, Rosa in France, Reny in São Paulo, and Armand in Montreal. Between 1948 and 1952 he pursued their cases with relentless energy. Despite his poor physical condition he traveled frequently to Hanau and Frankfurt, meeting with bureaucrat after uncooperative bureaucrat with little expectation of success. "In comparison to the German authorities," he noted wryly in April 1950, "even a snail is a jet fighter."[30] If one door was slammed in his face, he simply brushed himself off and knocked on the next one. He invested enormous energy in educating himself about the law and talking to advisors. Every month, he sent Rudolf minutely itemized accounts. His densely typewritten letters, often four or five pages long, contained detailed reports about his activities and recommendations for action. He sought out witnesses to give evidence of the Schwab family's property to the courts, and unlike other agents working for Rudolf in Worms and Cologne, he actively pursued all possible avenues in fighting his "paper wars."[31]

As payment Rudolf agreed to send parcels of coffee, the proceeds of which Karl would use to fund the claims and cover his own expenses. This remuneration was not just tokenistic. Postwar Germany was blighted by continued scarcity of food and heating material, and the official ration system was insufficient. As a result, trading on the black market was a means of survival for many, including the poverty-stricken Karl.[32]

After a while, however, Rudolf noticed that Karl had not been receiving enough remuneration for representing the family.[33] Karl replied that he was willing to wait until the claims had been successful before receiving payment. In a letter to Rosa he wrote:

> May I take the liberty of asking how you will be able to cover your share of the expenses for postage, paper, official fees, etc.? You see, I unfortunately am not in a position to cover these costs, having completely lost my health and all my belongings in the war, and consequently also find myself in a financially precarious situation. As for payment for the work I am doing, on the other hand, I am happy to wait until the process has been completed and your accounts in Germany are in credit once again.[34]

Karl surely knew better than anyone how protracted the claims process was likely to be, and how small were the chances of success. In response to Rudolf's repeated offers, Karl eventually proposed a share of 5 percent of the successful claims. Rudolf suggested 6.5 percent in addition to the parcels.[35]

Rudolf was persuaded by Karl's sincere investment in his cause, and he trusted him to defend his interests. Karl, in turn, vigorously guarded Rudolf against the many "witnesses" who were offering to give testimony in exchange for food parcels. One "typical case of ham parcel hunters" was a certain Mr. and Mrs. Schmitz:

> The man came to my house and talked to me for an hour about all the things he used to have but doesn't have any more and, when I asked him quite timidly what he had to report in relation to your case, he told me as if it were breaking news that Mr. Alex Boh had been in contact with you and I should ask him. He didn't know anything else. So let him ask Alex Boh to give him something from the parcel of ham that Boh himself is never going to receive. We've been expecting to get these types of people. Quite frankly, the Schmitz couple—although I've only ever met them once in my life—are the most dislikeable and unpleasant people in the world, but of course my personal views don't affect the work I do for you in any way.[36]

Karl entertained Rudolf with stories about other characters who told him nothing and then had the "cheek, impudence, effrontery and greed" to request parcels. A certain Miss Marion Krug wrote to say that she knows nothing whatsoever. But she wishes us every success with the rest of the case. As for her, she'd like a parcel of ham. You'd have to be running a pig farm and an oil well to satisfy all these requests.[37]

As work on the claims progressed, the two developed a shared approach to dealing with people, on the implicit understanding that pragmatism was sometimes necessary to get what one wanted. A particular witness or official would be privately assessed and ripped to pieces, and then receive a gracious letter requesting information or help. Disingenuous civil servants, lazy agents, and former Nazis were flattered and sweet-talked if they could provide testimony or help to progress a case. Even those whom Rudolf knew to be dishonest were sent food parcels if they offered useful information. Rudolf had confidence in Karl's judgment about who was genuine and who was not, and he told his relatives that he doubted he would ever find another representative to match him.[38]

Rudolf's family members, by contrast, were openly mistrustful of Karl's motives, describing him as a Nazi crook and a "good for nothing" who was likely to make off with their reparations money.[39] Aunt Rosa ranted:

> I received several documents from *Monsieur* Kipfer and a message about the garden. . . . What will be left for us after that thief has pocketed everything? . . . You must keep on top of him and demand that he send you a record of the accounts. I don't trust him.[40]

In response to Karl's request for postage expenses, Siegfried wrote to Rudolf:

> Do you know Mr. Kipfer well? It seems to me that he was a genuine Nazi who wants to exploit the Jews . . . and only wants to get money out of everyone entitled to the inheritance.[41]

Armand and Reny similarly doubted Karl's trustworthiness and abilities, and the fact that he had been Rudolf's friend "before" made little difference. Karl was well aware of their mistrust, and he and Rudolf often joked about the millions he was supposedly stealing from them.[42]

Rudolf defended his friend in the face of these persistent and often vicious claims. In February 1949 he wrote to Rosa:

> I'm no more in a position than you are to be 100% certain about Mr. Kipfer or indeed anyone in Germany these days. All of them were

definitely Nazis, some are honest about it and admit it openly but most now swear to high heaven that they never even knew there was a Nazi government in Germany. Just like old King Barbarossa, they were sleeping the sleep of the "just" during those years. The only thing I do know is that back then he was a very decent person despite his militaristic tendencies, and he was my best friend for years. I have no complaints whatsoever about his way of doing business, as he's managed to find things out for me and obtain witness statements that any normal person would consider impossible. Don't forget that I knew nothing whatsoever about my parents' property before. Among other things, he's found out that my father was buried in Frankfurt (even the exact number of the grave) and is going to send me a photo of the grave sometime soon. But that's just one of the smaller things he's discovered. All things considered, he seems to me to be more trustworthy than anyone else in Germany I've heard from. It's perfectly understandable that he can't cover all the expenses out of his own pocket, especially as his war injuries have left him 100% disabled. After all, we're going to need to obtain certificates of inheritance, for which we'll need dozens of documents such as birth certificates, marriage certificates, and God knows what else all the way down to the third generation. The authorities won't do all this for free—postage, paper, official copies, photocopies, all cost a lot of money. We have to make between 6 and 10 copies of the restitution claims in order to submit them, etc. And it's not as if, despite all of the above, he sent you a demand for payment; rather he inquired, with a gentle whimper, as to how you will be able to pay for your share of the expenses, since he himself has nothing and therefore can't do it. So far he's accounted for every single penny with great accuracy, and has sent me the original receipts for most of his expenses, even the smallest bus ticket, so as of yet I have no indication that he's exploiting us. If you want something done properly you'll have to pay for it in the end; by contrast, I have to ask my agent in Worms—who, because he's wealthy, it seems, still hasn't sent an expenses report for similar items—ten times before I get a reply, and I have to plague him constantly or he doesn't answer at all. Nevertheless he is the best-known and respected financial agent in Worms and the reports I've had of him say he is first class. That's why, so far, my preference has always been Kipfer. In any case, I've already written to him to say that I'm prepared to pay half the costs for both of you and for Alex if Armand pays the other half. If you can think of a better solution, I am more than willing to accept your proposal.[43]

Rudolf emphasized that Karl was completely trustworthy, and his work far more energetic than that of other agents.[44] To Alex he wrote in English:

It seems to me that he is the type of fellow who holds fast to everything like a bulldog, in spite of or perhaps on account of his disability. We ordinary human beings don't appreciate what an effort it is for such people to be as active as they are.[45]

He also stressed that his willingness to employ Karl was based solely on his efficient work, rather than on sympathy or misguided trust. "I am not particularly sorry for him," he repeatedly assured them, or indeed "for any German." But "right is right," he also emphasized: Kipfer was a disabled man in a precarious financial situation, and "if we want him to carry on as our representative, he is entitled to see something now and again." Karl's work was also "first class and tip top," and within just a few months of taking on their claims he had made "astonishing progress."[46] Rudolf also pointed out that although Karl had once "had a very nationalistic attitude," he was now

one of the very few people who admit it openly and honestly and he doesn't gloss over it in any way, even though he seems to have changed his opinion radically since then.[47]

Rudolf concluded that Karl was

by far the most reliable, and he tries everything humanly possible, or in any case much more than anyone else does, to squeeze every last penny out of the authorities. Thus far, I have not, unfortunately, found anyone better.[48]

Despite his relatives' continued misgivings, Rudolf ultimately persuaded them to give Karl power of attorney and allow him to manage their claims.

Although Karl referred frequently to his "undemocratic past," it was unclear precisely what Rudolf knew about it. How was he able to applaud Karl's frankness and honesty when, as far as we can tell from the letters, very few specifics about his past had actually been divulged?

I began to pursue the question. Karl had joined the Nazi Party when he was twenty-six, on 1 March 1937.[49] By that time, the Nazis had been in power for over four years. What were his motivations for joining? Since the early 1930s he had been an active member of a local fencing group, which would probably have been *gleichgeschaltet* (nazified) along with other associations and absorbed into the umbrella Nazi organization for sports. He had also been a member of the Nazi trade union from 1933, of the Nazi social welfare organization from 1934, and from 1942 of a Nazi war victims' welfare organization. In addition, he may have been encouraged to join the Party in order to keep his job at a local jewelry firm.

In all likelihood, these were the unremarkable reasons for his Nazi Party membership. When he reported for service in the *Wehrmacht* on 22 August 1939, he was a reluctant conscript. "Everyone came of their own free will," he later wrote to Rudolf; "I was the only fool who showed up because I'd received a draft notice." From September 1939 until April 1942, he served in various signals units of the *Luftwaffe* (air force), until he was discharged due to a severe disability and sent back to Hanau.[50]

The period from 1939 to 1942 was opaque. From Karl's oft-repeated mantra "We fly against England," a popular *Luftwaffe* slogan and song, Rudolf reasonably concluded that he had taken part in the aerial bombardments of Britain in the autumn of 1940, and that this is when he sustained his spinal injury. Karl later catalogued for Rudolf the exact details of his hospitalization: in the first week of October 1940 he was discharged from the *Lazarett* (military hospital) at Detmold, and on 2 December 1940 he was admitted for treatment at nearby Bielefeld-Bethel, where he convalesced for nine long months. On 30 August 1941 he was taken to Frankfurt, where he was housed in a former brothel that had been converted into a military hospital. "This," he bragged to Rudolf, "is what one calls a functioning memory."[51]

Pinning down the details of Karl's wartime role was more difficult than I had expected. I turned first to the *Bundesarchiv*, the German Federal Archives in Berlin, where I found his Nazi Party membership application and card, but the documents told me very little that I didn't already know.[52] Next I turned to the Hanau town archive. I had the enthusiastic support of Martin Hoppe, head of the Hanau historical society and assistant to the local mayor, who was intrigued by the story and put considerable energy behind my search. Yes, the archive had an entry for Karl Kipfer—but perhaps unsurprisingly for a local archive, it could offer little more than dates of birth, marriage, and death, and various addresses.[53] The local archive in Giessen, Karl's birthplace, also provided dates and addresses but no details from the Nazi period.[54] Inquiries with the Hanau historical society yielded only the vague recollections of neighbors, one of whom thought Karl might have earned money as an English teacher after the war, and most of whom could not remember him at all.[55]

Karl's widow, Elisabeth, was no longer alive, but Martin was able to locate one of his surviving stepdaughters, Elke Lorenz. Elke explained that her mother and Karl had met in Langendiebach, where they were evacuated after the bombing of Hanau in March 1945. She described him as a gentle and well-dressed man, and she recalled that he had been an avid amateur fencer. But she and her sister Paula had been young children when he came to live with them in 1951, and neither remembered much about him. When their mother died in 1977, they found as evidence of the union only three small photographs. One showed Karl and Elisabeth at their wedding. The other images captured a visit to the Castle Phillippsruhe in April 1954. By this time Karl was in bad health, and his frailty was clearly visible.[56]

A further archival lead was the Deutsche Dienststelle in Berlin, which preserves documentation relating to members of the former *Wehrmacht*. It took several months for my query to be processed, but eventually the archive sent a letter cataloguing everything that was known about Karl Kipfer, including his identification number, the units in which he served, and his ranks and promotions. Each division of the German army, I learned, included a signals battalion that was responsible for telephone, radio, and telegraph communications, and sometimes also for encoding and decoding secure messages or intercepting enemy radio communication.[57] Karl had served in various signals units as a *Funker* (Radio Operator) from March 1940. By September 1940 he had been promoted to *Gefreiter* (Junior Cadet), although the date of promotion was unknown. In April 1942, he was formally discharged. The archive also confirmed the dates of his hospitalization in Bielefeld and Frankfurt that he had so proudly recalled to Rudolf.[58]

I was intrigued by Karl's portrayal of his experiences. Was this really the substance of his "undemocratic past"? Scouring repeatedly through the letters, I could find only an unexceptional association with the Nazi Party (he was member number 3,867,957), conscription into one of the army's auxiliary support services, and a debilitating injury. Was this a sufficient explanation for the intense mixture of guilt, anger, and contrition that filled his letters?

Apart from Karl's powerful sense of complicity, a few unsettling comments in the letters encouraged me to persevere with my inquiries. In October 1948, a

Karl and Elisabeth Kipfer, 1953. Courtesy of Elke Lorenz.

few months after he and Rudolf had renewed contact, Karl had given the first of many long rants about Germany's refusal to take responsibility for its past. He also gave a frank appraisal of his own character:

> Indeed, my memory is the only thing that wasn't squished in the war, a fact that has, without doubt, already caused the state some anxiety. Admittedly, I would have been well suited to the role of corpse-in-charge

in a mass grave, and would have cut a fine figure if I had ended up in Hell reporting to the Devil on duty, but I prefer it here on this sinful earth, and if I have anything to do with it I'd like to stay here for a good few years yet. In short, they tried their very best to knock me one on the head during the war, but it didn't work out.[59]

Soon after this somewhat tasteless passing remark, Karl made another reference to a mass grave, this time more explicitly. In January 1949 he sent a long and mostly unremarkable letter summarizing his current work on the claims and mocking corrupt politicians. He and Rudolf had also been exploring import-export opportunities between South Africa and Germany, and Karl gave a report on his progress:

The direct inquiries I made with producers of tar, coal, and creosote were unsuccessful, and I'm worried that we'll have the same fiasco again if I proceed in the same way regarding semi-precious stones. So I'm going to do things a little differently. First I'm going to write to the Jewelry Industry Association in Hanau and get them to tell me the names of companies we could consider for exports. Only then will I send inquiries to the companies themselves. I think that way we'll have some success. I'll also make inquiries in Idar-Oberstein if appropriate. Unfortunately the addresses of the jewel suppliers have slipped my mind; after all, I haven't worked in the sector for almost ten years now, and in the meantime I spent several long weeks hovering at the edge of a mass grave myself, and it can't be ruled out that this has made my memory somewhat weaker. If any specialist issues should arise during the negotiations with the companies, I will of course consult Mr. Weigelt.[60]

Karl's letters were, in general, lucid and forthright. He had never been one to mince his words, as he reminded Rudolf early on in their correspondence. How, then, were these references to mass graves to be understood? Was this Karl's metaphorical way of describing the harrowing experience of combat, or life-threatening injuries? Or did he mean a literal mass grave? If so, he was being breathtakingly casual about it. Then again, if he had somehow been implicated in criminal activity, how else might he have communicated that information? Without being able to talk to his friend in person or gauge his response, was this perhaps a way of hinting at the nature of his "undemocratic past" without making it explicit? He had from the outset implied that it was known to Rudolf very well, but such details are not the type of thing one can easily convey in a letter.

An unexpected document unearthed at the International Tracing Service in Bad Arolsen added more ambiguity to the picture. The ITS is an enormous archive, successor to the Tracing Bureau established by the Allies and the British Red Cross, recording the fates of millions of victims of Nazi persecution. A search for "Kipfer" in the database turned up a statement from a thirty-two-year-old member of the *Waffen-SS* named Simon Kiern, given at a US military trial at Dachau on 30 October 1945.[61] Kiern had joined the German Army in 1932, and from 1937 until 1939 was employed at the Dachau concentration camp as a member of a signals unit. After a period in Czechoslovakia he returned to Dachau, where he was again active with a signals unit until July 1941.

According to his statement, Kiern was ordered to participate in the execution of fifteen "Russian Partisans" in November 1941, and in two further shootings of twenty-five Russians in January 1942. "At the time these executions took place," Kiern explained, "5 persons would be shot at once and the corpses would be removed by SS men." Among the fifteen men he listed as having participated in these executions was Karl Kipfer. Kiern added to his statement this caveat: "All of the men I have mentioned, with the exception of ENDRESS, BETZ and KIPFER, I know took part in the actual shooting, but of the three I cannot say for sure."[62]

Could Kiern's deposition be referring to the same Karl Kipfer? On one hand, it seemed impossible. The letter-writing Kipfer was fiery and quick-tempered, to be sure, but he was also disarmingly funny and engaging, and he expressed a strong sense of morality and personal responsibility. Whatever his faults, his heart was in the right place. On the other hand, why could it not have been him? For the most part, perpetrators were not evil monsters but ordinary men with diverse motivations, caught up in complex circumstances. Historians attempting to understand their behavior have had to ask difficult questions about how ordinary human beings can end up doing such inhumane things. Karl's name was clearly mentioned on the deposition, and the fact that Kiern worked with members of signals units during his many years in Dachau seemed an uncanny coincidence.

Research into the Dachau trials at the National Archives in Washington, DC, yielded another set of documents. Between 1945 and 1948, a total of 489 proceedings were held by the US Army Courts, mostly on the site of the former concentration camp. In May 1947, almost two years after Kiern testified, a different case brought charges against five individuals who had held assignments at Dachau at some point between January 1942 and January 1945, and who had

VOL IX

Before me, Lt. JOHN H. BOWSER, AC, being authorized to administer oaths, personally appeared SIMON KIERN, who after being duly sworn through the interpreter, made and subscribed to the following statement:

My name is SIMON KIERN. I am 32 years of age and resided until my arrest on 30 April 1945 at Hebertshausen, Wurmuhle 3. I was inducted into the German Army on 1 October 1932 and was discharged as a coporal on 1 March 1936. Then I became a civilian and remained one until 30 January 1937 and after that time I entered the organization of the Waffen SS. I first came to Dachau on 1 February 1937 and was employed there as a Signal Corps man. I remained in Dachau from 1937 until 1939 to train SS men as Signal Corps men and was thereafter sent to Czechoslavakia where I remained until the year 1941. Then I returned to Dachau and was active with the Signal Corps until July 1941. Then I was commanded to the Concentration Camp where I was employed as clerk in the office of Hauptsturmführer ZILL. My rank at that time was Unterscharführer. My duties in the office consisted of filling out the file cards of inmates, as well as writing N.S.V. post cards to the families and relatives of inmates. In November 1941 I was ordered for the first time to participate in the execution of Russian prisoners. I did not want to do that and told ZILL so. Thereupon he shouted at me and said that I had to execute his orders. Fifteen Russian Partisans were shot to death that month. These executions took place at the rifle range.
The next shootings I was ordered to participate in took place in January 1942. There were two executions that month, in each of which 25 or more Russians were shot. I was active in all three executions, taking part in the shooting. Untersturmführer JAROLIN was in command of these executions. The following named men have participated in one or more executions:

        Hauptscharführer PETER BETZ
        Scharführer HERTHA
        Scharführer ANGERER
        Hauptscharführer GEISBERGER
        Oberscharführer MÜLLER
        Hauptscharführer WOLFGANG SEUSS
        Rottenführer PHILIPP
        Scharführer STAEFL
        Oberscharführer KARL KIPFER
        Oberscharführer ENDRESS
        Scharführer PREISS
        Scharführer MAX BOOCK
        Scharführer JOSEF BOCK
        Scharführer SCHOPPMEIER

Furthermore I want to mention that at the time these executions took place 5 persons would be shot at once and the corpses would be removed by SS men. I broke my arm in February 1942 and spent 8 weeks in the hospital. After that time I never took part in any more executions. The only men of the above mentioned SS men that I can say were at all three executions were JAROLIN and PHILIPP, and due to the lapse of time I cannot say which men took part in the executions of November 1941 and which took part

ROS Ex 119a

226

Partial transcript of Simon Kiern's deposition, 30 October 1945. National Archives and Records Administration 581096, A1 2238, Box 289.

each committed "individual atrocities." Among the defendants was listed "Karl Kiepfer." A glance at Kiepfer's prisoner personnel file soon made clear, however, that this was not the same person. Neither the date of birth nor the Nazi Party membership number matched, though such inaccuracies were not unheard of in these documents. But Kiepfer had also served a prison sentence from 7 May 1945 until 6 May 1948, by which time Rudolf was already receiving letters from Karl in Langendiebach. The photographs in the file also left little doubt that this was not the same man.[63]

Could Kiern have been referring to a different person, someone who simply had a very similar name, when he made his statement in 1945? The two trials were unrelated, identifying entirely separate groups of co-conspirators. Frustratingly, research in the Dachau Archives yielded nothing whatsoever for either Kiepfer or Kipfer, and the fact that Kiepfer's name was frequently misspelled as Kipfer in the 1947 trial documentation only added to the confusion. The two men also held different military ranks, although Kiepfer's were SS or SA ranks that were unlikely to refer to Karl.[64]

Having reached an impasse with the Dachau documentation, I returned to Karl's *Wehrmacht* record. The information provided about his deployment was skeletal. The first unit into which Karl was drafted, and which identified him on his dog tag as "-216 - Lu. Fspr. Bau Kp. (m.) 3/9," was a *Luftwaffe* signals construction unit. This is probably where he received his basic training. On 11 March 1940, he was drafted into the battalion where he would serve for the next two years: *Luftnachrichten Abteilung* (air signals battalion) 32. He began in Company 2, and sometime before his discharge in April 1942 he was transferred to Company 4. His units' locations were not indicated, which left Dachau open as a possibility, even if not a verifiable or likely one.[65]

The only way to ascertain where Karl had been would be to track the activity of his units. Even for a historian accustomed to digging in archives, this was easier said than done. My multiple inquiries until this point had yielded few definitive results. It was at this juncture that I stumbled upon seventeen volumes, painstakingly compiled in the 1970s, cataloguing the organization and deployment of individual *Wehrmacht* formations during World War II. The volumes are not exactly user-friendly: a fair amount of specialist knowledge is needed to know where to even begin looking, and to make sense of the somewhat elliptical, abbreviated entries.

With the help of a military historian of World War II, I was able to ascertain that Karl's battalion, *Abteilung* 32, was attached to the II. *Fliegerkorps*, one of the sub-divisions of the German air force. Tracking the activity of the II. *Fliegerkorps*, we determined that Karl's unit was deployed in the invasion of France in May 1940, and then—as he had repeatedly stated—in the campaign against Britain in August 1940. As a support rather than a combat battalion, however, *Abteilung* 32 conducted its activities on the ground, and it seems to have been based in the region of Calais, where the *Fliegerkorps* had its headquarters. This corresponded with Karl's reflections in a 1949 letter to Rudolf about the time he had spent in "Ostend, Calais, Gent, Bruges, and Brussels," apparently milestones along the route from Germany to France. (For all Karl's gripes about the war, this part, at least, does not seem to have been so arduous: he fondly recalled to Rudolf his frequent outings to the Café Budapest in Ghent with a certain "Givette.")[66] On 22 June 1941, when Nazi Germany launched Operation Barbarossa against the Soviet Union, the II. *Fliegerkorps*—including *Abteilung* 32—was transferred to the eastern front.[67]

This was crucial. While the Nazis' war on the western front conformed largely to the conventions of warfare, at least in the early years when Karl served, the attack on the Soviet Union was conceived fundamentally differently. The historian Omer Bartov describes it as a "uniquely savage" war of extermination and enslavement, a conflict of unprecedented brutality during which twenty-four million Soviet citizens were killed, over half of them civilians. German soldiers shot, maimed, and murdered with impunity. They plundered resources with no regard for local populations. Not only Soviet commissars and POWs but also civilians of every undesirable stripe (Jews, Slavs, Roma) were taken to forced labor, tortured, or shot into mass graves. If mass graves were on Karl's mind, the eastern front was very likely the place where he had seen them.[68]

One question that arose was Karl's injury, which had led him to be hospitalized for long stretches. More than a year into his service, on 14 September 1940, he was taken to a *Luftwaffe* field hospital in Guînes, just outside Calais. His records, however, indicate the cause of hospitalization not as the spinal injury he claimed to have sustained during the Battle of Britain, but bronchitis. A few weeks later he was taken to a *Lazarett* back in Germany, in Detmold, though here again the cause listed was not a war injury but "Kinderlähmung" (poliomyelitis). None of his subsequent records indicate war injury of any kind.[69] Why then did Karl repeatedly insist that his spinal damage was a "souvenir" of the war? Was he ashamed of the otherwise unheroic reasons for his long periods in hospital? Or was this an expedient way of claiming postwar veterans' disability benefits?

The more interesting question, however, was the extent to which Karl's ill health affected his service. If he spent many months in hospital, perhaps he was never on the eastern front at all? It turned out, indeed, that when Operation Barbarossa was launched in June 1941, Karl was still in hospital at Bielefeld, where he had been transferred from nearby Detmold. From here, he was taken on 30 August 1941 to a military hospital in Frankfurt am Main. This, however, was Karl's last recorded hospitalization before his discharge seven months later. In early October 1941, he was back in action. *Luftflotte* 2, to which his battalion was attached, was still in the Soviet Union, based in the central sector of the eastern front. It would remain there for several more months before being transferred in January 1942 to the Mediterranean.[70]

More than this I was unlikely to establish. Where precisely his company was located in the large terrain that constituted the central sector, the daily tasks they were assigned over the course of several months, the people they encountered, the events they witnessed—all most likely eluded the historical record. But Karl's very presence on the eastern front was enough for me to begin to fathom his powerful sense of taintedness. He may not have been part of a shooting commando in Dachau (we would never know for sure), but complicity in the Third Reich took many forms.

At the time Karl was corresponding with Rudolf, a few years after the Nuremberg trials, popular perception was that Nazi atrocities were the work of a clique of die-hard individuals, confined to a handful of notorious camps. Today, we know the extent of "ordinary" German involvement to have been far greater. The categories of "perpetrator" and "bystander," once thought to distinguish neatly between those who had acted and those who had simply seen, are no longer helpful guides to understanding the nature and scope of individual involvement. Not only the SS but also police, civil servants, *Wehrmacht* soldiers, doctors, bureaucrats, and many others played a part in the Nazis' crimes. Some acted under orders, others on their own initiative; some watched from a distance, others were pulled in from the sidelines and asked to lend a hand. Mass shootings on the eastern front were not infrequently observed by crowds of bemused or fascinated onlookers.[71]

In the mid-1990s, the exhibition *Crimes of the German Wehrmacht* confronted an uncertain German public with the reality of ordinary soldiers' widespread participation in Nazi atrocities on the eastern front. The vast majority of German soldiers—close to twenty million served between 1939 and 1945—were at the very least aware of Nazi crimes, and sizeable numbers were actively involved. Relatively few were inspired by ideological commitment to the Nazi cause. Far more often, they were motivated by factors such as military discipline, careerism, and peer pressure, especially in the context of the barbarization of war on the eastern front, which carried with it a powerfully dehumanized notion of the Soviet enemy. Racism was not, it must be stressed, a Nazi monopoly. For many soldiers, the racial war against the Soviet Union was legitimated by conceptions of "an inferior people," "animals," and "members of a foreign race."[72] Karl shared the ardent anti-Bolshevik sentiments of his compatriots, and in his letters he made frequent unashamed references to Red Army soldiers who outdid the SS in their brutality.[73]

By the time Karl left the eastern front in early 1942, roughly two million Soviet POWs had already died, either directly or indirectly, at the Nazis' hands.[74] The *Wehrmacht* soldier Konrad Jarausch admitted to a friend in late August 1941 that even those posted far behind the front lines had "seen here the misery that war brings."[75] In short, the fact that Karl was a low-ranking Nazi soldier deployed in an unexceptional army support unit says little about what he heard, saw, or was even drawn into. During the many months he spent in the military hospital, he also encountered wounded soldiers who had been brought back to Germany for treatment. And in the spring of 1942, when he returned to Hanau, he would have seen Jews marked with the yellow star, among them perhaps Rudolf's mother Martha and his brother Hans, and men performing forced labor in the town's streets.[76] It is also entirely possible that he witnessed the deportation of Hanau's Jews from the *Hauptbahnhof* in late May and early September, which occurred in full view of the public. It is not easy to imagine what his response might have been.

Karl's application for denazification, the final bit of archival evidence, was unable to solve fully the mystery of his story.[77] Conceived by the Allied military authorities before the war's end, denazification was born of an idealistic American foreign policy aimed at reforming the enemy. Its objective was to remove Nazis from public and semi-public positions in Germany, and to replace them with "persons who, by their political and moral qualities, are deemed capable of assisting in developing genuine democratic institutions in Germany."[78]

From the outset the system was a shambles. The problem was the sheer number of people implicated in the Nazi Party and its affiliated organizations. The American military authorities vastly underestimated the time and resources it would take to process the cases, and by the end of 1945 around 3.5 million people were still waiting to be classified.

In June 1946 the jurisdiction for denazification was transferred to German hands, with the passing of the Law for Liberation from National Socialism and Militarism. The Law established five levels of culpability: Major Offenders, Incriminated, Less Incriminated, Followers or "Fellow Travelers," and Exonerated. Questionnaires called *Meldebogen* (Report sheets) were distributed to all adults in the American zone requesting information about past political activities and affiliations. Hundreds of denazification tribunals were set up to try Nazi officials, Party members, and members of Nazi organizations.

On his questionnaire, Karl indicated that he had been a member of the Nazi Party, and Nazi welfare, trade union, and sports organizations. He stated that he had not profited financially from his Nazi affiliations, nor held any prominent positions, nor belonged to other organizations such as the SS, the Gestapo, or even the Hitler Youth. He also indicated that he had served in *Luftwaffe* air signals regiment 32, and that in March 1942 he obtained the rank of *Unteroffizier* (Junior Non-Commissioned Officer). This last assertion was disproved by his *Wehrmacht* documentation, which indicated his rank at the time of discharge as the rank-and-file *Gefreiter* (Junior Cadet).[79] Asked in which category he would place himself, he responded *Mitläufer* (fellow traveler). He noted also that he was "helpless and incapable of working due to a war injury (in receipt of nursing-care benefits)."[80]

With millions of chargeable denazification cases it was impossible to adequately cross-check records, and it soon became clear to the occupation authorities that completing all the trials would take years. In an attempt to address the problem, several large-scale amnesties were extended. In December 1946, an amnesty was given to those whose chargeable status was not higher than "Follower" and who were either in a low-income group or at least 50 percent disabled (it was dubbed the "Christmas Amnesty"). On the basis of his severe disability, Karl was denazified under its provisions and exempted from "restrictions of any kind whatsoever."[81] His exemption meant that he was never brought to trial, and the details of his wartime participation were never documented or investigated. He had misrepresented at least one small detail about his past, but it would be impossible to establish with certainty whether he might have been dishonest about other things as well.

The amnesty measures removed almost 2.5 million pending cases from inquiry, significantly reducing the pressure on the tribunals, but also unquestionably exculpating many who deserved punishment.[82] The exoneration of these millions was the result not of careful scrutiny but rather of an impossibly overburdened system—a pardon by default that bore no relation to what they had actually done. It would be impossible to know how many of them were genuinely innocent, and how many simply slipped through the net.

Countless former Nazis also escaped punishment thanks to the tribunals' excessive leniency, corruption, and inconsistent implementation. The process of

102			W 279	K
Lfd. Nr.	Einlieferungsort	Einlieferungstag	Aktenzeichen	Buchstabe

Meldebogen

auf Grund des Gesetzes zur Befreiung von Nationalsozialismus und Militarismus vom 5. 3. 1946

Deutlich und lesbar ausfüllen (Druckbuchstaben)! Dick umrahmtes nicht ausfüllen! Jede Frage ist zu beantworten!

Zuname _Kipfer_ Vornamen _Karl_ Beruf _Kaufmann_
Wohnort _Langendiebach_ Straße _Engegasse 10_
Geburtsdatum _5. 7. 1910_ Geburtsort _Giessen_ Familienstand ledig/verheiratet/verwitwet/geschieden
Wohnorte seit 1933:
a) _Hanau/Main, Langstr. 47_ von _1933_ bis _6. 1. 1945_
b) _____ von _____ bis _____
c) _____ von _____ bis _____

1.	Waren Sie jemals Angehöriger, Anwärter, Mitglied, förderndes Mitglied der:	Ja oder Nein	Höchster Mitgliedsbeitrag monatlich RM	von	bis	Mit-glieds- Nr.	höchster Rang oder höchstes bekleidetes Amt oder Tätigkeit, auch vertretungsweise oder ehrenhalber Bezeichnung	von	bis	Klasse oder Teil B
a	NSDAP.	Ja	1.80	1.33	1945	3867957	Keine			
b	Allg. SS	Nein								
c	Waffen-SS	Nein								
d	Gestapo	Nein								
e	SD (Sicherheitsdienst der SS)*	Nein								
f	Geheime Feldpolizei	Nein								
g	SA.	Nein								
h	NSKK. (NS-Kraftfahr-Korps)	Nein								
i	NSFK. (NS-Flieger-Korps)	Nein								
k	NSF. (NS-Frauenschaft)	Nein								
l	NSDSTB. (NS-Studentenbund)	Nein								
m	NSDoB. (NS-Dozentenbund)	Nein								
n	HJ.	Nein								
o	BdM.	Nein								

*Hier ist auch nebenamtliche Mitarbeit, z. B. Vertrauensmann, aufzuführen.

2.	Gehörten Sie außer Ziffer 1 einer Naziorganisation gemäß Anhang zum Gesetz an?* Bezeichnung	von	bis	höchster Rang oder höchstes bekleidetes Amt oder Tätigkeit, auch vertretungsweise oder ehrenhalber Bezeichnung	von	bis	
a	DAF	1933	1945	Keine			
b	NSV	1934	1945	Keine			
c	NS-Kriegsopferversorgung	1942	1945	Keine			
d	Reichsbund f. Leibesübungen	1933	1945	Vorfechter	1933	1945	
e							
f							
g							

*Es ist jedem freigestellt hier auch die Zugehörigkeit zu anderen Organisationen nachzuweisen.

3. Waren Sie Träger von Parteiauszeichnungen (Parteiorden), Empfänger von Ehrensold oder sonstiger Parteibegünstigungen? _Nein_
Welcher?

4. Hatten Sie irgendwann Vorteile durch Ihre Mitgliedschaft bei einer Naziorganisation (z. B. durch Zuschüsse, durch Sonderzuteilungen der Wirtschaftsgruppe, Beförderungen, UK-Stellung u.ä.)? _Nein_
Welche?

5. Machten Sie jemals finanzielle Zuwendungen an die NSDAP. oder eine sonstige Naziorg.? _Nein_
an welche: _____ in welchen Jahren: _____ insgesamt RM: _____

Karl Kipfer's submission to the denazification authorities, April 1946. Courtesy of the Hessisches Hauptstaatsarchiv, Wiesbaden, Abt. 520/ WA Nr. 278.

denazification steadily lost public support, and within a few years, as Karl told Rudolf, "no one wanted to hear about it anymore." Although he was one of the beneficiaries of denazification, he recognized it to be a sham. He told Rudolf about a mutual friend who was imprisoned in 1945 because of his Nazi past but then "coughed up a little, paid the gentlemen off, and took a job with the Yanks."[83]

By the time the Federal Republic of Germany was established in 1949, there were widespread calls for the amnestying and integration of millions of former

6. Zugehörigkeit zur Wehrmacht, Polizeiformationen, RAD, OT, Transportgruppe Speer u. ä.

	Genaue Bezeichnung der Formation	höchster erreichter Rang	ab wann	Klasse oder Teil B
a	Ln.Rgt. 32	Unteroffizier	1.3.42	
b				

c	Waren Sie NS-Führungsoffizier (auch wenn nicht bestätigt)? Nein	von _____	bis _____
d	Waren Sie Generalstabsoffizier? Nein Rang _____	von _____	bis _____

7. In welchen **Organisationen** (Wirtschaft, Wohlfahrt) bekleideten Sie ein Haupt-, Neben- oder Ehrenamt?

	Bezeichnung	von	bis	höchster Rang od. höchstes bekleidetes Amt od. Tätigkeit, auch vertretungsweise od. ehrenhalber Bezeichnung	von	bis	
a	Keine						
b							
c							
d							
e							
f							

8. Angaben über Ihre **Haupttätigkeit**, Einkommen und Vermögen seit 1932

Ziff.	Jahr	Waren Sie selbständig oder Arbeitnehmer?	Falls selbständig, Zahl der Beschäftigt.	Stellung od. Dienstbezeichnung als Arbeiter, Handwerker, Angestellter, Beamter, Vorstand, Gesellschafter, Aufsichtsrat, Unternehmer, freier Beruf etc.	Firma des Arbeitgebers oder eigene Firma bezw. Berufsbezeichnung mit Anschrift	Steuerpflichtig. Gesamt-Einkommen des Betroffenen RM	Steuerpflichtig. Vermögen des Betroffenen RM
a	1932	Arbeitnehmer		Kfm. Angestellter	ohne Stellung	Keins	Keins
b	1934	desgl.		Kfm. Angestellter	Dt. Arbeitsfront, Hanau	2400.-	Keins
c	1938	desgl.		Kfm. Angestellter	M. Kreusel, Hanau	3500.-	Keins
d	1943	Arbeitsunfähig		durch Kriegsbeschädigung		Keins	Keins
e	1945	Arbeitsunfähig		durch Kriegsbeschädigung		Keins	Keins

9. Haben Sie Unternehmen oder Betriebe betreut oder kontrolliert? Nein
Welche? _____

10. Wurden Ihnen von Staat, Partei, Wirtschaft o. ä. Organisationen bisher nicht aufgeführte Titel, Dienstränge oder -bezeichnungen verliehen? Nein
Welche? _____

11. Läuft oder lief für Sie bereits ein Prüfungsverfahren? Nein Akt.-Zeich _____
Wo? _____ Mit welchem Ergebnis? _____

12. Ist Ihre Beschäftigung von der Militärregierung schriftlich genehmigt? Nicht betreffend
Vorläufig? _____ Endgültig? _____ Ist Ihre Beschäftigung von der Militärregierung abgelehnt? _____
Durch welche örtliche Militärregierung u. wann wurde Ihre Beschäftigung genehmigt oder abgelehnt?
Nicht betreffend
Ich versichere die Richtigkeit und Vollständigkeit der von mir gemachten Angaben. Falsche oder irreführende oder unvollständige Angaben werden gemäß Art. 65 des Gesetzes zur Befreiung von Nationalsozialismus und Militarismus mit Gefängnis oder mit Geldstrafe bestraft.

13. In welche Gruppe des Gesetzes gliedern Sie sich ein? Mitläufer
Falls Sie glauben, daß das Gesetz nicht auf Sie Anwendung findet, geben Sie Gründe an: _____

14. Bemerkungen: Ich bin durch Kriegsbeschädigung arbeitsunfähig und hilflos (Pflegezulage empfangen)

24.4.1946.
Datum

Unterschrift: Kipfer Karl
Name   Vorname

Karl Kipfer's submission to the denazification authorities, April 1946. Courtesy of the Hessisches Hauptstaatsarchiv, Wiesbaden, Abt. 520/ WA Nr. 278.

Party members punished by the Allies. The final years of Karl's life coincided with a critical period for the new German state, as it made the transition from years of war and occupation to a stable society. Key to that transition was marking the new West Germany off from the Nazi past. The amnesty program had widespread public and political support, and there was an obvious pragmatic motive behind it: if all former Party members were to be punished, then a large proportion of the adult population in West Germany would be removed from political and economic life "at a time when the country needed every productive hand and capable, experienced brain it could muster."[84] But even if the pardoning of millions of "minor" Nazis could be justified, the public's willingness to support even the most heinous perpetrators raised troubling questions about German attitudes toward guilt and responsibility after the war.[85] Karl's past, like that of so many others, quickly receded in the face of an inexorable current of denialism and forward progress.

Germany's reluctance to confront the past was a subject around which Karl and Rudolf found much common ground. They often talked sarcastically about the epidemic of "withered memory" they encountered in dealings with local authorities, and mocked those who claimed never to have supported the Nazis. Karl quipped:

> One gets the impression that the Nazi Party was the largest anti-fascist organization that ever existed, for if you listened to its former members now you'd think they were all opposed to it from the very beginning.[86]

He talked about how he had seen Hanau authorities and residents shamelessly pilfering Jewish property and profiting from the Jews, despite their later spirited claims to the contrary.[87] He had also seen the *Wehrmacht* and other organizations refuse to acknowledge their misdeeds:

> It is absolutely clear that some sections of the military and certain government offices and individuals disgraced themselves utterly through their behavior during the war. Increasingly, however, one sees many cases in which the newspaper correspondents who are now portraying this behavior as if it was universal are doing so to cover up their own misdeeds. There was an excellent example of this recently. There was a particular editor-in-chief at the *Mainpost* newspaper whose every line, by the time he had emptied his ink pot, was about how all German soldiers ate at least one child for breakfast. Around 8 weeks ago I was astonished to read a report, out of the blue, saying the Yanks had unceremoniously axed this man from his job, because it had turned out that during the war he had written inflammatory articles for the German newspaper in Belgrade. They were, it seems, the same sort of articles he writes now, but under different auspices. It's exactly the same with the "acquiring" and "organizing" of property that took place in the occupied countries. We who should supposedly hang our heads in shame

had very few opportunities to do any of it, although of course there were offenders among us too. But it was nothing in comparison to that rabble that came after us, or to those we later referred to as the occupying troops. That lot certainly never had it so good in their lives as they did in the army.[88]

Unlike others who claimed not to remember anything, however, Karl talked frequently about taking responsibility for what had happened. "Once your reputation's in the bin," he joked, "your best years can begin."[89] In October 1948 he wrote to Rudolf:

I think "convenient memory" is a very mild description of the condition afflicting people here in Germany. One might better describe it as amputation of the memory. It's odd, though, that one part of the memory has survived the amputation; namely the part that helps people remember how the Nazis forced them to join their ridiculous party by means of extreme and brutal violence. I have to say I don't entirely understand how one can lose only part of one's memory but apparently I am too simple-minded to comprehend it. Two years ago a relative came to visit me. When she saw me reduced to an eighth of my former size, as I am, she immediately launched into a tirade of curses against the Nazis. I, on the other hand, told her straight out that I couldn't join her in cursing them because I myself had been one, meaning that I would be describing myself as a marauding band of murderers, vagabonds, crooks, and criminals, etc. At first she nearly fainted from the shock of finding herself related to such a person, but then she admitted that she too had gone "with the times" back then. That, at least, was honest of her. Most people don't remember anything about it these days, and the most unpleasant of such people are those who protest loudly when you remind them that they did very well financially by going "with the times" back then.[90]

Karl ridiculed the opportunistic political shifts that he witnessed all around him:

Just between you and me, I haven't met a single German in the last three years apart from myself who was a Nazi, just as during the war I didn't meet a single German soldier apart from myself who wasn't a willing volunteer. The masses turn any way the wind blows. I want no part of it and I've already just told you what I think of it.[91]

In March 1949 he told Rudolf about the trial of Veit Harlan, director of several antisemitic propaganda films. Karl hadn't seen the notorious *Jud Süss* when it was released in 1940, but all his friends had raved about it.

> Now, exactly the same people are saying precisely the opposite. Harlan and all the actors are claiming in court that Goebbels forced them to make the film, and that if they hadn't they would have been locked up.... I know people who, on each of the three occasions on which state power has changed hands during the last 30 years, have had to run to whoever the new big-wigs were to have it certified that they always supported them.[92]

Another favorite target of Karl's invective was the new philosemitism sweeping Germany, as everyone suddenly sought out Jewish "friends":

> You should have seen what happened here after 1945. Everyone hurried to find themselves some Jewish friends and then scampered off to the denazification board with them to get themselves exonerated with their help. The bigger the big-wig, the more he had done, apparently, to help the Jews. Now I'm excited to see what people will do if the Reds arrive one day.[93]

Karl had emerged from the war with a profound disdain for politics. Everyone was singing the praises of Germany's so-called democracy, but the "voting-cattle" (*Stimmvieh*) kept reelecting the same corrupt leaders, blindly swayed by all the "election-lard, election-butter and election-bread" that was doled out. Since 1945 he had refused to vote, even in support of rights for disabled war veterans.[94] He had turned down the opportunity to stand for regional elections in 1946

> because I'm absolutely determined to maintain my abstinence from politics. In politics, as in war and at the cinema, the best places are at the back. That was certainly true in 14/18. There's another saying from those times that's also still applicable: you'll find the heroes in the mass graves, the suckers at the front lines, and the wise men at home. I've had my fill of politics once and for all.[95]

Karl savored any chance to mock authority, ranting at the swindle of currency reform and the hypocrisy of German rearmament, and condemning the disparity between rich and poor ("The people have it hard while the fat cats have the lard").[96] In July 1948 he offered Rudolf his cynical interpretation of current events:

> People everywhere are afraid there could be a war between the West and the East, especially here, because we would bear the brunt of it. After all, they promised the world eternal peace in 1945 but it hasn't lasted long, and things are already backfiring, first in Indonesia and China, then in Greece and Palestine. Who knows whether it'll start up again here tomorrow? Between you and me, I don't believe there'll ever be peace as long as there are generals. Anyone who has chosen soldiering as a profession will always strive for the opportunity to do his job. The higher his rank, the stronger his desire to use those professional abilities because doing so becomes less and less dangerous. Wars should be fought as duels between the highest ranking military men and politicians; the world would look a lot different then. But as long as one man can send millions of innocent people to their deaths with just a simple command, then nothing on this earth will change. Such men are reckless and brutal when it comes to achieving their goals regardless of which side they're on. . . . If there is to be a war between East and West . . . I'm just happy that I won't have to take an active part in it, as these days I couldn't even help them conquer a single flowerpot. But I'd like to know what the politicians of today who are shouting so loudly about the Bolshevik threat have to say. There are so many more important things going on in the world than the stuff that's sending them into convulsions. Instead of spending billions on rearmament they should use that money for river control and building railways, streets and housing, and then all mankind really would be satisfied and happy. But that's enough politics, I'll retreat back now into my non-political and peaceful existence.[97]

Karl ridiculed the hypocrisy of those who supported German remilitarization, noting drily that it was exciting to everyone, "except for those who will actually have the honor of serving as cannon fodder in the next war." As for himself, he had resolved that "if there really is going to be another war, since it's not as if anyone's going to ask us if we would like to have one, then I have only one wish: to have a huge boulder dropped on my head immediately."[98]

The state's mishandling of reparations claims was yet more grist to Karl's mill. He ranted that the whole thing was nothing more than an "empty gesture," and derided the authorities' claim to be working for the benefit of the victims. "Don't make me laugh!!!" he wrote in November 1948. "Have you ever known a state organization or a state-sponsored organization to throw a few crumbs to the citizens of the state? I haven't."[99] He was convinced that the state was deliberately exploiting legal get-out clauses to dodge its responsibility to the victims, and refused to be taken in by their evasion and lies. When one of Rudolf's claims for compensation was rejected in early 1949, Karl wrote directly to the reparations authorities in Frankfurt:

> All items made of precious metals or stones owned by Jews in Hanau am Main had to be handed over to the *Landesleihbank*. . . . It is grossly unreasonable that the *Landesleihbank* is now justifying itself on the grounds that its records were destroyed on 19.3.1945 due to the war, but nevertheless demands that people entitled to compensation produce the certificates of receipt they were given at that time. If even the *Landesleihbank* was unable to preserve its own records, then how could a victim of persecution have kept his receipts safe through persecution, deportation, concentration camps, crematoria and mass graves?[100]

Rudolf, like Karl, was exasperated by the rampant amnesia he encountered as he pursued his claims. No one remembered anything about the treatment of the Jews. No one would admit to confiscating Jewish property. All records had conveniently been destroyed in bombing raids. Bank officials and civil servants were deliberately elusive and uncooperative. The authorities demanded unreasonable proof of property ownership, and imposed unworkable deadlines for the submission of claims.[101]

In mocking the "swindle" of reparations, however, Karl was expressing not only Rudolf's grievances but also his own. The state's neglect of Jewish victims was, for him, parallel to its neglect of war veterans, and his anger stemmed from what he perceived to be the government's failure to provide for all its vulnerable citizens. "When it comes to emotional suffering," he wrote to Rudolf in August 1949,

> no one got off any easier than anyone else. In the East they poured petrol over Germans, set them alight and let them run around on fire. Here in the West they used phosphorous instead of petrol, which admittedly lightened the workload for the chaps on the other side as it meant they didn't need to light a match. Both methods have the same result. And, in the East, in the case of a mother holding her child's hand when the

child was blown into the air by a gunshot, upon which the Russian soldier burst into peals of laughter at his winning shot, that woman was certainly no less upset than were the two parents in Hanau obliged to watch as their daughter burned alive because she was stuck so fast in rubble they couldn't free her. There are no grounds for differentiating between these people; all the more so as everyone is supposed to be equal before the law according to the new constitution.[102]

Karl often described how, like Rudolf, he found himself constantly battling obstructive officials who refused to help him. Like Rudolf, he had been abandoned by a state that despite its noble public pronouncements did not care about its victims. All its lofty proclamations about helping war veterans were, as with reparations, "just a swindle."[103] While other former Nazis were paid generously, he received a paltry pension that barely covered his basic needs. Even police dogs were better provided for. Had the war cripples been "of decent character," he remarked sardonically, they "would have consented to being shot dead so now the state wouldn't have to pay their war pensions."[104] But it was the state's responsibility to ensure the injured had enough to live on, even if this meant there was less money for those who had been persecuted. "Big business profits and the small man pays," he fumed—and often he portrayed himself and Rudolf as equally small, similarly pitted against official corruption and stonewalling.

Amidst all of his raging and recriminations, the question of Karl's past lingered. He condemned the hypocrisy and amnesia that surrounded him, and yet for all his insistence on being honest about his past, he never spoke about it explicitly. There is no doubt that he recognized the suffering endured by Rudolf's family, but he was also endlessly preoccupied with his own persecution. What was the connection between his powerful feeling of taintedness—his repeated allusions to his "undemocratic past"—and his equally ardent perception of victimhood? And how did these seemingly opposing forces shape his renewed relationship with his Jewish friend?

In many ways, their friendship seemed basically to have taken up where it left off. They joked together, reminisced about the past, grumbled about women, shared intimate concerns. In their conversations about politics or reparations, the Nazi past was often implicit, but it was seldom the focus.

Some of the most puzzling pieces of their correspondence were their lengthy exchanges about poisons and pesticides. By 1948 Rudolf was working in the field of pest control, and he traveled widely in South Africa to advise retailers and manufacturers. He also offered advice in letters to relatives who had problems with insect infestations, and he discussed the topic frequently with Karl, too. Karl would complain at length about the bugs in the "dung pit" where he lived, and they would proceed to discuss which insects were killed most effectively by which poisons. DDT was fine for flies, wrote Karl in October 1949, but for spiders a product called Jacutin seemed to be better.[105] Two weeks later, Rudolf responded:

> It is absolutely true that DDT barely has any effect on spiders as it is a very selective poison. And thank God for that, because otherwise we wouldn't be able to use it as easily or as carelessly as we do. The Jacutin tablets sound very interesting. We have something similar here: smoke capsules of DDT and BHC. However, no smoke can last as long as a spray; in any case we've never seen one here that does. If some technical literature is indeed available on Jacutin I would be very interested in it, especially as they say the smoke can penetrate wood and destroy wood-worm. I can't see any possible explanation for that. Ordinary air can't even do that never mind air that's been thickened with smoke. I've been using a gas for some time now that penetrates particularly well and has exceptional properties in this regard. But the minimum time required for it to be effective on wood is now 6–8 hours, and the house has to be 100% sealed up, much more carefully than when using ordinary potassium cyanide gas. . . . Of course I'm aware that during the war and in the period shortly before it the Germans made progress with phosphorous insecticides. But these are usually very dangerous substances and can have unpleasant side effects on humans and animals.[106]

In a series of later letters, Karl also told Rudolf in detail about a spate of Hanau murders and suicides using a poison called E605. Rudolf responded with great interest.[107] Their conversation about poison gas was entirely devoid of irony or insinuation: indeed, the most remarkable thing about it is how unremarkable it was to them. If anything, it was an indication of how normal their relationship was, seemingly untouched by everything that had happened in between.

Neither Karl nor Rudolf ever explicitly addressed the significance of their reconnection. Perhaps this was unsurprising. What would they have said? For both, the past was still too raw, the losses too recent, and the present difficulties too great to warrant the luxury of extended reflection. Both nonetheless clearly derived comfort from their relationship as the months passed. On the face of it, Rudolf's reparations claims were an opportunity for Karl to supplement his meager income. They also served as an outlet for his anger, and provided him with some human contact, if only with truculent officials. Over time, however, the claims also assumed a more profound significance than either Karl or Rudolf could have foreseen, and that perhaps neither even recognized.

Part of the appeal for Karl was undoubtedly the opportunity the claims afforded him to take on the German state. He took pleasure in raging at the "pack of insolent, lying fat cats" in the reparations office and "blowing sugar up their arses" in order to elicit the responses he wanted.[108] He was determined to take the state for what it was worth, and went to great lengths to do so. But he had no confidence that the claims would amount to anything and knew that the chances of success were minimal. Why, then, did he pursue them with such dogged fervor, particularly given his physical state? Within a year, he had even quietly stopped asking for payment for his work. Remuneration, in other words, quickly ceased to be a motivating factor.

If the Jewish refugees saw the reparations claims as a way to force Germany to acknowledge their suffering, for Karl, too, pursuing the claims was a moral necessity, a fundamental matter of principle. Germany could not be allowed to get away with what it had done to its victims. That Karl perceived himself as a victim simply added to the intensity with which he worked. His determined and relentless commitment to the claims laid bare something deeper, if less quantifiable, than merely legal or financial motivations. Was this his attempt to seek absolution, even if only from his own conscience, for his "undemocratic past"?

Karl's attitude echoed a larger narrative of German victimhood that characterized the postwar memory culture of West Germany. Until at least the late 1950s, Germans were preoccupied with the massive suffering they had endured in the final phases of the war and its aftermath: aerial bombardments with huge civilian casualties, military defeat, millions of soldiers who remained "missing" or in captivity in the Soviet Union, the violent expulsion of German-speaking civilians from eastern Europe, and Allied occupation. Many believed they had fought a legitimate war of national defense, and saw soldiers as unwitting victims who had simply done their duty at the front. Karl certainly felt that he had been mere cannon fodder in a war not of his own making, and his own victimhood, like that of many of his fellow countrymen, overshadowed any concern he might have felt about the genocide of the Jews.[109]

It might be tempting to dismiss this narrative as offensively self-centered, a simple and stubborn refusal on the part of ordinary Germans to acknowledge what their country had done. But memory cultures are rarely so straightforward. While the narrative of victimhood may have been shaped in part by political expediency, Germans were also not inventing their suffering, nor were they only avoiding guilt, as the historian Neil Gregor has stressed: they "were also seeking to make sense of an unprecedented set of experiences which no obvious language existed to describe."[110] It was not until the 1960s, long after Karl's death, that critical dialogue on this question began to emerge in any meaningful form.

What Karl endured during the war was devastating. In August 1939 he was a fit, gregarious twenty-nine-year-old. Less than three years later, he returned to his hometown severely disabled and virtually unable to work. The state offered meager support. Left homeless by an Allied air raid in the spring of 1945, the incapacitated thirty-four-year-old was then forced out to a tiny nearby village, surrounded by people he despised, with little to fill his time, and few friends or family members for company.

Karl was undoubtedly angry. He was angry at the state for its indifference to his suffering. He was angry at the corrupt leaders and generals who were oblivious to the lives that could be destroyed by their fickle actions. He was angry about selective amnesia. But it is one thing to be angry, another to be morally outraged—and this Karl was not. He remained a committed anti-Bolshevist until his death, convinced that the Soviet Union would provoke the next world war. He also seemed surprisingly unmoved by what had happened to Rudolf's family, although he gathered enough shocking details while he pursued their claims. He even joked with Rudolf that he would have made a top-notch corpse-in-charge in a mass grave.

In her book *The Mark of Cain*, the theologian Katharina von Kellenbach studies the postwar responses of perpetrators convicted of direct involvement in Nazi atrocities. Many of her subjects were willing to talk about their actions, but most would not acknowledge guilt, and their testimonies were "purposefully and tenaciously obtuse, their writing convoluted, their recollections deceitful, and their thinking twisted."[111] Some adopted the language of religion or even underwent conversion, but often these expressions of Christian piety were precisely what enabled them to deny responsibility. Confession and conversion served as "get out of purgatory free" cards that allowed them to evade genuine contrition. Many perpetrators claimed ignorance of the camps and blamed Nazi brutality on a few bad apples, emphasizing instead their own devotion to the fatherland. Even when they admitted to carrying out heinous acts, most denied moral agency and refused to accept personal responsibility or to express remorse for what they had done.[112]

Biblical phrases, invoked sarcastically, were Karl's favorite weapon for mocking the hypocrisy of German officialdom. Was this a conscious gibe at how others were hiding behind religious language? Another means by which he could distinguish his own sincere contrition from their mendacious prevarications? Or was he, like others, more preoccupied with his own victimhood than with acknowledging the harm he might have caused others?

Another recurring theme was Karl's contempt for the state and his pacifism, both borne of his experience as a foot soldier forced to do someone else's dirty work. This, too, could be read in different ways. In postwar Germany, the peace movement was an unlikely meeting point for leftists, war-weary veterans, and perpetrators alike. For the latter it served as an "opportunity to fold genocide into the general devastation of war"—in other words, to find easy exoneration using the widely sanctioned moral language of the time.[113] Was Karl's pacifism a response to his harrowing experiences as a soldier, or was it yet another way of avoiding personal responsibility?

Karl was not an ideologically committed Nazi, and he was almost certainly not a hands-on killer. Perpetrators such as those described by von Kellenbach, who were convicted criminals, denied their actions to avoid obvious punishment, and perhaps because they needed to distance themselves psychologically from what they had done. The position of someone like Karl was more ambivalent. He had, by his own admission, been a longtime supporter of "undemocratic" politics, and he joined the Nazi Party of his own accord. He had also served in the *Wehrmacht* for two and a half years, including several months on the eastern front, and was at the very least an onlooker, if not an accessory, to some of the war's crimes.

If Karl was a cog in the Nazi machine, he was a minuscule and utterly unremarkable one. Paradoxically, however, it was precisely his insignificance in the larger Nazi system that led him to feel a shameful guilt and taintedness, a sense that he had participated, however marginally, in perpetuating a genocidal system. Karl's responses do not exactly constitute taking responsibility, but he persistently acknowledged his feelings of complicity, and found an intriguing, if not entirely conscious, way of expressing his contrition.

Over the course of Karl and Rudolf's almost seven years of correspondence, there was a significant shift in the way Karl came to terms with his "undemocratic past." It was almost certainly not calculated, and never explicitly articulated; it was also impossible to pin down the moment at which it crystallized. Despite his dire condition, Karl obstinately hobbled on, pursuing onerous and fruitless legal claims with unremitting energy. He was undeterred by obstructive bureaucrats and even by Rudolf's thankless relatives, who never forgot his Nazi past and never ceased to mistrust his motives. His work on Rudolf's claims was perhaps a way to process his sense of complicity, and restore his moral agency—

as he put it, to "relieve the sorrows of my existence." He never mentioned the question of guilt to Rudolf, nor did he likely consider it consciously himself. Rather, he quietly devoted the remainder of his life to the project of "making good," though he would never have articulated it as such, and would have balked at such sentimental language.

A small offhand reference revealed in a similar way Karl's ongoing pursuit of moral recovery. In May 1951, he mentioned to Rudolf a young boy with whom he had struck up a friendship. The boy had fled from his home in East Prussia and had been detained in a camp for two years. Since his return to Germany he had been suffering badly from rheumatism, and he now attended the same facility where Karl was undergoing treatment. Without being asked to do so, the boy had begun to help Karl with various odd jobs. He had also now started coming to Karl's house to help him with difficult physical jobs like chopping wood. Karl, in turn, was helping him with his school work. But the child had been so generous, Karl told Rudolf, that he wanted to recognize him in a more substantial way. He had thus decided to name him as sole heir in his will.[114] Karl did not have much to put in his will in the first place, but his gesture was moving in its symbolism.

How did Rudolf, for his part, deal with his friend's "undemocratic past"? Despite the personal devastation the Holocaust had wrought, Rudolf was reluctant to talk about it until the day he died. Like many refugees, he spent the early postwar years trying to rebuild his life, and it was only toward the end of the 1960s that he began to talk about the importance of "occasionally" reminding the public "that these things did happen."[115]

Rudolf's anger at Germany and the Nazis did, however, spill over into the pages of his letters. From afar he followed the Nuremberg trials and other investigations into Nazi crimes, and remained resolute that no punishment could compensate for what had been lost. His anger was at its rawest in the immediate postwar years, and it was not only the "mass murderers" who were its targets. For him, ordinary Germans had followed the Nazis like sheep, and should be held equally responsible for what had happened.[116]

In their responses to Rudolf's advertisement in January 1948, former neighbors and acquaintances had described their valiant efforts to help his family. Sepp Weigelt highlighted his devoted friendship and refusal to succumb to Nazi intimidation:

> As you know I was always a good friend of your family; even the Nazis couldn't change that. . . . I wasn't afraid of them and didn't let them stop me visiting your parents every evening until I was called up for military

service in June 1942. When I was on leave I brought your mother and Hans something to eat every evening, the entire time I was there.[117]

Rudolf, however, maintained a deep-seated skepticism about Germans' behavior during the Nazi period. He dissected his German correspondents' claims in order to evaluate their reliability, and often asked them secretly to report on one another. He did the same with Karl, asking two contacts in strict confidence to investigate his reputation and his handling of the family's claims. To Rosa and Siegfried he confessed that "despite all these wonderful assurances I don't believe a single word anyone says. I can't escape the feeling that they're all hiding something."[118] In August 1947 he wrote in English to his uncle Phillippe in Belgium:

> I have no pity for German "victims." They also seem to have forgotten, that some six Million jews [*sic*] alone were killed by these beasts and that sixty million Germans did very little to stop this and the innumerable other atrocities committed in their name. There is a very apt German proverb "If you're caught alongside them, you hang alongside them!" and I am not in the very least sorry for them.[119]

Upon hearing about the almost complete devastation of Hanau in 1945, he wrote in his newfound English: "it did my heart good to know, that there was some kind of judgment, very grim and thorough [*sic*], I admit, executed and they do realize to-day how it is to be on the receiving end."[120]

To what extent did Rudolf's views about Germany shift after his reconnection with Karl? In defending his Nazi friend to his relatives, Rudolf emphasized not only that he was an effective and devoted agent, but also that he was one of those rare Germans who had sincerely faced up to what he had done. But without knowledge of Karl's experiences, how did Rudolf reach this conclusion? Did he simply trust Karl and believe in his transformation? Did he perhaps reason that Karl was his best hope of success for compensation? Or was this explanation a way of getting his relatives to co-operate? In July 1951 he wrote to Alex:

> Kipfer really seems to be the best, we can get under the circumstances, but, I don't trust a single one of these B. . . . . ds over there, implicitly. I can't forget what they have done to our Dear ones and us.[121]

Rudolf may just have been appeasing his relatives with such remarks, but there is enough evidence to suggest that this is also what he genuinely felt. While he expressed concern, for example, that Karl be fairly remunerated for his work, he was paying him far less than his other agent in Worms, who was providing a terrible service. He thought highly of Karl's work, but obviously realized that he could get away with paying him less.

Rudolf also strongly rejected Karl's narrative of victimhood. In response to the remark that "there are no grounds for differentiating" between victims, Rudolf retorted that "if compensation payments are to be calculated based on the severity of emotional and psychological suffering, then we Jews without doubt have the biggest claim."[122] At heart, Rudolf seems never to have dispelled entirely his doubts about Karl's Nazi past.

Rudolf's ambivalence was not dispelled when Karl died suddenly in January 1955, at the age of forty-four. The obituary was published in the *Hanauer Anzeiger*:

> Today, suddenly and unexpectedly, incomprehensibly to all of us, my dear, kind-hearted husband passed away; our beloved Papa, son-in-law, brother-in-law, uncle and friend
>
> Mr. Karl Franz Josef Kipfer
> aged 44 years
> in Hanau, 5 January 1955, at 11 Sandeldamm
>
> with deep sorrow,
> Elisabeth Kipfer, widowed Preuß, née Vaupel, her children
> and all the family[123]

In April 1955, Rudolf conveyed the news to Alex and Rosa:

> I don't know whether you have already heard from Germany, that Kipfer passed away on 5 January. As you no doubt remember, he was very badly paralyzed, and I presume, that his war injuries eventually caught up with his energy during this particularly serious winter. I am particularly sorry about this, now we have to look for a new agent in our claims. It is not very easy these days to find somebody as reliable and conscientious as he was. I wrote his widow a very long and feeling letter of condolences, which she so far has not yet answered.[124]

Given what his relatives thought about Karl, it was perhaps not surprising that Rudolf did not offer a more heartfelt response. In another letter to Rosa he wrote: "I was very amused now that Kipfer's dead to see that you have such a good opinion of him. While he was alive neither of you did anything but complain about him."[125] But his real feelings toward Karl remained ambiguous. The "very long and feeling letter" to Karl's widow, the one tantalizing document that might have given more insight into his feelings, was nowhere to be found in his otherwise meticulously preserved collection, nor had Karl's stepdaughters found it among their mother's possessions. Rudolf was also not overly disappointed that Elisabeth never responded. "Perhaps it's better this way," he concluded coldly, "as we don't have any moral obligations toward her."[126]

How can we explain the inconsistency between the warm and intense correspondence between them and Rudolf's apparent indifference to Karl's death? It is difficult to gauge Rudolf's response from the letters alone. Who knows what private grief he might have felt? But the letters also suggest other possibilities. Rudolf and Karl had not seen one another since 1933, and the prospect of meeting again never entered their conversations. Neither had enough money to make this possible in the first place, but something about the distance between them seems paradoxically to have enabled their renewed closeness. Rudolf's letters to Karl were far longer, more comfortable, and more open than those he wrote to any of his other correspondents. He revealed personal intimacies and shared unashamed opinions. Perhaps it was only someone detached from his everyday life, whom he was unlikely ever to see again, in whom he could confide in this way. Perhaps, also, the warmth and intensity was directed not so much at Karl as at an idea, at a memory of who Rudolf had been at a particular time of his life. Karl was Rudolf's link to his idealized youth of fencing and beer, to the unknowing twenty-one-year-old he had been before he left Germany. Karl was also a good partner with whom to battle the German state, with whom to rant about its deceits and injustices. Perhaps, ultimately, Rudolf didn't wonder about what Karl had done because he didn't really care, and because his life had taught him to be sparing with his loyalty and trust.

The final lingering mystery was a document dating from August 1956, a year and a half after Karl's death. This was one of the first documents the Schwab family had shown me: a claim for compensation that Rudolf had submitted to the authorities in Wiesbaden. Now that Karl was no longer around to deal with the family's claims, Rudolf had decided to take matters into his own hands and was beginning a fresh round of submissions.

Before setting out his claims for damages to health, freedom, property, wealth, and professional advancement, Rudolf provided a summary of the persecution he had suffered at the hands of the Nazis. When he had left Germany in May 1933, he explained, he had done so "hurriedly, because I had been warned by a friend, Mr. Kipfer, who was a Party official, that I was going to be arrested."[127] Nowhere in the letters was there another reference to this arrest, nor was there an obvious explanation for it. In addition, Karl was only twenty-three years old in 1933, and archival records confirmed that he had only joined the Nazi Party in 1937. His father had died many years earlier, and so there was no other Party official named Mr. Kipfer in Hanau to whom Rudolf could have been referring. I wondered initially whether this was an allusion to some kind of "undemocratic" cause in which Karl had been involved, which might have given him access to privileged police information. I suspect, however, that Rudolf wrote it simply because it made for a more convincing claim. It was further proof that Rudolf was only guessing at the substance of Karl's Nazi past, and that in all their years of friendship, Karl never divulged the details.

At the core of Rudolf and Karl's story is a stubborn kernel of the unknown, details that the archives cannot yield, questions that no surviving family members or relatives or neighbors or friends are able to answer. We will never establish for certain what Karl saw or did. We can also only guess at what Rudolf thought about him, his cantankerous fencing and drinking pal, long-lost friend and confidante, one-man anti-establishment warrior, former Nazi.

If we knew without doubt that Karl was a murderer, his story would perhaps have been even more remarkable—or so it seemed to me early on in the project. In fact, were it not for Karl's very marginality in the Nazi system, his responses would most likely not have been as profoundly conflicted and astonishing as they were. At first, I imagined that in taking on the Schwabs' compensation claims with such passion and resolve, Karl was enacting a kind of penance. But penance is too strong a term, suggesting a deliberate and conscious atonement that simply does not fit with what we know about 1950s Germany and Karl's own circumstances. The reality was, as reality often is, much messier and more opaque. Karl's outraged insistence on German guilt was uncommonly outspoken, and far beyond what any convicted perpetrator would have expressed, though it was partial and underpinned by a sense of his own victimhood—a product of the in-between, grey zone of peripheral complicity that he inhabited. His friendship with Rudolf, remarkable for its effortless reawakening, was unquestionably part of Karl's coming to terms with the past, though never in a straightforward or intentional way. His life, like Rudolf's, obstinately resists our attempts to categorize it. At the same time, it is precisely lives such as theirs, in all their ordinary, motley unpredictability, that bring us closer to understanding the complex choices and motivations and inclinations that—even in extreme situations, or perhaps then more than ever—make us human.

4

A Refugee in South Africa

When Rudolf arrived in South Africa in 1936 he knew little about the country that would become his new home. Most German Jewish refugees were, like him, full of wild imaginings about what they would find. His relatives warned him to beware of snakes, lions, and elephants, and fretted about the availability of "modern" accommodations.[1] In his replies, Rudolf offered long descriptions of the unfamiliar landscape and weather, and complained about the "unbearable" heat ("In the last few days it has started to rain a bit, but not long enough to make any impression on plants, animals, or people").[2]

South Africa was not a significant destination for refugees fleeing Hitler's Germany. Between 1933 and 1939, around 6,000 Jews landed on its shores, scarcely 2 percent of the total number who left. They came to South Africa not because of particular opportunities or connections, but simply because—for a time at least—it was one of the few places that would let them in. Upon their arrival, they found a community of over 72,000 mostly eastern European Jews who had migrated at the turn of the century, concentrated in the centers of Johannesburg and Cape Town.[3]

The existing community did not make life easy for the newcomers. The antagonisms between eastern and western European Jews had deep-seated historical roots, in the period of emancipation more than a century before, when new Jewish identities began to be forged in the struggle between modernity and tradition.[4] These hostilities played themselves out with renewed energy in the 1930s, as German Jews sought refuge in communities that were often populated, as in South Africa, by eastern European Jews whose arrival preceded them by only a few decades. Gus Saron, secretary of the South African Jewish Board of Deputies, wrote to a friend that "the older South Africans in the Jewish population had shown very little desire to welcome the German Jews into their social life."[5] The Board itself even at points discouraged German Jewish organizations from sending refugees to South Africa, because of concerns about exacerbating antisemitism.[6]

During the 1920s, the idea of Jews' "unassimilability" had found growing support in South Africa, especially in Afrikaner nationalist circles. January 1930 saw the passing of the Quota Act, which radically curtailed immigration from (among others) Latvia, Lithuania, Poland, Russia, and Palestine, on the basis of eugenicist ideas. Although not explicitly named, eastern European Jews were the chief target.[7] German Jews were free of the Quota Act's restrictions, although few came before the mid-1930s. Worsening conditions under the Nazi regime and fresh immigration restrictions in Palestine combined to swell the numbers of immigrants in 1936—a development that intensified openly antisemitic hostility within South Africa, emanating from the Afrikaner nationalist opposition as well as the government itself. A further set of restrictions was imposed in late 1936, and in February 1937 a new Aliens Act came into force, reducing Jewish immigration from Germany to a trickle.[8]

By the 1938 general election, antisemitism had become a central aspect of several mainstream parties' platforms. The Nazi Party established local branches in the country, and Nazi-inspired political movements including the South African Gentile National Socialist Movement and the *Ossewabrandwag* (Oxwagon Sentinel) began to find popular audiences. Nationalist newspapers minimized or refuted the Nazis' antisemitism and aggressive expansionist policies. The Aliens Registration Act of June 1939 classed refugee Jews as "enemy aliens," and when war broke out in September, only a very narrow parliamentary majority supported the decision to join the fighting on the side of the Allies.[9] This eruption of political antisemitism was alarming for South African Jews, and it did little to assuage the newcomers' fears about this remote, unknown refuge.

"We were a German clique and we stuck to it," recalled Hilda Jeidel, who arrived in South Africa from Breslau as a refugee in 1933, aged twenty-eight.[10] The refugees' separation was partly a result of the existing community's lack of interest, and partly the natural inclination toward the familiar. It was also undoubtedly a symptom of the perceived cultural superiority of German Jews to so-called *Ostjuden* (eastern European Jews). "Predominantly middle class, and devotees of German high culture," writes Michael Burleigh, "German Jews had next to nothing in common with Jews from the backward 'East,' who seemed like the incarnation of some earlier embarrassing self."[11] Rudolf used the term *Ostjuden* liberally and without irony. The settled community may have laughed at the ways of the *Yekkes* (German Jews), but the *Yekkes* in turn were often critical of South Africa's second-rate cultural and social life as compared with western Europe.[12]

The newcomers established connections with any fellow German Jews they could find, from distant relatives and acquaintances of acquaintances to contacts recommended by a hairdresser. The shared ship journey to South Africa was the beginning of many lifelong friendships. They held social gatherings in one another's homes, where they spoke German and sang German songs. They settled in the same neighborhoods, established their own organizations, and opened their own shops and restaurants.[13] More than material help, the organizations that the German Jews created provided what refugees everywhere yearn for: a sense of identity and belonging in the face of displacement and loss.

But if they themselves were "more German than Jewish," the refugees did not pass that identity on to their children.[14] They learned English well and spoke it at home. They also contributed to Jewish communal life and particularly to the growth of Reform Judaism in the country.

There were also those, like Rudolf, who shied away from communal life, perhaps because it reminded them of things best forgotten. Rudolf dutifully kept in touch with acquaintances and distant relatives who had also ended up in South Africa, and conveyed their news in his letters to the refugee diaspora, but they remained on the margins of his existence. While others married within the German Jewish community, Rudolf married a South African woman, Rachel, with whom he spoke only English (though he assured his aunt Rosa that his wife was "naturally a local Jewish girl (not Black!!!)").[15] Discussing with his uncle Alex their common struggle to begin life again in a new language, he wrote in English:

> From the first day, I associated very little with Germans and Foreigners generally, stayed from the first day in an English boarding house, cultivated English friends etc, and was for nearly 12 years married to a South African. We have never spoken German at home, so that even the children do not speak a word of it. That has its ovious [*sic*] disadvantages for them, but it helped me a lot to learn English quicker and better then [*sic*] some of my friends did.[16]

Rudolf was proud of his acquired English, and within just a few years of his arrival was claiming that he spoke it better than his mother tongue, though he retained a German accent until the end of his life.[17]

Rudolf threw himself determinedly into the project of becoming South African. When war broke out in 1939, he attempted twice to sign up for military service. He explained to Rosa that all Jews "worthy of the name" willingly signed up,

> especially the ones who had emigrated in the few years right before the war, as we had a particular bone to pick with that pack of bastards.[18]

Military service also had important implications in German Jewish conceptions of citizenship. Jewish communal leaders, for their part, were concerned to pre-empt antisemitism, and encouraged refugees to "show to the utmost of their ability that they are prepared to play their part in the defense of the country."[19] According to existing records, over 10 percent of the total Jewish population of South Africa served in the Union Defence Force.

Rejected from the army because of a knee injury, Rudolf found an alternative outlet in the National Volunteer Brigade. For almost three years he did night-time guard duty at gas depots, armaments factories, and strategic government buildings. He often turned up to his day job still in uniform—out of convenience, perhaps, but one suspects also out of quiet pride. Thanks to his war service and some prominent friends, Rudolf became a naturalized South African citizen in 1946, which he proudly announced was "better than being stateless or a German Jew."[20]

Rudolf's relatives' letters were full of far-fetched impressions about a land distant from civilization where wild animals roamed freely. In response he enthusiastically described South Africa's modern transport facilities and world-class doctors. He wrote positively about Johannesburg's cultural life, even if it could not compare with cities like London or Milan ("That is beyond a young country like ours, especially as the State does not subsidize the Arts"). He learned to speak Afrikaans and studied South African history.[21] He offered detailed descriptions of the country's gold mining industry, agriculture, and tourism. In a letter to Armand he hailed the sixtieth anniversary of Johannesburg's establishment:

> It is something to be proud of, I suppose, a town of over 600,000 inhabitants where there was nothing but bare veldt 60 years ago and still increasing at a tremendous pace.[22]

After World War II, South Africans experienced their fair share of difficulties, including food shortages, rising costs, and widespread labor unrest. For the most part, however, Rudolf emphasized how much better he had it than his relatives in Europe.[23] To his friend Iris Braby in London he wrote:

The war has passed us very lightly here in South Africa, and although there are some small disappointments here, we can be highly satisfied with our lot. The miners are busy with a strike at the moment, we are still blessed with various Controls, a lot of food and other commodities are still scarce, but this is nothing in comparison to how you in Dear, Old England still "have to take it."[24]

To a relative in New York he wrote: "I am very happy to have come here to this sunny country and thank God and the Belgium [sic] Government every day."[25]

Rudolf cannot have been unaware of antisemitism in South Africa in the late 1930s. In his letters, however, it never arose as a serious concern. When the Afrikaner National Party came to power in 1948 and began to implement its policy of apartheid, Jews remained doubtful of its intentions, not least given its earlier association with Nazi-inspired parties. By the late-1940s, however, Afrikaner antisemitism had dissipated in the wake of a new push for unity amongst so-called "Europeans": as one right-wing politician put it, "We place the saving of White South Africa first."[26] In 1949, the communal leadership was able to report confidently that the political atmosphere was generally favorable toward Jews.[27]

Rudolf came to love his adopted homeland and saw himself as a kind of ambassador. He urged friends to visit and promoted the country's virtues to potential immigrants. He wrote to Iris in January 1948:

> In spite of all our troubles this is a great country with space for counless [sic] millions more, in every walk of Life. Haven't you changed your mind yet about coming out here? If necessary pack up your whole school and bring them all with you, we need new blood here.[28]

In August 1946 he wrote to his uncle Phillippe in Belgium:

> Now something that should prove of great interest to all young people in old, ungrateful and wartorn Europe. South Africa is to throw her doors wide open to immigration of young people of the right type from Europe; I am sure, you have read reports of last weeks [sic] speech by Field Marshall Smuts to this effect. The type of immigrant contemplated includes skilled artisans in any trade, people who can set up industries, professional men, in short any body decent hardworking and the normal complement of reliability, steadyness and brains will be only too welcome.... So if any friends of old ... feel the spirit of adventure

strong enough in them, and are sure, that they are hardy enough to carve a future for themselves in a country, that will only now begin to develop properly, here is their chance! . . . I expect the waitinglists [*sic*] will be long. And of course I am only too pleased to do whatever I can from this side.[29]

Rudolf's references to "new blood" and immigrants "of the right type" revealed not only the influence of the chauvinistic South African milieu, but also the legacy of his conservative upbringing. His childhood Hanau home was firmly nationalistic and anti-Bolshevik, and in his youthful involvement with fencing groups and the anti-Zionist *Kameraden*, he revealed similar political inclinations to his father. In South Africa, Rudolf's implicit sense of cultural superiority—manifest in his ideas about politics, Jewish life, leisure activities, and social interaction—was a reflection of his traditionalist background as much as it was evidence of his embracing the attitudes and values of his new homeland.

Rudolf fell in love with South African wildlife, and portrayed his encounters in the bushveld with endless delight. "I don't think I'll ever get over the thrill and excitement I feel when I see an elephant near the road," he wrote to cousin Reny.[30] His first trip to the Kruger National Park, taken with his nine-year-old son, Norman, was a revelation:

We went in a truck because I don't have a passenger car and started off in the northern part of a massive wildlife reserve, 430 miles away from the civilization of Johannesburg; this was after a peaceful and pleasant drive from Pietersburg to Tzaneen through the ravines, hills and valleys of the north-eastern Transvaal, some of which were incredibly beautiful. The reserve's bushveld area alone (there isn't any real tropical jungle there) is between 25 and 50 miles wide and almost 300 miles long from north to south, and is home to almost every type of South African wildlife still in existence; and, apart from some dirt tracks and a few camp sites, it's still in the same natural state that it's been in for thousands of years. We were there for almost three weeks during which we saw—in addition to the herds, some of them enormous, of various types of gazelle and antelope, for example: impala, kudu, sable, blue wildebeest, duiker, steenbok, nyala, klipspringer and waterbuck—elephants, lions, leopards, cheetahs, giraffes, warthogs, bushpigs, hippopotami, crocodiles, hyenas, jackals, wild dogs, zebras, eagles, vultures, and many other wild animals and birds walking around freely in their natural habitat; animals one would normally be able to see only in the zoo. But in this strange, gigantic zoo, it's the people who're put behind bars (in their vehicles), and the animals are the ones free to roam around. . . . The journey back through the fruit and vegetable gardens of the eastern Transvaal, with thousands of orange and grapefruit trees, etc., was extraordinarily beautiful, until slowly but surely we approached the bleak, craggy mountains of the Witwatersrand, our home.[31]

His letters were also filled with lyrical descriptions of South Africa's natural beauty and vast open spaces.

But when finally we arrived in the subtropical climate of the Soutpans-berg, the difference was so striking that we thought we were seeing one of those famous desert mirages. Everything was fresh and green, and if the vegetation hadn't been so very subtropical we'd have thought ourselves in the most fertile region of Switzerland. You can't imagine all the different types of fruit that grow there in addition to what you get in Europe (oranges, lemons, bananas, pineapples, rice, etc.) because the other kinds aren't easy to transport. The view from the mountains over the fertile valleys is indescribably beautiful, even just the drive through a few of the beautiful forests is worth the long trip.[32]

Rudolf's passionate descriptions revealed both his endearing devotion to South Africa, and—in effortless shifts to memories of childhood fruits and Switzer-land—the enduring Europeanness he never quite left behind.

If Rudolf's travels featured prominently in his letters to relatives, the bulk of his time was spent engaging in more prosaic pursuits. First was earning a stable living. In Holland he had attended a vocational training camp in order to acquire portable skills, and by night he had also pursued informal studies in building engineering. When he arrived in South Africa, however, it became clear that he could not compete with qualified tradespeople. The years after his arrival were tough, "an uphill struggle all the way," as he drifted from job to job and struggled to make ends meet. To his worried family back in Hanau, however, he wrote that he was "very happy, and satisfied that this is the only complaint I have."[33] Over the years he explored a variety of entrepreneurial possibilities, including imports and exports drawing on the family's trans-continental diaspora.[34]

Amidst his life's upheavals Rudolf had remained committed to self-education, and already in the 1930s he had become fascinated by the challenge of preserving wood against termites and rot, a pressing issue in South Africa's temperate climate. For several years he spent every free moment pursuing his studies, and by the late 1940s he had become a local expert. In later years he proudly told people about his ground-breaking work as "Wood Preservation Engineer & Consultant Entomologist." He established the first commercial enterprise in the field in South Africa, and in 1968 merged his business with Rentokil, "the largest and most reputable firm in Pest Control in the world." Invoking the legacy of his father, he emphasized that he had achieved his success legally and honestly, with a reputation built on quality products and excellent customer service. In the last decade of his life he advised the South African government on public health issues and played a prominent role in his professional association. Although his entrepreneurial pursuits caused him great difficulties for many years—unlike most of his friends, who had pursued more traditional routes "and can now sit back and take it a bit easier"—he saw himself as a pioneer, and cheered himself with the knowledge that he enjoyed his work and was satisfied with his achievements.[35]

Rudolf's personal life brought challenges of its own. The early years of marriage with Rachel seem to have been happy ones, providing him with some comfort from his family's painful experiences. But in early 1948 Rachel began to suffer from a debilitating illness of which specialist doctors were unable to ascertain the cause. Rudolf wrote to Phillippe:

> Unfortunately my dear wife is suffering rather badly from pains in the back and legs at the moment and the doctors can't make it out. The one calls it Fibrositis, the other one Neurosis and the third lumbago, but with all that she has terrible pains night and day and there appears to be nothing to relieve it. She has hardly slept at all at nights for several days now.[36]

To his confidante Karl, Rudolf vented his frustration and impatience in less polite terms. Rachel was physically healthy, he insisted; "her 'illness' is the difficulty she has with relationships and getting on with the people around her." Norman, now aged eight, was sent to boarding school and returned home once a month, mostly to Rudolf's care. The marriage collapsed under the strain, and the divorce was finalized in September 1951, though it was several months before Rudolf felt able to break the news to his relatives.[37]

During this time Rudolf also suffered health complaints, most of them the result of his overworked existence. He had skin problems that required ongoing intervention, and in the winter of 1950 he was confined to bed with a lung infec-

Rachel and her son Louis from her previous marriage, 1941. Courtesy of Daniel Schwab.

tion, which his heavy smoking did not help. He and his cousin Reny found much pleasure over the years in grumbling together about their ailments.[38]

Rudolf spent the next few years living in guest houses and rented accommodations, surviving on a shoestring. One or two short-term relationships petered out quickly. But in July 1957, he reported to his stepson Louis that he was "in the lucky position of being at present very much in Love myself, and my Love is returned fully." Almost seven years after his divorce, Rudolf remarried in June 1958. Miriam Mandelstam was a former high school teacher, the daughter of a large, warm Johannesburg family, and actively involved in Jewish communal affairs. When she married Rudolf, she was the director and only employee of the local Jewish Telegraph Agency. A widow, she brought to the marriage three children: two daughters already in their twenties, and a son, David, aged twelve. Norman, now fifteen, moved in with them in late 1958, an arrangement to which Rachel reluctantly acceded. "The main point, of course," Rudolf wrote to Alex, "is that after 8 years of boarding school, Norman has the right to live in a proper family." The marriage lasted until Rudolf's death in 1971.[39]

In the years after his arrival in South Africa, Rudolf went through the motions of Jewish life without much enthusiasm. Rachel had little interest in religion, and they held Passover Seders "only for the children's sake and never [for] more than half an hour, maximum." When Rudolf began to rediscover Judaism after his divorce, he turned not to Orthodoxy but rather to the tiny and marginalized Reform community. Norman later suspected that this was Rudolf's way of tacitly rejecting the Judaism that he believed, rightly or wrongly, had led to his family's persecution. Reform of course had a rich history in Germany, and this may also have been Rudolf's way of re-creating a connection with his home-land, as so many other German Jews did across the refugee diaspora.[40]

Rudolf developed a lifelong commitment to the Reform movement. In 1953 he joined the board of Temple Israel in Johannesburg, later serving on the Executive of the United Jewish Progressive Congregation. One of his biggest motivations for participation was that Norman be able to "[integrate] into a large community such as ours quickly and painlessly," and Reform's focus on children was why "I feel much better in it than with the Orthodox community." As chairman of Temple Israel he occupied a prominent seat in synagogue and took an active role in services. During the 1960s he expanded his work for the movement to include publicity and fundraising. He gave lectures, led conference delegations, and met with visiting dignitaries. In 1967, he was elected president of the national Reform organization.[41]

To understand a person's religious identity is not straightforward, even if in this case we have unusually rich evidence of how Rudolf's ideas shifted over the years. Thanks to his Orthodox upbringing he was very knowledgeable about Jewish practice. He considered it an honor to lead services and placed great importance on reciting the mourner's *kaddish* for distant relatives who had no one else to say it for them. At the same time, he ate non-kosher food without compunction ("Oysters, lobster and knuckles of pork . . . I eat with great pleasure when they aren't too expensive"), and was openly irreverent about Orthodox leadership.[42] In February 1949 he told Karl about the Chief Rabbi of South Africa, Louis Rabinowitz, the only rabbi to have ever won his admiration:

As you well know, I too have never thought much of rabbis, priests, etc. . . . but our Chief Rabbi here at the moment is the first I've ever respected in all my life. He was the Jewish senior chaplain for the English troops during the last war and one of the first of the men to do a parachute jump. The first week he was here, some cretin jostled him in the street calling him a "dirty Jew," whereupon he took off his black hat and gave the chap such a hiding that he'll definitely be giving men with long beards and black hats a wide berth for the rest of his life.[43]

For Rudolf, the ultimate purpose of Jewish leadership was not to dictate supposedly God-given laws, but rather to lead by moral example. His Jewish identity
was at core communal rather than spiritual: Jewishness was a source of stability and belonging, most successful when "everyone feels they're part of a big
family."[44] Explaining his move away from Orthodoxy to Reny in November 1953,
he wrote:

> I can already hear you asking in astonishment, why "reform"??? More
> than 20 years ago when I was still religious orthodox, under the influ-
> ence of my deceased father, I attended services in many orthodox syna-
> gogues in different countries around the world, but only occasionally
> and with very long gaps in between. With the laudable exception of our
> local orthodox Chief Rabbi, who is an excellent speaker, these services,
> including the sermons, were always so prescribed that it's no surprise
> to me that Jewish communities throughout the world lost, in a spiritual
> sense, not just their adults but also their children a long time ago. But
> our reform community here is a laudable exception. Our rabbi under-
> stood all this a long time ago, as did the rest of the community, so
> he made the services so interesting—though admittedly, just as few
> adults come to *Shabbat* and *Yom Tov* services as before, as is the case
> everywhere in world—that the children adore him and lead almost the
> entire service all by themselves in Hebrew and English; that is to say,
> the boys getting ready for their bar mitzvah do most of it. The result
> is that we regularly have between 350 and 400 members in attendance
> at an ordinary *Shabbat* service, most of them children of course, aged
> between six and 18 years old. It's interesting for the children because
> they can participate, and the parents come for the children's sake if they
> come at all.[45]

In the years after his divorce, Reform Judaism provided Rudolf with a sense of
community and purpose. After his marriage to Miriam, some of his happiest
times were celebrating *Shabbat* and Jewish festivals at large family gatherings in
their home.[46]

For all his attempts to separate himself from other German Jewish refugees,
the new identity that Rudolf fashioned for himself reflected ideas about citizenship and social responsibility that had clear origins in his German Jewish past.
His efforts to integrate into South Africa were driven especially by an impulse
to emulate his father, who had been a devoted contributor to Hanau's communal

life, although Rudolf admitted to Alex that he was "very far from being able to compete with my late father" in that respect.[47]

Whether he was writing to new friends, old relatives, financial agents, or German bureaucrats, Rudolf endlessly recalled his father's contributions to German society. In seeking to become South African, he instinctively chose as his model the way in which his father had been German: articulate in the language, passionate about the landscape, and active in public life. In addition to his leadership in the Reform movement, over the years Rudolf assumed positions in diverse Jewish organizations, from the Zionist movement to the South African Jewish Board of Deputies, the Bnai Brith Lodge, and a local school board. He proudly informed his many correspondents about the responsibilities he held and meetings he attended, while also frequently complaining that he was harried and overworked. In November 1954 he reported that he "had countless meetings to attend for the various organizations of which I am a member of the board. This took up every minute of the day and half of the night. I have barely slept for a full night for months." But he defended himself to a friend: "As a businessman ought to be well-informed about what is going on in his community, and I could, after all, have refused to accept these honorary offices, I have nothing to grumble about. But, it does explain, why I have so little time."[48] Though Rudolf's involvement in public life sprang from genuine interest and dedication, it was also a way of perpetuating his father's values, principles, and legacy.

Rudolf was also committed to political engagement. "'By the people, from the people and for the people' can work only if the people take a particular personal interest in all governmental processes and every man takes the time to keep a close eye on the fat cats," he wrote to Karl in July 1949.

> Only when every voter, instead of following the herd, writes a strongly worded letter to his so-called representatives at least once a week to remind them that the only source of their power is him, and that they can be replaced at the drop of a hat if they don't behave properly, will democracy become a reality.[49]

Rudolf took his own advice seriously. In the mid-1940s he joined the ruling United Party, which had been formed in 1934 as an amalgamation of Jan Smuts's South African Party and the Afrikaner-dominated National Party led by J.B.M. Hertzog. He energetically supported United Party election campaigns, and offered earnest advice to parliamentary candidates.[50] His closest contact was a member of parliament named Sarel Tighy, to whom he first wrote in May 1947:

I have read quite a bit about you lately between the lines of the local papers and occasionally in Hansard, and as I saw from an advert the other day that you are interested in what your constituents think and would like to increase your "fan mail," I am addressing these few lines to you.

The ordinary man-in-the-street is rather fed up with the way things are going, or rather not going, and from what I hear all over the show, our staunch supporters are rather worried at the prospects for the United Party at the next General Election. What are the Party bosses, The UP organisers and you M.P.'s doing? Don't you fellows know what the country is thinking? I know you as a sound fellow and from your record during this last session particularly you appear to have a good political future, if . . . IF our constituency will not be too sick and tired of the whole way things are being run, or rather allowed to slide in this beautiful country of ours and vote for the other fellow. . . . It is five minutes to midnight and if it is not done soon, you might as well throw in the sponge now and invite Malan and his crow [*sic*] to take over without a fight.

Sarel Tighy, these things must be done. The Country has got a right to demand them of you. And when you have done them, HIT THE HEADLINES, go to the voters and tell them WHAT YOU BOYS HAVE DONE AND WHY YOU HAVE DONE IT!!!!!

If I have made a few mistakes and spoken rather strongly, I know you will excuse me, because you realise it is only because I have Our Cause so much at heart.[51]

In the 1948 election, as Rudolf had feared, the United Party narrowly lost to D. F. Malan's *Herenigde Nasionale Party* (Reunited National Party), an earlier right-wing Afrikaner breakaway.[52] Rudolf continued to be involved with the UP, now in opposition, as the Nationalist government began to cement the foundations of apartheid in the late 1940s and early 1950s. He was a fierce opponent of the government and was convinced the UP would reassume power, not least because it enjoyed the popular support of the White electorate (the National Party's election victory in 1948 was due to unequal weighting in the electoral system).[53] In a glowing testimonial, Johannesburg mayor J. F. Oberholzer described Rudolf as a "highly respected, civic-minded citizen," "an energetic, vigorous organizer," and

a man of diplomatic skill who managed his team to such good effect that our opponents' majority in the 1953 Parliamentary Elections was

City of Johannesburg
Stad Johannesburg

Management Committee,
Room 105,
City Hall,
JOHANNESBURG.

<u>TESTIMONIAL</u>

I have known Mr. Ralph Schwab since we first met at meetings of the Witwatersrand Executive and General Council of the United Party almost twenty years ago. We worked together in various election campaigns in those days. He is an energetic, vigorous organizer, who gets on well with his colleagues.

This was probably one of the main reasons why Ralph Schwab was elected to the office of Regional, and later Divisional Chairman. Here he proved himself a man of diplomatic skill who managed his team to such good effect that our opponents' majority in the 1953 Parliamentary Elections was almost halved in this area, the exact opposite to the general trend in the rest of the country.

During my many years in the City and Provincial Council, and particularly while I was Mayor of Johannesburg, Mr. Schwab was very active in communal affairs, and for that matter continues to be so.

Mr. Schwab is a highly respected, civic-minded citizen, and it is only with the interest of people of this calibre that our city can continue to flourish.

J. F. OBERHOLZER, M.P.C.

Testimonial from Johannesburg mayor J. F. Oberholzer. Courtesy of Yad Vashem.

almost halved in this area, the exact opposite to the general trend in the rest of the country.[54]

Rudolf eventually served on some of the United Party's highest boards, including the Witwatersrand Executive and the General Council.[55]

In describing the National Party to his friends and relatives abroad, Rudolf often made reference to the Nazis. For a German Jewish refugee, this was undoubtedly an emotionally charged parallel to make. Ahead of the 1948 elections he warned repeatedly that the National Party "is not much better than the Nazis":[56]

> we have also our own troubles here in South-Africa [*sic*] what with Natives, Coloureds and Indians, who all perfectly legitimately ask for better treatment, the right to vote and generally more equality with the White population. . . . That is difficult even for such a clever statesman as General Smuts and his liberal Government, as the Europeans want to cling to their rights as long as possible, and are frankly afraid of what would happen to them, in a four to one contest. Therefore if this Govt. moves too fast they will not be the ruling party any more after the next elections and we would get a Nazi government by the opposition.[57]

Rudolf was not the only German Jewish exile to draw such analogies. Several refugees were outspoken against what they perceived to be Nazi-style racism in their own backyard, and were impelled to political action by their personal experience of victimization. One of these was Franz Auerbach, an educator and activist who arrived in Johannesburg in 1937. Auerbach often drew parallels between Nazism and apartheid, and he pointed repeatedly to the "similarities between some present features of life in South Africa and life under Hitler." In his diverse activities, which ranged from research on Christian-National education to activism in Jews for Social Justice, he perceived a clear link between the Holocaust and South African racism. Like other Jewish activists, he deliberately invoked the comparison in urging his co-religionists to protest apartheid's injustices: "To be silent is to betray our history, our religion and our duty to the land that gave us refuge."[58]

Another of apartheid's prominent German Jewish opponents was the lawyer and politician Harry Schwarz, who arrived in South Africa in 1934. His long political career began, like Rudolf's, with campaigning for the United Party in the 1948 election, and his energetic anti-apartheid work brought him to national prominence in the 1960s, when he emerged as the leader of the liberal offshoot of the United Party, which fought aggressively against the government's racial policies. Explaining his lifelong devotion to anti-racist activism, Schwarz declared: "I know what the word discrimination means, not because I've read it in a book, but because I've been the subject of it."[59]

It was not only Jewish refugees who identified parallels between Nazism and the new Nationalist government. Malan's National Party was widely referred to as the "Malanazis." In a "Declaration to the Nations of the World" drafted shortly after the war's end, one of the most significant anti-racist movements of the time proclaimed: "The life of a Non-European is very cheap in South Africa. As cheap as the life of a Jew in Nazi Germany."[60] Such analogies were intended to explain the nature of the racist regime and the struggle against it, and to mobilize the world's support.

In his letters, Rudolf echoed some of this language. He enjoyed ridiculing the Nationalist government and its policies, particularly in anti-establishment repartee with Karl. After the new government took office, he often used Nazi language to explain its absurdities and inconsistencies. Just as in Nazi Germany, he reported, "the mixing of blood in South Africa is strictly forbidden," despite the obvious fact that "there are no pure races left in the world." He empathized with those who lost their social standing and livelihood because a court arbitrarily pronounced them a "*Mischling*."[61] In a letter to Karl, he mocked the government's attempts to criminalize *Rassenschande*:

> For example, at the moment they're pushing through a "Law Against Immorality." Under this law, marriage and sexual relationships between Whites, half-castes and Indians will be strictly prohibited. These things have already been forbidden between Whites and Blacks for a long time. Their intention in and of itself is very laudable. But in practice, of course, and given that we have neither a residents' registration office nor any kind of official population register, it's completely impossible to differentiate accurately between farmers, sailors and fishermen who've been browned by the sun (to name but a few crass examples) and the entirely white-skinned children of half-caste parents. The whole business is laughable and impossible to implement. Nevertheless the poor old pastors and marriage officials will be obliged by law to guess which race someone belongs to based on his or her general appearance and skin color and, of course, if they make a mistake and insult a European by labeling him a half-caste, that would be a punishable offense too. The government knows just as well as everyone else that it's impossible to implement this law, but the most ridiculous thing about it is when it comes to extra-marital relations of which there's no evidence for a public prosecutor to scrape together. Nevertheless they'll push the law through so that the Nationalists can show their hangers-on in the countryside how much they're doing for them in parliament.[62]

At first glance, Rudolf's early political involvement makes for a neat redemptive story of the victim of Nazism turned anti-racist campaigner. The underlying reality, however, is more complicated. Like most South African Jews, Rudolf saw few connections between the antisemitism he had witnessed in Europe and the anti-Black racism he encountered in his new homeland. For all that he ridiculed the Nationalist government's laws, he affirmed that "their intention in and of itself is very laudable." His objection, in other words, stemmed not from ethical principles but rather the difficulty of classification. Similarly, his opposition to the new National Party government was based not so much on its racial policies as on the declining economic situation. He recognized that "people abroad now equate a Nationalist government with a Nazi government," but the chief fear for him was that this was causing the withdrawal of foreign investment. For a small business owner struggling to keep his enterprise going, the impact of politics on the country's economy was worrying. The National Party was managing to keep hold of the reins of power, but in Rudolf's eyes a small country like South Africa could not afford to isolate itself through "ridiculous hysteria" and "petty laws": "Soon it will all go wrong."[63]

According to the historian Gideon Shimoni, "Casting the lot of Jews with that of 'non-Europeans' was absolutely inconceivable for the mind-set of all but the tiniest minority of Jewish communists who had long been alienated from Jewish identification and were peripheral to Jewish affairs." While there were some prominent Jews who participated in left-wing and anti-racist causes, they were few and far between. The South African Jewish Board of Deputies, the community's chief representative body, followed a policy of non-involvement in politics save where the rights of Jews as Jews were directly affected.[64]

Rudolf quickly accepted the values and vocabulary of White South Africa. When his twenty-two-year-old stepson Louis wrote to him from England in December 1954, expressing his distress at finding "natives slandering S.A. etc. to their hearts' content" at London's Hyde Park corner, and seeing mixed-race couples "waltzing in the street hand in hand," Rudolf responded: "I can well imagine, what your feelings must be, when you see natives and coloureds associating with White women." He often complained about the laziness and unreliability of his native "boys"—or worse still, in the parlance of the day, "kaffirs."[65] Immigrants from Europe were desperately needed, he wrote to his correspondents back in Europe, because

it is extremely difficult to get decent employees here; we have to chop and change about every now and again and if it is not travelers, it is workmen, or unskilled laborers (natives—Darkies to you, I presume) or youngsters fresh from school.[66]

People outside the country, he often grumbled, simply did not understand the complexity of its racial problems.

The whole question of domestic servants is rather more trying here and very difficult for Mrs. Schwab. She has just now had to dismiss another native boy, because he did not do the work she told him to do. His only duties were to attend to the small garden we have got and cleaning the floors in our small house. As even that was too much for him, it was no use. It is only some families who still have devoted servants, and can afford to pay them fabulous wages, that are well cared for. But this is the exception rather than the rule. In business it is differrent [*sic*], because once a boy is trained in his duties and shows that he is prepared to work well, we can afford to pay him better. My best boy, per instance, earns now £3.—a week, plus free lodging, at my house. But he drives my small 1 ton lorry, starts at 6.30 a.m. to 7 a.m. and we seldom get home before 6 p.m. He is dependable and reliable as far as natives go, has learnt to read and write, as well as driving and servicing his van in the army, and when something difficult has to be done or overtime to be worked he is always there. I have, on his good army record and his own good behaviour while he was with me, obtained excemption [*sic*] for him from carrying a pass (much like the carte d'identitee) and this raises him to the status of a respectable man amongst his race. But cases like this are very rare indeed, even my leading hands, one of whom has been with me for over four years now are still on the whole rather independable and unless they are watched all the time, their work slacks off. A great improvement will occur once they all are able to go to school properly from early childhood and are properly trained. This imposes a heavy strain on the pockets of the comparatively small White population here as well as a great responsibility, after all there are more than 4 coloured persons here to every White, and the great majority have only started coming in to towns for work during the last 10 years or so and return for two to six months out of every year to their tribe or Kraal in one of the reserves to help their tribe with sowing, reaping or tilling the land or just for lazing around. It is difficult to properly train and educate such a shifting and unsettled population. To get enough of their number well enough trained to become teachers alone is a herculean task. I wonder whether the delegates at UNO thought about some of our problems here when they told us how to run our country!!?!67

Writing here at the height of his involvement in United Party campaign work, Rudolf was defending the merits of his "best boy," who was literate, competent, and reliable, but a "rare" find among the generally "independable" natives. His efforts to obtain exemption for his "boy" from carrying a pass betrayed an attitude that was condescending and paternalistic, to be sure, but one that was also commonplace at the time.

Rudolf's loyalty to the United Party can be understood against the background of divisions between English- and Afrikaans-speaking Whites, which had long-standing roots in South African history and politics. For Afrikaners, memories of British concentration camps during the South African War (1899–1902) remained fresh for much of the twentieth century, and fed a powerful anti-British sentiment. During that war Jews had largely kept neutral, but they had long been inclined toward the commercial, Anglo-dominated urban centers of the country, and in the war's aftermath they overwhelmingly supported the British.[68] In 1939, when Smuts led the country into war against Germany, the choice of loyalty was obvious for Jews, whereas most Afrikaners fiercely opposed the alliance with Britain. Apart from the National Party's anti-British position, its leader Malan was also widely reviled among Jews as the champion of legislation that had slammed the gates of South Africa shut on refugees.

The National Party, in other words, was seen as an exclusivist antisemitic party that had supported the German war effort. The United Party, predominantly English- rather than Afrikaans-speaking, was a more comfortable political home for South Africa's Jews. Despite its more reform-minded policies, however, it was firmly predicated on White dominance. Smuts was a well-regarded statesman and peacemaker, credited with introducing the phrase "human rights" into the preamble of the UN Charter in 1945, but he was also a firm advocate of racial segregation, a supporter not of equality but rather of trusteeship, where White society had an obligation to care for the social and material welfare of less advanced races.[69] His ideas were reflected in the paternalistic discourse of the UP, which was in turn reflected in Rudolf's ideas as well.

Liberal elements in the UP, including German Jewish refugee Harry Schwarz, later broke with the party to pursue more progressive political reforms. Rudolf's closest ally in parliament, Sarel Tighy, was not among them. Rudolf's relationship with Tighy does not necessarily mean that Rudolf supported racist apartheid policies, but it does point to his conservative political leanings, which echoed those of the mainstream Jewish community. In the 1940s Tighy became renowned for his energetic campaign to remove non-White populations ("black spots") from Johannesburg. He was widely recognized as the principal architect

Rudolf (back right) at a function with Sarel Tighy (front center). Courtesy of Yad Vashem.

of the Western Areas Removal Scheme implemented by the apartheid government in the 1950s, which "resettled" non-Whites from what were now decreed White-only areas.[70] Tighy was far from an isolated example, but their relationship suggests something of Rudolf's political inclinations. Tighy later interceded with the German government to expedite Rudolf's claims for reparations, an effort that reveals at least a degree of personal allegiance.

As apartheid took root in the 1950s, Rudolf withdrew into a more domestic world. In earlier years, his attitudes toward Israel had mirrored those of his anti-Zionist father, who criticized Jewish behavior in pre-state Palestine and was skeptical about the inhospitable landscape. Rudolf wrote to Rosa and Siegfried in August 1947:

> Some of our coreligionists in Palestine are behaving wonderfully, it seems to be something they've learned from the Nazis. What they think they can achieve this way is a mystery to me; in my opinion it can only harm the poor people still in Germany. Hasn't the world had enough mass murder and death in the last 10 years?[71]

In time, however, Rudolf yielded to the Zionist consensus of South African Jewry. Toward the end of his life he became actively involved in the Zionist movement, serving on the councils of local and national associations. When South African Jews rallied to Israel's cause during the 1967 war, he proudly described his stepson

David's exploits as a volunteer in the Sinai desert and the hopeless failures of the Egyptian army. His retreat from politics and into Jewish community issues like religion and Zionism echoed that of the community as a whole.[72]

Rudolf's accommodation to local mores was also evident in his political engagement. His status as a small business owner had earlier fueled his opposition to the National Party government, but like many South African Jews he enjoyed the economic benefits of White domination. The extent to which economic concerns shaped Jews' political attitudes toward apartheid is an open question, but their participation in economic life was undoubtedly a key aspect of their comfort and success in South Africa.[73] Rudolf's political involvement flagged after the United Party's 1953 election defeat, and he turned his attention to the Jewish community and caring for his young son and stepson. He later wrote to his cousin Reny that despite its "Christian-Nationalist" government he preferred South Africa to so-called culture in Europe, since he was physically safe and had managed to create a stable existence: "After all, I came here 13 years ago as a poor immigrant, so I'm satisfied with the progress I've made." To a friend in Germany, he remarked without irony, "Even to-day this is by far still the best country to live in if you are a European."[74]

Rudolf was well aware of the international community's condemnation of apartheid. "I know what the feeling in some parts of the very biased Press all over the world is, in regard to South Africa," he wrote to his stepson Louis in London, but their criticism was "incomprehensible." While South Africa had its problems, he insisted that they were mild compared to what was going on in the rest of the world.[75]

In his view, the gravest threat to peace was the Soviet Union. Over and over he ranted in his letters about the urgency of restraining "Uncle Stalin," whose dictatorship was "different to Hitler's in name only." Rudolf's views were partly a carryover from his nationalistic and anti-communist upbringing: Max's thinking informed his political consciousness until the end of his life. Rudolf's attitudes were also undoubtedly influenced by the extreme anti-communism of the apartheid government, which used the Suppression of Communism Act (1950) to justify draconian action against any political opposition.[76] He wrote to Karl:

> But unfortunately the Reds have learned their methods watching Hitler/Mussolini and now they want to rape the world just like those two tried to for the last 15 years. It seems the only thing they respect is the iron fist. But of course you don't need me to tell you anything about them. You love them even more than me, if that's even possible. Which

is why anyone who doesn't want to live under the Russians' thumb must choose the lesser evil and stand with those who are ready to defend themselves against them.[77]

Such standard Cold War fare pervaded their correspondence. For Rudolf, the main lesson to be learned from the Nazis was the need to act quickly against the Soviet Union, which threatened to unleash "the next war; this time to put the 'world revolution' into action."[78]

Should South African Jews, especially those who suffered under the Nazis, be held to a higher moral standard than other Whites as far as their responses to apartheid are concerned? Before rushing to judgment, it is worth understanding the context in which attitudes such as Rudolf's were formed. In today's world, the Holocaust is regularly invoked as a benchmark for talking about human rights abuses, from genocide to slavery, colonialism, and, indeed, apartheid. It is tempting, but mistaken, to assume that these connections were obvious to observers sixty years ago as well. Before the 1980s at the earliest, few South African Jews understood antisemitism to be related in any meaningful way to anti-Black racism, and most accepted the reigning order with little compunction.[79] That German Jews were victims of what we would now call a racialized system was at the time neither evident nor especially significant. While a handful of German Jewish refugees were drawn by their experiences to political activism, most drew other conclusions. If they had political inclinations they were overwhelmingly toward Zionism, which flourished in a political landscape premised on distinct group identities.

Rudolf's attitudes toward "race" were also shaped by his conservative German upbringing. He had always gravitated toward the political right, and it is not surprising that the ideas of the marginal Jewish left made little impression on him. Rudolf's prejudiced views on South Africa's "problems" were less a manifestation of ideological conviction than a reflection of his desire to become fully South African—an extension of his efforts to learn local history and languages. Decades before, Max had advised him of the importance of integrating and making connections in his new homeland: "Even in South Africa certain political views will hold sway," he had written, but "these concern you only in so far as you must show loyalty to your English host country so you can become a respectable English citizen as quickly as possible."[80] (South Africa withdrew from the British Commonwealth in 1961.) The political views that Rudolf expressed were widespread at the time, and were regarded as quite different from the "die-hard" ideas of Afrikaner nationalists—those who sought the legislated separation of the races, and what some saw as Nazi-like purity of blood.

Beyond politics, refugees like Rudolf also had countless challenges to confront, from surviving on meager resources to finding a job and housing, learning a new language, and establishing new lifelines of social support. Like refugees everywhere, they came to South Africa with emotional baggage: rejection, uncertainty, loss of social and economic status, and loneliness borne of leaving behind everything known and loved. Most were too preoccupied with the basic concerns of existence to be concerned about institutionalized racism.[81]

For Rudolf, South Africa was first and foremost a land of refuge. He had arrived as a vulnerable twenty-four-year-old, stripped of his livelihood and possessions, bombarded by a maze of unfamiliar laws and practices. His decision to leave Germany in 1933 was spurred not only by political events, but also by his difficult relationship with his parents, whose letters in the ensuing years expressed a fragile mix of advice, anger, longing, and recriminations. Rudolf had obviously strayed from the Jewish fold, and his parents felt that he had strayed from them, too. His letters became less and less frequent, and as his parents' predicament grew gradually worse, it is perhaps inevitable that they felt abandoned. Rudolf's later insistence that he fled Hanau to avoid arrest was almost certainly fabricated, perhaps because it was a more palatable explanation for why he had left his family given what happened afterward. The connection to his father and the values of his upbringing nonetheless remained with him throughout his life, taking on a special importance as he struggled to find his feet so far from home.

Just as Karl's actions do not fit neatly into the category of "perpetrator," so, too, Rudolf's life is not easily subsumed under the label of "victim." His children remembered him as a firm and unsentimental man, reserved in company, with a strong sense of morality but uncomfortable with demonstrations of warmth and affection. He was "meticulous, controlled, and very much the Boss," recalled his stepson David. "I remember for instance one winter night when he would not eat a pear because they were 'too cold,' and [Norman] warming a pear for him by twirling it in front of the heater. He took the offering as his due." Others had similar recollections about the elaborate work involved in preparing Rudolf's coffee to precisely the right temperature. He had high expectations of academic performance from his son and stepsons, and he dispensed outspoken and sometimes harsh advice. He also had his moments of anger and unkindness.[82] Max's patriarchal voice is clearly reflected in Rudolf's remoteness, quick temper, and exacting demands.

Rudolf's troubled first marriage was also probably shaped, in part, by the ordeal he had suffered. Whatever the source of Rachel's health challenges, Rudolf was not always sympathetic or supportive, as reflected in his rancorous and sometimes vicious tirades about her to Karl.[83] The two friends' attitudes toward women were a clear legacy of their fencing days, but Rudolf's tough disposition also perhaps made him a more demanding spouse than most. Partly this might be explained by personality, partly by upbringing; but partly also by the experience of extraordinary loss and displacement in his youth.

Rudolf's relationship with Karl adds another interesting piece to the puzzle of his character. Despite Karl's scrupulous work on the family's claims, Rudolf was content to pay him far less than he did his other agents. He also seemed to be remarkably little affected by Karl's death. Rudolf may have defended Karl to his relatives and reminisced about their shared past, but he was not sentimental: Karl was German, after all. Rudolf may have been a victim, but he was also a survivor: focused on self-preservation and the pragmatism necessary to achieve it.

In the decades after the war, Rudolf struggled to make a life for himself while also coming to terms with everything he had lost. If he carried a moral burden, it was that he had not been able to save those closest to him, even if he had tried. He established a reputation for himself as a reliable businessman, a loyal citizen, and a committed family man, devoted to his son and stepchildren. And every Sunday, dressed in his finest, he would sit at his Johannesburg writing desk, chafing in the dry heat of the African Highveld, holding together the fragile threads of his existence with its immoveable heart in Hanau. He was proud to have set down roots in a land of natural beauty, of curiosities and contradictions, where despite the political situation he was free from worry about his physical safety. He also always remained, consciously and resolutely, a Schwab: the last in a distinguished line of Schwabs to have been born in Hanau, bound to the centuries-long abode of his ancestors, and to their legacy.

Epilogue

Legacies

On Sunday, 22 July 1962, Max Schwab's ashes were interred in the Jewish cemetery in Hanau. In his eulogy, the rabbi officiating at the ceremony described Max as an upstanding citizen and an observant Jew, a prominent figure in both the town's Jewish community and its civic life. Also delivering addresses at the funeral were representatives of the Hanau sports association, the geological society, and the historical society, all of which Max had once enthusiastically led. The Lord Mayor Herbert Droese, representing the town council, declared that he was deeply moved by the occasion, and stressed that simply remembering victims like Max was not enough. It was imperative, he said, that people speak to their children "of the heavy guilt with which the German people covered itself [*sic*] during the Nazi period. This was a crime which filled everybody with deep shame, and for which there was no adequate atonement." The message of the ceremony was one of tolerance and reconciliation, and Rudolf later affirmed that he had found it "solemn and dignified." He was given the honor of lowering his father's urn into the grave.[1]

More than twenty years earlier, watching his community disintegrating around him, Max had explained to Rudolf in anguished terms why he would not contemplate leaving Hanau:

> I feel isolated and lonely; I long to get away from here but at the very moment the thought crosses my mind I can already feel the terrible homesickness I'll be slave to, come rain or shine, from the minute I shake the dust of my old homeland off my shoes. Just think about it: our forefathers have lived in Hanau, uninterrupted, for the last 335 years, and they're all buried in the same graveyard.[2]

According to Rudolf, Max had purchased plots in the cemetery, and his final wish was to be laid to rest alongside his ancestors.

Max Schwab's grave in the Hanau cemetery, July 1962. Courtesy of Yad Vashem.

After Max's death in February 1942, his ashes—or at least what the Sachsen-hausen camp command claimed were his ashes—were sent to the Jewish cemetery in Frankfurt for burial. The Jewish cemetery in Hanau had been closed in February 1939, and no amount of pleading on Martha's part could persuade the local authorities to honor her husband's final request.[3]

At the end of World War II, Hanau was in ruins. Allied bombings had reduced the town center, including the Schwab family home, to rubble. No memorial indicated where the Jewish school or synagogue had once stood. Virtually no Jewish presence remained—apart, paradoxically, from the cemetery, the last remaining link to the community that had once thrived there.

Rudolf's attempts to cope with his loss, in the immediate postwar years, found him returning again and again to the idea of burying his father's ashes, to what seemed the only concrete trace of his family's illustrious past. His mother and brother were irretrievably gone, but he clung to the notion that at least something of his father had remained: a tangible, material object that could be placed in the cemetery and honored. The implausibility of a camp official overseeing a Jewish prisoner's cremation—even more, the careful return of his ashes to his relatives—was not something that Rudolf allowed himself to ponder.

In 1948, shortly after their reconnection, Rudolf asked Karl to find out where his father was buried. Within a short time, Karl had located Max's grave at

B1 2-A-4 in the Frankfurt Jewish cemetery. It had not been well kept since 1942, he reported, but he would now ensure that everything was "in good order," beginning with arranging for a gardener to remove the weeds and plant fresh flowers. He would also deal firmly with the cemetery management, who were proposing exorbitant rates for maintenance. Rudolf was impressed by Karl's efficiency and lavished him with praise: "This clearly shows, again, the difference between an ordinary mortal and one who knows why he has 'grey matter' in his skull."[4]

Rudolf was fairly convinced, however, that his mother had paid in advance for ten to twenty years' upkeep of Max's grave. He had found bank statements showing payments Martha had made to the Frankfurt Jewish community shortly before her deportation, which made "very clear that my mother, who knew what was ahead of her, bravely and courageously made all the preparations she thought necessary."[5] A dignified burial site, a physical place where her husband's existence could be marked—even if it wasn't the Hanau grave he had imagined; even if she knew that she would probably never visit the grave herself—was Martha's urgent priority as she awaited her own departure for the unknown in May 1942.

In Hanau, as throughout Germany, there was never a real *Stunde Null* (zero hour), a radical new beginning, after Hitler's defeat. Much of the civil service, especially the middle and lower echelons, remained intact after 1945.[6] But as time passed the politics of memory shifted, and in 1960 Rudolf received a letter from Oskar Schenk, a town councilor and enthusiastic amateur historian. Delegated with documenting the fate of Hanau's Jewish community, Schenk tracked down as many former residents as he could, requesting information about their families' ancestry in the town, their involvement in public life, and their experiences under the Nazis. His was one of the initiatives responsible for bringing former residents back to visit Hanau, a trend evident across Germany from the early 1960s as Jewish survivors and their descendants began to return to their hometowns. Schenk's committed work resulted in a rich archive of testimonies and photographs, the basis for several important publications in the years that followed. Thanks to Rudolf's efforts, the Schwabs' story featured prominently in their pages.[7]

Rudolf met with Schenk in the summer of 1960, on his first visit back to Germany since he had left more than a quarter of a century before. Given his vociferous opposition to the idea of living in Germany, and his refusal to contemplate visiting sooner, I imagine that it was only an invitation of this kind that could entice him back: official and dignified, to satisfy the descendant of one of Hanau's most illustrious Jewish families that he was wanted again in his beloved hometown. Before arriving in Hanau, Rudolf traveled to Heidelberg, where he was finally reunited with his aged aunt Rosa. She was living in a home for survivors run by the small Jewish community, but was confused, incoherent, and almost completely deaf and blind. He would never see her again.[8]

Following his visit to Hanau, Rudolf wrote to Alex:

> Everything has changed, lots of new buildings, especially in the area of Französische Allee. I naturally also went to the cemeteries in Hanau and Frankfurt, and said Kaddish. Of our old friends I only met Jos. Weigelt and H. Mitterer.—I felt more at ease in England and in France than in Germany, and cannot understand people who want to return to Germany.[9]

In January 1961, Rudolf sent the first of a series of parcels to Schenk documenting his family's story. Here was his motivation to finally reopen the papers his father had sent him twenty-five years earlier, to begin work in earnest on the family tree, to research the centuries-long family lineage, to fill in the gaps.

It was in his correspondence with Schenk that Rudolf first raised the question of Max's burial wishes. "If you, Mr. Councilor, would use your influence in this exceptional case to correct this injustice from the Nazi period," Rudolf wrote, "I would be very much in your debt." Schenk moved quickly, and within three months the matter had been approved by the town council. Rudolf was overcome with gratitude for "this noble and humane deed." Schenk wanted to organize the transfer of the ashes as soon as possible, but Rudolf insisted on attending the ceremony in person. In July 1962, his father was finally laid to rest in the Hanau Jewish cemetery, between the graves of his beloved parents Regina and Samuel.[10]

More initiatives to honor the Jewish inhabitants of Hanau followed. On 19 March 1964, the nineteenth anniversary of the town's near-destruction, a small memorial was placed opposite the site of the former synagogue. The town of Hanau took on the responsibility of maintaining the cemetery in accordance with Jewish law, and an index was compiled so that descendants would be able to locate their relatives' graves.[11]

The story has not been without its setbacks. Like other towns in Germany, Hanau has had its share of antisemitic incidents, including several occasions on which the cemetery was desecrated. In January 1982, one of the graves affected was that of Rudolf's great-grandmother Jeannette Schwab.[12]

The town nonetheless also has a host of energetic individuals working to document and commemorate its Jewish past. On 30 May 2006, the sixty-fourth anniversary of the first deportation of Jews from Hanau, a commemorative panel was erected on Platform 9 of the town's *Hauptbahnhof*, using some of the archival photographs taken by photographer Franz Weber.[13] Some interest has also been shown in the *Stolpersteine* (stumbling stones) project by the Cologne artist Gunter Demnig, which remembers victims of Nazism by installing commemorative plaques in the pavement in front of their last addresses. The project is limited in Hanau by the fact that much of the town center was destroyed, leaving few Jewish homes in front of which to place a plaque. The local Jewish community, restored to a fraction of its former size, also objects to the project on the basis that treading on commemorative plaques runs counter to Jewish traditions of memorialization.[14] Rudolf's grandson Daniel shares this reservation, and while several plaques have been laid to commemorate former Jewish residents of Hanau, the Schwab family is not included on this list.[15]

On 30 May 2010, a new memorial was unveiled on Hanau's former ghetto wall, consisting of 228 bronze plaques inscribed with the names of murdered Jewish children, women, and men from Hanau. The names of Max, Martha, and Hans Schwab appear there, as do those of Max's sisters Helene Demuth and Erna Heymann. Several esteemed guests participated in the memorial's unveiling ceremony, among them the local mayor and town council chairman, representatives of local and national Jewish organizations, and invited descendants of Hanau's Jewish community.[16] Rudolf's grandchildren Daniel and Ricci were there that day to witness the town's first commemoration of individual Jews who had perished at the Nazis' hands. Daniel presented their family's story to sympathetic audiences, and the family has continued to receive unstinting support from the local authorities in tracing and remembering its past.

If the impact of the Holocaust in Hanau is evident in the landscape itself, the legacy of the genocide is more difficult to trace in the survivors and their descendants. Rudolf left Germany at the age of twenty-one and lived most of his adult life in South Africa. It was here that he married, had children, and started a business. He worked hard to integrate, and he engaged in local causes. To speak of recovery would be facile, but notwithstanding his ordeals he managed to establish a comfortable existence and to raise capable children.

Close to the end of his life, Rudolf explained to his cousin Armand his decision to change his name upon his arrival in South Africa. He wrote:

It is so many years ago, that anybody called me Rudi, and at my age a pet name somehow does not seem to be suitable, that I have dropped it long ago. As Ralph is the nearest translation for Rudolf, it has been that for a long time.[17]

Early on, it became apparent to me that Rudolf's name change held a particular significance.[18] When I spoke with Norman, Daniel, and Ricci about their father and grandfather, they talked about Ralph. But when I spoke with the assistants who were working on cataloguing the letters, he was unequivocally Rudi. At first I moved indiscriminately between the two names. As I became more and more absorbed in the letters, it seemed to me that it was not only the names that were different, but also that the Ralph of our conversations and the Rudolf of the letters were quite distinct characters: that the person perceived by his descendants as hard, reserved, and quick to anger was distinct from the refined, industrious, and occasionally dry-witted personality who emerged in the letters.[19]

There were obvious convergences, of course. Rudolf had never been a sentimental man, even in the earliest letters to Martha and Max, and the "school of emigration," as he called it, hardened him considerably.[20] But the separation between his lived and virtual existences was stark. His acculturation to South Africa was, in some respects, seamless: his involvement in local causes; his business success; his impeccable English, replete with idiomatic phrases and local slang. Other elements of his identity, however, remained inaccessible outside his correspondence, which for most of his adult life constituted a parallel world of reminiscence and anger and unshakable longing. In the course of tracing Rudolf's life, I increasingly had the sense of a man who never entirely felt at home anywhere, and who despite himself, perhaps not intentionally or even consciously, found an alternative life in his letters—a space in which to perpetuate his father's legacy, to be a devoted community man and patriarch, to remain connected to the past and the sense of rootedness and self that came with it.

Although Norman remembered his father as detached and aloof, it seemed to me that Rudolf did in fact try, in his quiet way, to draw his son into his world. His attempts came, as these things so often do, in the prosaic and improbable form of stamp collecting, that quintessentially German middle-class activity. Rudolf's own father, Max, had been an enthusiast for many years—he amassed a noteworthy collection, valuable enough for Rudolf to include in his reparations claims—and they had spent many pleasant afternoons together at the Hanau dining table sorting and classifying stamps from around the world.[21] The young Norman could not have grasped the deep-rooted significance of this activity for Rudolf, but he recalled nonetheless that his father had often tried to include him in his hobby:

Rudolf and Norman, c. 1944. Courtesy of Yad Vashem.

My father used to collect stamps diligently and everybody that he ever wrote to he would have asked to send him stamps. He used to work on his collection on a Sunday in the dining room on the table dressed in a tie and sports jacket!!! He always tried to involve me but I was not very interested. Nevertheless I would oblige and do some of the work that was necessary such as soaking the used stamps in a basin of water in the bathroom. Then I would take the stamps out of the water after floating the paper of the envelope off the stamp. After this the stamps had to be put on a sheet of blotting paper after rubbing as much of the gum off the stamp as possible (in the water). Sometimes I would put the stamp upside down on the blotting paper. Then the stamps were put in an empty cigarette tin from "Men of the World smoke Max" or some other brand. My father was of course a cigarette smoker. From time to time I would then sort out the stamps according to the country of origin and put them in an album. The part I liked the most was looking up the stamp in a large catalogue of stamps to see if it was worth anything!!! Also I used to like receiving the stamps from various people all over the world—mostly relatives of my father.[22]

Despite its undemonstrativeness, Rudolf's devotion to Norman was plain. In a letter to a family friend in 1945 he wrote that Norman was "a great comfort to me after everything that's happened to my family over the past six years." He regularly updated his relatives about Norman's progress at school ("He is healthy, strong and a good Mixer, the exact opposite to what his father was as a boy"), and later told them proudly about his exploits at university and in the army. As Norman grew up, Rudolf also involved him in the pastime of letter writing, encouraging him to add short notes of his own to his relatives across the world and, in time, their children. They responded with messages and stamps for Norman's budding collection.[23]

Perhaps unsurprisingly, the connections between the refugees' children—the so-called second generation—did not progress far beyond these occasional exchanges of notes and stamps. The fragile global web that had served for their parents as such a vital source of sustenance and identity seems to have been, for them, little more than an amusement, a source of exotic gifts and birthday cards.

The impact on the third generation is even more diffuse, and yet if the last decade is anything to go by, the victims' grandchildren are beginning to engage with the past in fresh and provocative ways. It is no coincidence that it was Rudolf's grandson Daniel who rediscovered his letters—their presence in the garage was not a secret; they were simply not, for a long time, of interest—and that it is Daniel who has devoted himself so untiringly to having the collection archived, catalogued, and studied. He recalls growing up with very little knowledge of Germany ("Germany was just like Mars," he quipped to an amused audience in Hanau), or of what had happened to his family. He also remembers being captivated "by the large and impressive family tree that hung at the entrance to my parents' home. I used to gaze at this family tree but never really understood it." Daniel's work has been spurred by his desire to recover his family's past as well as his broader concern about antisemitism. When we spoke soon after his first visit to Hanau in 2010, he spoke animatedly about how beautiful the town was, "like in a fairy tale," and how he could even imagine himself living there were he not so committed to his life in Israel.[24] On some level I was not surprised at his response, given his family's longstanding history. At the same time I found it a little uncanny, a hint of the persistent weaving of identity and belonging through the generations.

Not all grandchildren of victims experience the same intensity of connection, but many feel a link to the past and a compulsion to preserve its memory. I, like Daniel, am one of them. Though the Schwabs' story is very different from that of my own Polish grandparents, I have been driven by a similar commitment to unravel its details and to understand its implications. As a Jew who grew up in South Africa during the final years of apartheid, I have also repeatedly been drawn to the question of how the experience and perception of victimhood shapes our identities, though I have regularly had to remind myself that that question is far more mine than it was ever Rudolf's.

At first glance, the Schwabs' story is simply that of an ordinary family. Such ordinary stories, however, are at the same time far-reaching in their significance, opening up vital new perspectives on how we write the history of the Holocaust itself. The family's vacillations between hope and despair in the face of extreme uncertainty, Max's paranoia, Martha's stoic submission, their crumbling marriage, Rudolf's quiet defiance—all are everyday responses we recognize only too well, yet they still play surprisingly little role in our explanations of historical change, perhaps because they are so difficult to quantify or pigeonhole. Everyday lives nonetheless can, indeed should, fundamentally inform our perspectives: on questions of how societies acclimatize to violence, for example, or how people take the decision to become refugees, or how war transforms marriages and families. The refugees' stories similarly have much to teach us about how displaced people construct and sustain identity, not only as individuals but also as communities of affinity or circumstance. The refugees' struggles left a profound impression on their countries of refuge and the birthplaces they so reluctantly left behind, just as they did on their immediate circles.

The friendship between Rudolf and Karl is another important viewpoint from which we should rethink human behavior during and after the Holocaust. Their story reminds us that people are complicated, unpredictable, and stubbornly resistant to categorization, exposing a landscape of responses that is unexpected and unlikely, and also entirely human. Rudolf's life in South Africa in turn prompts troubling questions about the persistence of racism after the Holocaust, not only in abstract laws but also in the lives of individuals unwittingly propagating some of the ideas that spawned their own victimhood. Such thorny issues cannot be confronted without taking into account the countless private, everyday interactions through which racism endures and spreads.

In recent years, more and more family troves have begun to emerge from forgotten storage places. Some are modest in size; others preserve detailed records spanning continents and epochs. The worlds they chronicle are different from those we might seek in government or institutional archives, but they should be taken equally seriously: they, too, are the fragments of which history is made. Ordinary people's stories, by definition subjective and idiosyncratic, deepen and nuance our understanding of history's most challenging questions.

Over the six years that I have spent researching and writing Rudolf Schwab's story, the image that has stuck with me most persistently is that of the Hanau Jewish cemetery. Again and again my mind returns to my first visit to the town, and the feeling, on a sunny July afternoon, of standing outside the cemetery's high stone walls, locked out by imposing iron gates, powerless to access what seemed to be the only concrete remains of the town's Jewish past. The cemetery was the final stop on my carefully planned route; I had already spent several hours that morning encountering apartment blocks, pharmacies, and empty spaces where the Schwab family home, the synagogue, and the community center had once stood. I had simply assumed that the cemetery would be open, not that special permission would be needed to walk inside. I scoured the faces of passersby to see whether they registered any traces of the cataclysmic events that had taken place here decades before. But life in Hanau continued as normal, as if Max and Martha and Hans and Rudolf had never existed. That would be the case anywhere, I supposed, though in most other cases the past would not have been severed so violently and irrevocably.

Understandably, I think, we cling to these sites of memory. When they are not enough, we bring to them our strongest forces of imagination—not to contrive, but to reconstruct what was, even if we can only ever do so imperfectly; and to remember.

Acknowledgments

This book began its life as a small side project. When I initially encountered Rudolf Schwab's remarkable collection, I imagined editing and annotating a selection of the letters for publication, to enable other academics to make use of them in their research and teaching. Within a few weeks of beginning to read through the correspondence, however, it became clear that forty years of a person's life can hardly be reduced to a selection of representative documents. In the letters I saw identities, attitudes, and relationships evolving in incremental and often barely perceptible ways as years and decades passed. Talking with my friends and family, I would often use the analogy of a slow indie film, where nothing very dramatic happens from scene to scene, but somehow, by the end of it, entire worlds have transformed. I concluded that in order to do justice to such a rich record I would need to explore other avenues of expression, and I experimented with multiple ideas before settling on the current form. It has been one of the most enriching and moving pieces of research that I have had the privilege to do.

My first debt of gratitude is to the Schwab family, who entrusted me with their father and grandfather's story. Norman, Daniel, Ricci, and Lori: thanks for answering my many questions, providing anecdotes and photographs, and supporting my work with such enthusiasm and generosity of spirit. Carol Schwab sadly passed away while the book was in its final stages; she, too, was unstintingly supportive from the outset.

Bronagh Bowerman has been a key player in this project from the beginning. Soon after the discovery of the letters, in 2010, she was engaged by the Schwab family to produce a detailed catalogue, including information about writers and recipients, dates, places, and topics. The mammoth database she produced was of inestimable value as I navigated my way through more than 4,000 pages of written documents. As the only other person who has studied the entire collection of the letters, she was also a much-appreciated interlocutor as I worked to make sense of Rudolf, Max, Karl, and the extended Schwab family. Although I analyzed the letters in their original languages, I felt strongly that the translations in the book should do justice to the elegance and idiom of the correspondents' prose. Bronagh is a far more accomplished translator than I, and I am grateful to her for producing such beautiful translations of the letters, and for refining my own translations from the German. Omer Vanvoorden gave generously and extensively of his time early on in the project, producing translated outlines that allowed the Schwab family to access much of Rudolf's story for the first time.

In Hanau, I had the indefatigable assistance of Martin Hoppe, head of the Hanau historical society and assistant to the local mayor. I also benefited from the unparalleled local knowledge of Monica Kingreen and Eckhard Meise. Thanks to the many archivists and experts who helped me to locate elusive bits of information: in particular, Felix Römer of the German Historical Institute in London, Dick de Mildt of Ex Post Facto, Monika Rademacher at the Stadtarchiv Hanau, Christiane Kleemann of the Hessisches Hauptstaatsarchiv Wiesbaden, and Susanne Urban at the ITS. Frank Bajohr kindly offered advice during my pursuit of Karl's past. For research assistance, I am grateful for the meticulous work of Dorothee Lottmann-Kaeseler, Claudia Sandberg, and Lars Fischer. Thanks also to Robert Fallenstein for his transcriptions of Martha, Max, and Rosa's sometimes indecipherable prose, and to Barbara Kreuzer for her kind advice on a vexing question of translation. For their willingness to be interviewed for the project, thanks to Rudolf's stepsons Louis Prades and David Mandelstam, and also to William Schwabe, Madeleine Fane, and Elke Lorenz. I'm not normally in the habit of thanking inanimate objects, but without the amazing ATLAS.ti, this book would not even approximate what it has turned out to be.

My work on this book was supported by a number of generous funders. The Kaplan Centre has been committed to the project from the beginning, and I am grateful to Oren Kaplan in particular for his trust and encouragement. Thanks also to Milton Shain and Adam Mendelsohn of the University of Cape Town, and to Gavin Morris of the South African Jewish Museum, for their interest in pursuing projects alongside the book's publication. A grant from the Memorial Foundation for Jewish Culture, New York, and two semesters of research leave at the University of Southampton enabled me to complete much of the research and writing. I am honored and still somewhat astonished to have received unsolicited support from Elizabeth Ewing Stanford.

Much of my time writing this book has been spent imagining my correspondents' lives and responses from the quiet of my library or office desk. Like most historians I enjoy a fair bit of solitude, but my thinking is also vastly enriched in conversation with colleagues and friends. I am privileged to have the Parkes Institute at the University of Southampton as my intellectual home. I have learned enormously from my colleagues Tony Kushner, Joachim Schlör, Helen Spurling, Claire Le Foll, James Jordan, Devorah Baum, Dan Levene, Andrea Reiter, Sarah Pearce, François Soyer, and Mark Levene. I am also grateful for the support of my many history colleagues, including especially David Brown, Anne Curry, Priti Mishra, Mark Stoyle, and Mark Cornwall. Thanks to seminar participants and audience members at the University of Sussex, the Wiener Library, the Institute for Historical Research at the University of London, the University of Cape Town, and the Edinburgh Jewish Literary Society for their incisive comments on early drafts. Friends near and far, particularly the exceptional communities at Eden and Assif in London, are an unfailing source of support, from playdates and meals to sharing in the joys of success and discovery. Clive Marks is a constant and tireless supporter.

Huge thanks to those who took the time to read the manuscript at various stages, and to offer their invaluable insights: Nick Stargardt, Joachim Schlör, Tony Kushner, Konrad Kwiet, Esther Jilovsky, Hannah Holtschneider, Richard Mansell, Oren Kaplan, Dave Gilbert, Leah Gilbert, Susan Heitler, Jesse Heitler, Yzanne Mackay, Daniel Schwab, Paul Israel, and two anonymous reviewers for Wayne State University Press. Thanks to Tali Nates for supporting the idea of including a display on Rudolf in the new museum at the Johannesburg Holocaust and Genocide Centre. Kathy Wildfong understood the project completely from the outset, and together with the team at WSUP—Emily Nowak, Kristin Harpster, Eric Schramm, Rachel Ross, Jamie Jones, Carrie Downes Teefey, and Kristina Stonehill—has done a sterling job of sheperding the manuscript to publication. Thank you all.

As always, my most profound gratitude is to my family. To my parents, siblings original and acquired, in-laws and outlaws, and especially to Jesse, Noah, Eliana, and Sam: Not a day goes by when I don't think about how extraordinarily fortunate I am to be surrounded by such unflagging love, loyalty, good humor, and inspiration.

Notes

Introduction

Epigraph taken from "Anno dazumal in Hanau," *Frankfurter Rundschau*, 23 March 1961.

1. Yad Vashem File Number 1589: Collection of Rudolf Erwin Alexander Schwab (hereafter Schwab Collection), 58.
2. Email correspondence with Ricci Lyons and Norman Schwab, 9 July 2012.
3. Schwab Collection, 3542.
4. See for example Rebecca L. Boehling and Uta Larkey, *Life and Loss in the Shadow of the Holocaust: A Jewish Family's Untold Story* (Cambridge: Cambridge University Press, 2011); Oliver Doetzer, *"Aus Menschen werden Briefe": Die Korrespondenz einer jüdischen Familie zwischen Verfolgung und Emigration 1933–1947* (Köln: Böhlau, 2002); Christopher R. Browning, Richard S. Hollander, and Nechama Tec, eds.. *Every Day Lasts a Year: A Jewish Family's Correspondence from Poland* (Cambridge: Cambridge University Press, 2007).
5. Schwab Collection, 582.
6. See Doetzer, *"Aus Menschen werden Briefe,"* 2.
7. Schwab Collection, 1232.
8. Schwab Collection, 633.
9. On letters as a genre and historical source, particularly in the context of migration, see among others David Barton and Nigel Hall, eds., *Letter Writing as a Social Practice* (Amsterdam: John Benjamins, 2000); Julia Creet, "The Archive as Temporary Abode," in *Memory and Migration: Multidisciplinary Approaches to Memory Studies*, edited by Julia Creet and Andreas Kitzmann (Toronto: University of Toronto Press, 2014), 280–98; Bruce S. Elliot, David A. Gerber, and Suzanne M. Sinke, *Letters across Borders: The Epistolary Practices of International Migrants* (New York: Palgrave Macmillan, 2006); Esther Jilovsky, "Grandpa's Letters: Encountering Tangible Memories of the Holocaust," in *In the Shadows of Memory: The Holocaust and the Third Generation*, edited by Esther Jilovsky, Jordana Silverstein, and David Slucki (Portland, Ore.: Vallentine Mitchell, 2015), 135–48; Margaretta Jolly and Liz Stanley, "Letters As/not a Genre," *Life Writing* 2, no. 2 (2005): 91–118; Barbara Kirshenblatt-Gimblett, "Objects of Memory: Material Culture as Life Review," in *Folk Groups and Folklore*

Genres: A Reader, edited by Elliott Oring (Logan: Utah State University Press, 1989), 135–48.

Chapter 1

1. Naftali Bar-Giora Bamberger and Eckhard Meise, eds., *Der jüdische Friedhof in Hanau* (Hanau: Hanauer Geschichtsverein 1844 e.V, 2005), 298; email correspondence with Eckhard Meise, 16 October 2012.

2. www.deutsche-maerchenstrasse.com/en/?lang=en_US (accessed 21 August 2014).

3. This overview section is drawn from the following sources: Paul Arnsberg, *Die jüdischen Gemeinden in Hessen: Anfang, Untergang, Neubeginn* (Frankfurt am Main: Societäts-Verlag, 1971); Paul Arnsberg, *Die jüdischen Gemeinden in Hessen: Bilder, Dokumente* (Darmstadt: Eduard Roether Verlag, 1973); Gerhard Flämig, *Hanau im Dritten Reich*, 3 vols. (Hanau: Magistrat der Stadt, 1983); Monika Ilona Pfeifer and Monica Kingreen, *Hanauer Juden 1933–1945: Entrechtung, Verfolgung, Deportation* (Hanau: CoCon, 1998); Baruch Z. Ophir, Chasia Turtel-Aberzhanska, Shlomo Schmiedt, Joseph Walk, and Bracha Freundlich, eds., *Pinḳas Ha-ḳehilot. Entsiḳlopedyah Shel Ha-Yishuvim Ha-Yehudiyim Le-Min Hiẏasdam Ṿe-'ad Le-Aḥar Sho'at Milḥemet Ha-'olam Ha-Sheniyah: Germania*. vol. 3 (Jerusalem: Yad Vashem, 1972), 427–34; Shulamit Volkov, *Germans, Jews, and Antisemites: Trials in Emancipation* (Cambridge: Cambridge University Press, 2006). I have also drawn on the following testimonies of former Jewish residents of Hanau, all accessed at the USC Shoah Foundation Visual History Archive on 23 August 2013: Gerhard Levi, Interview 40707, 10 February 1998; Manfred Strauss, Interview 5279, 7 August 1995; Meir (Manfried) Fulda, Interview 38086, 8 January 1998; Sophie Marum, Interview 21094, 11 October 1996; Henry (Heinz) Hirschman, Interview 47904, 12 November 1998.

4. On the significance of Worms as a German Jewish city, see Nils H. Roemer, *German City, Jewish Memory: The Story of Worms* (Waltham, Mass.: Brandeis University Press; Hanover, N.H.: University Press of New England, 2010).

5. Schwab Collection, 2269, 2300–2301.

6. Schwab Collection, 3623, 2428.

7. Schwab Collection, 2646.

8. Schwab Collection, 3626–27.

9. Schwab Collection, 2269, 3455.

10. Schwab Collection, 60.

11. Schwab Collection, 25; Arnsberg, *Die jüdischen Gemeinden in Hessen: Anfang, Untergang, Neubeginn*, 331; Eckhard Meise, "Die Hausnamen der Hanauer Judengasse," in Bamberger and Meise, *Der jüdische Friedhof in Hanau*, 191–286.

12. Jacob Katz, *Out of the Ghetto: The Social Background of Jewish Emancipation, 1770–1870* (Cambridge, Mass.: Harvard University Press, 1973), 34–36; Gerhard Flämig, *Hanau im Dritten Reich*, vol. 2, 276–77; see also the introduction to Monika Richarz, ed., *Jew-*

ish Life in Germany: Memoirs from Three Centuries, translated by Stella P. Rosenfeld and Sidney Rosenfeld (Bloomington: Indiana University Press, 1991).

13. Nils H. Roemer, "Between the Provinces and the City: Mapping German-Jewish Memories," *Leo Baeck Institute Yearbook* 51, no. 1 (2006): 61–77.

14. Arnsberg, *Die jüdischen Gemeinden in Hessen: Anfang, Untergang, Neubeginn,* 327; Pfeifer and Kingreen, *Hanauer Juden 1933–1945,* 69; Steven Lowenstein, "Decline and Survival of Rural Jewish Communities," in *In Search of Jewish Community: Jewish Identities in Germany and Austria, 1918–1933,* edited by Michael Brenner and Derek Penslar (Bloomington: Indiana University Press, 1998), 223–42, here 236; Jacob Borut, "Religiöses Leben der Landjuden in westlichen Deutschland während der Weimarer Republik," in *Jüdisches Leben auf dem Lande: Studien zur deutsch-jüdischen Geschichte,* edited by Monika Richarz and Reinhard Rürup (Tübingen: Mohr Siebeck, 1997), 231–48. See also Paul Mendes-Flohr, *German Jews: A Dual Identity* (New Haven, Conn.: Yale University Press, 1999). Hanau does not classify as rural, but a growing literature offers helpful insight into Jews living in smaller towns and cities as well; see for example other essays in Richarz and Rürup, *Jüdisches Leben auf dem Lande.*

15. Ruth Pierson, "Embattled Veterans: The Reichsbund jüdischer Frontsoldaten," *Leo Baeck Institute Year Book* 19 (1974): 139–54.

16. Schwab Collection, 72.

17. Schwab Collection, 171–72.

18. Arnsberg, *Die jüdischen Gemeinden in Hessen: Anfang, Untergang, Neubeginn,* 322–23.

19. Max Schwab, "Die Freiheitskriege von 1813/15 und die Kurhessischen Juden," *Hanauisches Magazin* no. 4 (1930): 27–32, and continuation in *Hanauisches Magazin* no. 5 (1930): 33–37. See also Eckhard Meise, "Leopold Löwenstein, Max Schwab und Hanau," *Neues Magazin für Hanauische Geschichte* (2005): 78–95.

20. Victor Klemperer, *The Diaries of Victor Klemperer 1933–1945: I Shall Bear Witness to the Bitter End,* translated by Martin Chalmers (London: Phoenix, 2000), 128 (6 October 1935), 507 (30 May 1942).

21. Michael Wildt, *Hitler's Volksgemeinschaft and the Dynamics of Racial Exclusion: Violence against Jews in Provincial Germany, 1919–1939,* translated by Bernard W. Heise (New York: Berghahn Books, 2012), 118.

22. Gerhard Flämig, *Hanau im Dritten Reich,* vol. 1, 175.

23. Carl Schwabe, in Richarz, *Jewish Life in Germany,* 327–28.

24. Pfeifer and Kingreen, *Hanauer Juden 1933–1945,* 36–38.

25. Wildt, *Hitler's Volksgemeinschaft,* 2.

26. Schwab Collection, 3468.

27. Richarz, *Jewish Life in Germany,* 4. For an introduction to the rich and nuanced historiography on Jews in Germany, see Amos Elon, *The Pity of It All: A Portrait of Jews in Germany 1743–1933* (London: Penguin, 2004); Marion A. Kaplan,, ed., *Jewish Daily Life in Germany, 1618–1945* (Oxford: Oxford University Press, 2005); Michael

A. Meyer and Michael Brenner, eds., *German-Jewish History in Modern Times* (New York: Columbia University Press, 1996).

28. Wildt, *Hitler's Volksgemeinschaft*, 130; Ophir et al., *Pinḳas Ha-ḳehilot*, 429.

29. See for example Mendes-Flohr, *German Jews*.

30. David Cesarani, *Final Solution: The Fate of the Jews 1933–1949* (London: Macmillan, 2016), 72.

31. Schwab Collection, 756.

32. See Marion A. Kaplan, *Between Dignity and Despair: Jewish Life in Nazi Germany* (New York: Oxford University Press, 1998).

33. For many German Jewish refugees, the chief reason for going to South Africa was "because we could." See, for example, Wolfgang Benz, ed., *Das Exil der kleinen Leute: Alltagserfahrung deutscher Juden in der Emigration* (München: Beck, 1991), 102; Lotta M. Stone, "Seeking Asylum: German Jewish Refugees in South Africa, 1933–1948," Ph.D. dissertation, Clark University, 2010, 50.

34. Schwab Collection, 604–7.

35. Jonathan C. Friedman, *The Lion and the Star: Gentile-Jewish Relations in Three Hessian Communities, 1919–1945* (Lexington: University Press of Kentucky, 1998), 29.

36. Derek Penslar, "The German-Jewish Soldier: From Participant to Victim," *German History* 29, no. 3 (2011): 423–44, here 439–40. For a historical overview, see Peter C. Applebaum, *Loyal Sons: Jewish Soldiers in the German Army in the Great War* (Portland, Ore.: Vallentine Mitchell, 2014). See also more generally Derek Penslar, *Jews and the Military: A History* (Princeton, N.J.: Princeton University Press, 2015).

37. Francis R. Nicosia, "The End of Emancipation and the Illusion of Preferential Treatment: German Zionism, 1933–1938," *Leo Baeck Institute Year Book* 36 (1991): 243–65, here 254; Tim Grady, "Fighting a Lost Battle: The Reichsbund jüdischer Frontsoldaten and the Rise of National Socialism," *German History* 28, no. 1 (2010): 1–20, here 18; Pierson, "Embattled Veterans," 148. Although the organization's leaders were firmly conservative in their political leanings, its members undoubtedly represented a much wider range of orientations, since this was the only Jewish veterans' organization. Arnold Paucker, "Researching German-Jewish Responses and German-Jewish Resistance to National Socialism: Sources and Directions for the Future," *Leo Baeck Institute Yearbook* 51, no. 1 (2006): 193–208, here 198.

38. Grady, "Fighting a Lost Battle," 9, 13–15.

39. Klemperer, *The Diaries of Victor Klemperer*, 472 (16 March 1942).

40. Schwab Collection, 38.

41. Schwab Collection, 609.

42. Schwab Collection, 612–13.

43. Schwab Collection, 710.

44. Flämig, *Hanau im Dritten Reich*, vol. 2, 303; Pfeifer and Kingreen, *Hanauer Juden*, 42.

45. Schwab Collection, 582–83.

46. Schwab Collection, 771, 620.

47. Schwab Collection, 653.

48. Menahem Kaufman, "The Daily Life of the Village and Country Jews in Hessen from Hitler's Ascent to Power to November 1938," *Yad Vashem Studies* 22 (1992): 147–98, here 184–85; Richarz, *Jewish Life in Germany*, 7, 18; Friedman, *The Lion and the Star*, 18; Michael A. Meyer, "Gemeinschaft within Gemeinde: Religious Ferment in Weimar Liberal Judaism," in Brenner and Penslar, *In Search of Jewish Community*, 15–35; Borut, "Religiöses Leben," 242–43. Many Jews found ways of balancing their identities as Jews, Germans, and members of their local communities: Benjamin Maria Baader, Sharon Gillerman, and Paul Lerner, eds., *Jewish Masculinities: German Jews, Gender, and History* (Bloomington: Indiana University Press, 2012), 8.

49. Lowenstein, "Decline and Survival," 227. See also Arnsberg, *Die jüdischen Gemeinden in Hessen: Anfang, Untergang, Neubeginn*, 326; Friedman, *The Lion and the Star*, 18.

50. Ophir et al., *Pinkas Ha-kehilot*, 430. From the sparse information available, it is not clear whether Rudolf belonged to the *deutsch-jüdischer Wanderbund "Kameraden"* (founded 1916) or the *Jugendverband jüdischer-deutscher Kameraden* (founded 1919); given his background the former seems more likely. See Paul Mendes-Flohr, "Rosenzweig and the Kameraden: A Non-Zionist Alliance," *Journal of Contemporary History* 26, no. 3/4 (1991): 385–402. On Jewish youth movements more generally, see Michael Brenner, "Turning Inward: Jewish Youth in Weimar Germany," in Brenner and Penslar, *In Search of Jewish Community*, 56–73.

51. The family was not unique in maintaining its religious observance. See Jacob Boas, "The Shrinking World of German Jewry, 1933–1938." *Leo Baeck Institute Year Book* 31 (1986): 241–66.

52. Schwab Collection, 642.

53. Schwab Collection, 768.

54. Schwab Collection, 582; author interview with William Schwabe, 1 August 2013.

55. Schwab Collection, 678.

56. Schwab Collection, 682–83.

57. On analyzing the material objects of emigration, see Joachim Schlör, "'Take Down Mezuzahs, Remove Name-Plates': The Emigration of Objects from Germany to Palestine," in *Jewish Cultural Studies, Vol. 1: Jewishness: Expression, Identity and Representation*, edited by Simon J. Bronner (Oxford: Littman Library of Jewish Civilization, 2008), 133–50.

58. Schwab Collection, 633.

59. Deborah Dwork and R. J. van Pelt, *Flight from the Reich: Refugee Jews, 1933–1946* (New York: Norton, 2009), 94–95; Boas, "The Shrinking World of German Jewry," 244; Schwab Collection, 590.

60. Otto Dov Kulka and Eberhard Jäckel, eds., *The Jews in the Secret Nazi Reports on Popular Opinion in Germany, 1933–1945*, translated by William Templer (New Haven, Conn.: Yale University Press, 2010), lvi.

61. Schwabe, in Richarz, *Jewish Life in Germany*, 331–32.

62. Kulka and Jäckel, *The Jews in the Secret Nazi Reports*, 303–4.

63. Flämig, *Hanau im Dritten Reich*, vol. 2, 294, 299, 310–11.

64. Kulka and Jäckel, *The Jews in the Secret Nazi Reports*, 302-5.

65. Kulka and Jäckel, *The Jews in the Secret Nazi Reports*, lviii.

66. Schwabe, in Richarz, *Jewish Life in Germany*, 332.

67. Kulka and Jäckel, *The Jews in the Secret Nazi Reports*, 303–4.

68. Flämig, *Hanau im Dritten Reich*, vol. 2, 326.

69. On Kristallnacht in general, see among others Martin Gilbert, *Kristallnacht: Prelude to Destruction* (New York: HarperCollins, 2006); Alan E. Steinweis, *Kristallnacht 1938* (Cambridge, Mass.: Belknap Press, Harvard University Press, 2009).

70. Information on *Kristallnacht* in Hanau has been taken from Arnsberg, *Die jüdischen Gemeinden in Hessen: Anfang, Untergang, Neubeginn*, 334; Flämig, *Hanau im Dritten Reich*, vol. 2, 311–21; Ophir et al., *Pinkas Ha-kehilot*, 431–32; Pfeifer and Kingreen, *Hanauer Juden*, 56–71.

71. Schwab Collection, 1176–81.

72. Schwab Collection, 3435.

73. Flämig, *Hanau im Dritten Reich*, vol. 2, 311–14; Gerhard Levi, Interview 40707, *USC Shoah Foundation Visual History Archive*, 10 February 1998, accessed 23 August 2013; Ophir et al., *Pinkas Ha-kehilot*, 432.

74. Schwab Collection, 3511.

75. Schwab Collection, 3435, 3454.

76. Flämig, *Hanau im Dritten Reich*, vol. 2, 324; Schwab Collection, 758, 748.

77. Pfeifer and Kingreen, *Hanauer Juden*, 79.

78. Schwab Collection, 1178–79.

79. Schwab Collection, 3455.

80. Pfeifer and Kingreen, *Hanauer Juden*, 80–81; Ophir et al., *Pinkas Ha-kehilot*, 432.

81. Schwab Collection, 3465–67; 3470–77.

82. Schwab Collection, 1749.

83. Schwab Collection, 765–66.

84. Schwab Collection, 759, 752.

85. Dwork and van Pelt, *Flight from the Reich*, 257–59; William Kaczynski and Charmian Brinson, *Fleeing from the Fuhrer: A Postal History of Refugees from Nazi Germany* (Stroud: History Press, 2011); Hester Vaizey, *Surviving Hitler's War: Family Life in Germany, 1939–48* (Basingstoke: Palgrave Macmillan, 2010), 43–55.

86. Schwab Collection, 784.

87. Schwab Collection, 693.

88. Schwab Collection, 773, 780, 3623, 651.

89. Schwab Collection, 666.

90. Arnsberg, *Die jüdischen Gemeinden in Hessen: Bilder, Dokumente*, 87.

91. Schwab Collection, 658, 759, 1110–11.

92. Schwab Collection, 600.

93. Schwab Collection, 775, 779.

94. Schwab Collection, 765–6.

95. Schwab Collection, 2536.

96. See Kaplan, *Between Dignity and Despair*; Vaizey, *Surviving Hitler's War*.

97. Schwab Collection, 985, 661.

98. Work on sexual violence in the Nazi camps and ghettos is more developed. See, among others, Sonia M. Hedgepeth and Rochelle G. Saidel, eds., *Sexual Violence against Jewish Women during the Holocaust* (Waltham, Mass.: Brandeis University Press, 2010).

99. Kaplan, *Between Dignity and Despair*; on the non-Jewish family, see Vaizey, *Surviving Hitler's War*.

100. Kaplan, *Between Dignity and Despair*, 16.

101. Mark Roseman, "'Der Dank des Vaterlandes': Memories and Chronicles of German Jewry in the 1930s," paper delivered at the Lessons and Legacies Conference, Florida Atlantic University, 2010.

102. Nicosia, "The End of Emancipation," 255.

103. Schwab Collection, 620.

104. Schwab Collection, 657.

105. Schwab Collection, 764.

106. Nicholas Stargardt, "The Troubled Patriot: German Innerlichkeit in World War II," *German History* 28, no. 3 (2010): 326–42, here 342.

107. Nicholas Stargardt, *The German War: A Nation under Arms, 1939–1945* (London: Bodley Head, 2015), 16–17.

108. Schwab Collection, 787.

109. Schwab Collection, 659, 723, 1098, 664.

110. Schwab Collection, 666, 764, 674, 747.

111. Schwab Collection, 667.

112. Schwab Collection, 696.

113. Schwab Collection, 705. On conduits, see Dwork and van Pelt, *Flight from the Reich*, 246.

114. Schwab Collection, 675.

115. Schwab Collection, 693, 717.

116. Schwab Collection, 716.

117. Information drawn from Flämig, *Hanau im Dritten Reich*, vol. 2, 319–28; Ophir et al., *Pinkas Ha-kehilot*, 432; Pfeifer and Kingreen, *Hanauer Juden*, 86–95. On *Judenhäuser*, see Konrad Kwiet, "Without Neighbors: Daily Living in Judenhäuser," in *Jewish Life in Nazi Germany: Dilemmas and Responses,* edited by Francis R. Nicosia and David Scrase (New York: Berghahn Books 2010), 117–48.

118. Schwab Collection, 699.

119. Schwab Collection, 725.

120. Schwab Collection, 728.

121. Schwab Collection, 732.

122. Schwab Collection, 710.

123. Schwab Collection, 698.

124. Schwab Collection, 705, 712, 726.

125. Schwab Collection, 649.

126. Schwab Collection, 691.

127. Schwab Collection, 705.

128. Schwab Collection, 740.

129. Schwab Collection, 727.

Chapter 2

Epigraph from Schwab Collection, 1382.

1. See Dwork and van Pelt, *Flight from the Reich*.

2. There is a rich literature on the exile of German Jews after 1933. See, among many others, Eckart Goebel and Sigrid Weigel, eds., *"Escape to Life": German Intellectuals in New York: A Compendium on Exile after 1933* (Berlin: De Gruyter, 2012); Anderson, *Hitler's Exiles*; Steven E. Aschheim, *Beyond the Border: The German-Jewish Legacy Abroad* (Princeton, N.J.: Princeton University Press, 2007); Claus-Dieter Krohn, Patrik von zur Mühlen, Gerhard Paul, and Lutz Winckler, eds., *Handbuch der deutschsprachigen Emigration 1933–1945* (Darmstadt: Wissenschaftliche Buchgesellschaft, 1998); Alexander Stephan, ed., *Exile and Otherness: New Approaches to the Experience of the Nazi Refugees* (Bern: Peter Lang, 2005); Joachim Schlör, *Endlich im gelobten Land? Deutsche Juden unterwegs in eine neue Heimat* (Berlin: Aufbau, 2003); Benz, ed., *Das Exil der kleinen Leute*; Krista O'Donnell, Renate Bridenthal, and Nancy Reagin, eds., *The Heimat Abroad: The Boundaries of Germanness* (Ann Arbor: University of Michigan Press, 2005); Marion A. Kaplan, *Dominican Haven: The Jewish Refugee Settlement in Sosúa, 1940–1945* (New York: Museum of Jewish Heritage, 2008). An interesting reflective piece is Atina Grossmann, "German Jews as Provincial Cosmopolitans: Reflections from the Upper West Side," *Leo Baeck Institute Yearbook* 53, no. 1 (2008): 157–68.

3. Transnationalism offers a potentially fruitful interpretive framework for thinking about the in-between spaces where German Jewish refugees imagined their identities. For some preliminary ideas, see Joachim Schlör, "Irgendwo auf der Welt: German-Jewish Emigration as a Transnational Experience," in *Three-Way Street: Jews, Germans and the Transnational*, edited by Jay Geller and Leslie Morris (Ann Arbor: University of Michigan Press, 2016). For a helpful clarification of the concept of transnationalism, see Patricia Clavin, "Defining Transnationalism," *Contemporary European History* 14, no. 4 (2005): 421–39.

4. On refugees and their representation in historiography, see Tony Kushner, *Remembering Refugees: Then and Now* (Manchester: Manchester University Press, 2006); Tony Kushner and Katharine Knox, *Refugees in an Age of Genocide: Global, National, and Local Perspectives during the Twentieth Century* (London: Frank Cass, 1999).

5. Dwork and van Pelt, *Flight from the Reich*, 94.

6. Schwab Collection, 1083.

7. Schwab Collection, 829.

8. Gertrude van Tijn, "Werkdorp Nieuwesluis," *Leo Baeck Institute Yearbook* 14, no. 1 (1969): 182–99. See also Bernard Natt, "Growing Up in Nazi Germany: Experiences and Memories," *Leo Baeck Institute Yearbook* 51, no. 1 (2006): 267–85.

9. Schwab Collection, 3470.

10. For an overview of Jewish emigration from Nazi Germany, including the Evian conference of July 1938, see Dwork and van Pelt, *Flight from the Reich*.

11. Schwab Collection, 614–15, 696.

12. Balmoral Castle passenger list, departing Southampton 24 April 1936, National Archives, BT27/1461.

13. Stefan Zweig, "House of a Thousand Destinies," Jewish Museum London, catalogue number 1984.143.2., www.jewishmuseum.org.uk/?unique_name=search-our-collections -new&adlibid=10759 (accessed 14 June 2012), p. 5.

14. Schwab Collection, 592.

15. Schwab Collection, 618.

16. Louis Hotz, "South Africa and the Refugees en Route," in Frieda H. Sichel, *From Refugee to Citizen: A Sociological Study of the Immigrants from Hitler-Europe Who Settled in Southern Africa* (Cape Town and Amsterdam: A. A. Balkema, 1966); Linda Coetzee, Myra Osrin, and Millie Pimstone, eds., *Seeking Refuge: German Jewish Immigration to the Cape in the 1930s including Aspects of Germany Confronting Its Past* (Cape Town: Cape Town Holocaust Centre, 2003). On the general profile of Jewish refugees arriving in South Africa at this time, see Stone, "Seeking Asylum," 45–48.

17. Dwork and van Pelt, *Flight from the Reich*, 269–70; Sichel, *From Refugee to Citizen*, x, 27–29, 72–97; Franz Auerbach, "German Jews and Their Baggage," *Jewish Affairs* 60, no. 4 (2005): 16–19; author interview with Madeleine Fane, 6 February 2012.

18. Schwab Collection, 1105, 3470, 3354.

19. Schwab Collection, 3470.

20. Schwab Collection, 2416.

21. On the history of Breitenau as an early concentration camp and later *Arbeitser-ziehungslager*, see Gunnar Richter, ed., *Breitenau: Zur Geschichte eines nationalso-zialistischen Konzentrations- und Arbeitserziehungslagers* (Kassel: Verlag Jenior & Pressler, 1993); Gunnar Richter, *Das Arbeitserziehungslager Breitenau (1940–1945): Ein Beitrag zum nationalsozialistischen Lagersystem* (Kassel: Verlag Winfried Jenior, 2009); Dietfrid Krause-Vilmar, *Das Konzentrationslager Breitenau: Ein staatliches Schutzhaftlager 1933/34* (Marburg: Schüren Presseverlag, 1998). In a later letter, Karl suggested to Rudolf that Schilling was never arrested and lied about this in his account (Schwab Collection, 2613).

22. Max Schwab death notice from Sachsenhausen, Stadtarchiv Hanau; International Tracing Service archive (hereafter ITS), BA-23922. On Sachsenhausen, see Günter

Morsch and Astrid Ley, eds., *Das Konzentrationslager Sachsenhausen 1936–1945: Ereignisse und Entwicklungen* (Berlin: Metropol, 2008); Nikolaus Wachsmann, *KL: A History of the Nazi Concentration Camps* (Boston: Little, Brown, 2015).

23. Schwab Collection, 734.

24. Schwab Collection, 1176.

25. Schwab Collection, 746.

26. Rudolf initially calculated the date of Martha and Hans's deportation from the date Sal received his mother's letter (5 June 1942), as opposed to the day Martha wrote it (29 May 1942): see Schwab Collection, 2612. In later accounts to friends and various reparations offices, he clarified 30 May 1942 as the date of deportation. By the time a reparations application was submitted for Hans in June 1950, the date of deportation was given correctly (HHStAW, file AZ 518-7312).

27. Schwab Collection, 764. For a comprehensive account of the Kitchener camp, see Clare Ungerson, *Four Thousand Lives: The Rescue of German Jewish Men to Britain, 1939* (Stroud: History Press, 2014).

28. Ungerson, *Four Thousand Lives*, 165–66.

29. Schwab Collection, 843–50.

30. Schwab Collection, 911–12.

31. Schwab Collection, 1564–65; 1753.

32. Irene Eber, ed., *Voices from Shanghai: Jewish Exiles in Wartime China* (Chicago: University of Chicago Press, 2008), 9.

33. Walter Laqueur, *Generation Exodus: The Fate of Young Jewish Refugees from Nazi Germany* (London: I. B. Tauris, 2004), 227.

34. On general conditions for Jewish refugees in Shanghai, see Barbara Geldermann, "'Jewish Refugees Should Be Welcomed and Assisted Here!': Shanghai: Exile and Return," *Leo Baeck Institute Year Book* 44 (1999): 227–43; Eber, *Voices from Shanghai*; Avraham Altman and Irene Eber, "Flight to Shanghai, 1938–1940: The Larger Setting," *Yad Vashem Studies* 28 (2000): 51–86; Georg Armbrüster, *Leben im Wartesaal: Exil in Shanghai 1938–1947* (Berlin: Stiftung Stadtmuseum, 1997); Ernest G. Heppner, *Shanghai Refuge: A Memoir of the World War II Jewish Ghetto* (Lincoln: University of Nebraska Press, 1993); Audrey Friedman Marcus and Rena Krasno, *Survival in Shanghai: The Journals of Fred Marcus 1939–49* (Berkeley, Calif.: Pacific View Press, 2008); Marcia R. Ristaino, *Port of Last Resort: The Diaspora Communities of Shanghai* (Stanford, Calif.: Stanford University Press, 2001); James R. Ross, *Escape to Shanghai: A Jewish Community in China* (New York: Free Press, 1994); Evelyn Pike Rubin, *Ghetto Shanghai* (New York: Shengold, 1993).

35. Schwab Collection, 665, 701, 702–3, 731, 743.

36. Eber, *Voices from Shanghai*, 24; Schwab Collection, 986, 942, 1106.

37. Schwab Collection, 1042–43.

38. Schwab Collection, 1133.

39. Schwab Collection, 1285–86.

40. Schwab Collection, 1498, 1611, 29-30, 1956.

41. Schwab Collection, 838. On Gurs, see Walter Laqueur, ed., *The Holocaust Encyclopedia* (New Haven, Conn.: Yale University Press, 2001), 271; Martin Gilbert, *The Dent Atlas of the Holocaust* (London: J. M. Dent, 1993), 48; www.ushmm.org/wlc/en/article.php?ModuleId=10005298 (accessed 9 May 2016).

42. Schwab Collection, 860–63, 1716.

43. Schwab Collection, 860–63.

44. Schwab Collection, 1838–43, 1786–88, 910, 938, 1005.

45. Schwab Collection, 878.

46. Schwab Collection, 1055, 1435.

47. Schwab Collection, 1459, 2101, 959.

48. Schwab Collection, 1648.

49. Schwab Collection, 1772, 1782.

50. Schwab Collection, 1791.

51. Schwab Collection, 2167.

52. Schwab Collection, 1791–96, 2149.

53. Schwab Collection, 804–7.

54. Schwab Collection, 3443, 1542, 1559.

55. Schwab Collection, 797.

56. Schwab Collection, 2818. Rudolf was initially informed in June 1947 that his grandmother Johanna Hausmann was deported on 24 June 1942 to Mausbach and a few days later to Theresienstadt (Schwab Collection, 2244), but he later ascertained that she had in fact been deported to Riga on 6 December 1941 (Schwab Collection, 2586). David Cesarani, *Final Solution: The Fate of the Jews 1933–49* (London: Macmillan, 2016), 431.

57. Schwab Collection, 2264. See also International Tracing Service (ITS), 85088233#1.

58. ITS, 85088252#1, 85088263#1, 85088266#1, 85088253#1, ITS 85088254#1, 85088218#1, 85088225#1.

59. ITS, 85088220#2.

60. "Hanau erinnert an Deportation seiner Juden," *Frankfurter Allgemeine Zeitung*, 31 May 2006.

61. Pfeifer and Kingreen, *Hanauer Juden*, 98–135.

62. Hannah Arendt, "We Refugees," in *The Jewish Writings / Hannah Arendt*, edited by Jerome Kohn and Ron H. Feldman (New York: Schocken Books, 2007), 264–74.

63. Schwab Collection, 1370.

64. Author interview with Norman Schwab, 4 February 2012.

65. Schwab Collection, 1025.

66. Schwab Collection, 817, 1079.

67. Schwab Collection, 1559, 1535.

68. Schwab Collection, 1278.

69. Schwab Collection, 1716.

70. Schwab Collection, 1006, 1150, 1750.
71. Schwab Collection, 1860, 903, 1160, 2071.
72. Schwab Collection, 915.
73. Schwab Collection, 2319.
74. Schwab Collection, 851.
75. Schwab Collection, 982.
76. Schwab Collection, 1613, 1321, 1411.
77. Schwab Collection, 900.
78. Schwab Collection, 866, 871, 2416, 1610, 1680, 1630.
79. Schwab Collection, 1439, 1055, 2416.
80. The family submitted both restitution and reparations claims. For a helpful discussion of the use of the terms "restitution," "reparation," and "compensation," see Regula Ludi, "The Vectors of Postwar Victim Reparations: Relief, Redress and Memory Politics," *Journal of Contemporary History* 41, no. 3 (2006): 421–50, here pp. 427–28.
81. Leora Auslander, "Beyond Words," *American Historical Review* 110, no. 4 (2005): 1015–45. See also Jilovsky, "Grandpa's Letters," 135–48.
82. HHStAW, 7/525.
83. Schwab Collection, 2568–69, 2847–48.
84. Schwab Collection, 1280.
85. Schwab Collection, 2488, 2497, 2604.
86. Schwab Collection, 3543.
87. Schwab Collection, 2418, 2430.
88. Schwab Collection, 1140.
89. Schwab Collection, 894, 1081, 2847, 2877, 2512.
90. Schwab Collection, 3255.
91. Schwab Collection, 2670.
92. Schwab Collection, 2906.
93. Schwab Collection, 2981.
94. See related discussion in Auslander, "Beyond Words."
95. Ludi, "The Vectors of Postwar Victim Reparations," 449. For a useful range of perspectives see Michael J. Bazyler and Roger P. Alford, eds., *Holocaust Restitution: Perspectives on the Litigation and Its Legacy* (New York: New York University Press, 2006).
96. Schwab Collection, 1430.
97. HHStAW, files AZ 518-2796/07 (Max Schwab), AZ 518-2831/09 (Martha Schwab), AZ 518-2789/13 (Rudolf Schwab), and AZ 518-7312 (Hans Schwab). Most of the Schwab family's claims stalled in 1951–52, probably because Rudolf's chief agent in Germany had fallen ill, and they were resumed only in 1958–59 by the United Restitution Organization. The Legal Department of the Jewish Restitution Successor Organization subsequently attempted to resolve matters, but by the late 1960s some of the family's claims had still not been resolved.

98. See for example Mark M. Anderson, ed., *Hitler's Exiles: Personal Stories of the Flight from Nazi Germany to America*, 317–24.

99. Schwab Collection, 1915.

100. Schwab Collection, 3625.

Chapter 3

Epigraph from Aleksandr Solzhenitsyn, *The Gulag Archipelago 1918-56: An Experiment in Literary Investigation,* translated by Thomas P. Whitney and Harry Willets (London: Harvill Press, 2003), 75.

1. Schwab Collection, 2264.

2. Schwab Collection, 2264.

3. Schwab Collection, 2320.

4. Schwab Collection, 2319.

5. This favorite phrase of Karl's was drawn from a famous *Luftwaffe* slogan.

6. Email correspondence with Martin Hoppe, 19 July 2012 and 23 July 2012.

7. Sonja Levsen, "Constructing Elite Identities: University Students, Military Masculinity and the Consequences of the Great War in Britain and Germany," *Past & Present* 198 (2008): 147–83. See also Richard Cohen, *By the Sword: Gladiators, Musketeers, Samurai Warriors, Swashbucklers, and Olympians* (London: Pan Books, 2003); Robert A. Nye, "Fencing, the Duel and Republican Manhood in the Third Republic," *Journal of Contemporary History* 25, no. 2/3 (1990): 365–77.

8. Schwab Collection, 2307–9.

9. Schwab Collection, 2325–26.

10. Schwab Collection, 2338–39.

11. Schwab Collection, 2363.

12. Schwab Collection, 2432.

13. Schwab Collection, 2584.

14. Schwab Collection, 2563.

15. Schwab Collection, 2394.

16. Schwab Collection, 2775, 2347.

17. Schwab Collection, 2606.

18. Schwab Collection, 2836.

19. Schwab Collection, 2755.

20. Schwab Collection, 3033–34.

21. Schwab Collection, 3033.

22. Schwab Collection, 2363.

23. Schwab Collection, 2608, 2620, 3304, 2432, 2552.

24. Schwab Collection, 3078, 3084, 3102, 3053, 3280, 3066.

25. Schwab Collection, 3057, 3234.

26. Schwab Collection, 2578.

27. Schwab Collection, 2462.

28. Schwab Collection, 2712, 2781.

29. Schwab Collection, 2448.

30. Schwab Collection, 2856.

31. Schwab Collection, 2523, 2804, 2442, 2492, 2533, 2692.

32. Schwab Collection, 2325. See Paul Steege, *Black Market, Cold War: Everyday Life in Berlin, 1946–1949* (New York: Cambridge University Press, 2007).

33. Schwab Collection, 2859.

34. Schwab Collection, 2597.

35. Schwab Collection, 2946, 2984.

36. Schwab Collection, 2484.

37. Schwab Collection, 2526.

38. Schwab Collection, 2291, 2517, 1594, 1634.

39. Schwab Collection, 1397.

40. Schwab Collection, 1368.

41. Schwab Collection, 2597.

42. Schwab Collection, 3343, 2597, 1368, 2598, 2836, 3193.

43. Schwab Collection, 1196–97.

44. Schwab Collection, 2450, 1544.

45. Schwab Collection, 1241.

46. Schwab Collection, 1213, 1215, 2637, 2517.

47. Schwab Collection, 1305.

48. Schwab Collection, 1388.

49. Bundesarchiv, Berlin, NS 5 I/430.

50. Schwab Collection, 2678, 2307.

51. Schwab Collection, 3348, 2613.

52. Bundesarchiv, Berlin, NS 5 I/430.

53. Email correspondence with Monika Rademacher, 1 August 2011; Stadtarchiv Hanau, Bestand D3C Standesamt: Sterberegister 1955/8.

54. Email correspondence with Martin Hoppe, 19 July 2012.

55. Email correspondence with Martin Hoppe, 14 September 2012.

56. Email correspondence with Martin Hoppe, 8 September 2011.

57. Michael E. Haskew, *The Wehrmacht, 1935–1945: The Essential Facts and Figures for Hitler's Germany* (London: Amber, 2011), 177–78.

58. Correspondence from Deutsche Dienststelle, 21 January 2013.

59. Schwab Collection, 2477.

60. Schwab Collection, 2609.

61. ITS, 82311416#1.

62. ITS, 82311416#1. The full trial materials are located at the National Archives in College Park, Maryland, War Crimes Case Files (Cases Tried), 1945-1949, Case No. 000-50-2, RG 549, Entry A1 2238; box 289.

63. Prisoner personnel file for Karl Kiepfer, National Archives at College Park, Maryland, RG 549, USAREUR, War Crimes Records, Released Prisoner File, box 39.

64. The name Kiepfer is misspelled many times in the 1947 trial document and personnel file, and it appears as "Kipfer" several times (see pp. 11, 32, 33). The Kipfer identified by Kiern in 1945 was an *Oberscharführer*. By contrast, the 1947 trial documents frequently referred to Kiepfer as *Unterscharführer* and then, after his promotion, as *Hauptscharführer* (see pp. 7, 15, 16, 19, 26, 32).

65. Correspondence from Deutsche Dienststelle, 21 January 2013.

66. Schwab Collection, 2613.

67. Georg Tessin, *Verbände und Truppen der deutschen Wehrmacht und Waffen-SS im Zweiten Weltkrieg 1939–1945*, vol. 14 (Osnabrück: Biblio Verlag, 1980), 336.

68. Omer Bartov, *Germany's War and the Holocaust: Disputed Histories* (Ithaca, N.Y.: Cornell University Press, 2003), chap. 1.

69. Correspondence from Deutsche Dienststelle, 21 January 2013.

70. Schwab Collection, 2756, 2613; Militärgeschichtliches Forschungsamt, ed., *Germany and the Second World War* (Oxford: Clarendon Press, 1990), vol. 4, map 1; Tessin, *Verbände und Truppen*, vol. 14, 336.

71. On perpetrators, see among many others Olaf Jensen and Claus-Christian W. Szejnmann, eds., *Ordinary People as Mass Murderers: Perpetrators in Comparative Perspectives* (Basingstoke: Palgrave Macmillan, 2008); Ernst Klee, Willi Dressen, and Volker Riess, *"Those Were the Days": The Holocaust through the Eyes of the Perpetrators and Bystanders* (London: Hamish Hamilton, 1991); Jürgen Matthäus, "Historiography and the Perpetrators of the Holocaust," in *The Historiography of the Holocaust*, edited by Dan Stone (Basingstoke: Palgrave Macmillan, 2004), 197–215.

72. Hamburger Institut für Sozialforschung, ed., *The German Army and Genocide: Crimes against War Prisoners, Jews and Other Civilians in the East, 1939–1944*, translated by Scott Abbott (New York: New Press, 1999); Omer Bartov, *Hitler's Army: Soldiers, Nazis, and War in the Third Reich* (New York: Oxford University Press, 1991); Christopher R. Browning, *Ordinary Men: Reserve Police Battalion 101 and the Final Solution in Poland* (New York: HarperCollins, 1992); Sönke Neitzel and Harald Welzer, *Soldaten: Protokolle vom Kämpfen, Töten und Sterben* (Frankfurt am Main: Fischer, 2011), 77, 98; Ben Shepherd, "The Clean Wehrmacht, the War of Extermination, and Beyond," *Historical Journal* 52, no. 2 (2009): 455–73.

73. Schwab Collection, 2439, 2857, 2766, 3029.

74. Christian Streit, "Soviet Prisoners of War in the Hands of the Wehrmacht," in *War of Extermination: The German Military in World War II*, edited by Hannes Heer and Klaus Naumann (New York: Berghahn Books, 2000), 81.

75. Konrad H. Jarausch, ed., *Reluctant Accomplice: A Wehrmacht Soldier's Letters from the Eastern Front* (Princeton, N.J.: Princeton University Press, 2011), 272.

76. Flämig, *Hanau im Dritten Reich*, vol. 2, 333.

77. Karl Kipfer application for denazification, HHStAW Abt. 520/ Ha WA Nr. 279.

78. Office of Military Government, Civil Administration Division, *Denazification, Cumulative Review*, Report, 1 April 1947–30 April 1948, http://digital.library.wisc. edu/1711.dl/History.denazi (accessed 13 September 2015). Overview of denazification based on Perry Biddiscombe, *The Denazification of Germany 1945–48* (NPI Media Group, 2007); Norbert Frei, *Adenauer's Germany and the Nazi Past: The Politics of Amnesty and Integration* (New York: Columbia University Press, 2002); Fred Taylor, *Exorcising Hitler: The Occupation and Denazification of Germany* (New York: Bloomsbury Press, 2011).

79. Haskew, *The Wehrmacht*, 45–46.

80. Kipfer application for denazification.

81. Schwab Collection, 2360.

82. Biddiscombe, *The Denazification of Germany*, 65.

83. Schwab Collection, 3068, 2465.

84. Taylor, *Exorcising Hitler*, 255.

85. Frei, *Adenauer's Germany*, xiv.

86. Schwab Collection, 2667.

87. Schwab Collection, 2485, 2488.

88. Schwab Collection, 2563.

89. Schwab Collection, 2845.

90. Schwab Collection, 2477.

91. Schwab Collection, 2346.

92. Schwab Collection, 2677–78.

93. Schwab Collection, 2522.

94. Schwab Collection, 2766, 2752, 2775, 2752.

95. Schwab Collection, 2360.

96. Schwab Collection, 2752, 2347, 2705.

97. Schwab Collection, 2396.

98. Schwab Collection, 2872, 2610.

99. Schwab Collection, 1370, 2526.

100. Schwab Collection, 2697. The *Landesleihbank* became part of the *Sparkasse* bank chain in 1955.

101. Schwab Collection, 2379, 2418, 2430.

102. Schwab Collection, 2766.

103. Schwab Collection, 2543.

104. Schwab Collection, 2704, 2707, 2789.

105. Schwab Collection, 2790.

106. Schwab Collection, 2791.

107. Schwab Collection, 3327, 3330.

108. Schwab Collection, 3005, 2827

109. R. M. Douglas, *Orderly and Humane: The Expulsion of the Germans after the Second World War* (New Haven, Conn.: Yale University Press, 2012); Neil Gregor, *Haunted*

City: Nuremberg and the Nazi Past (New Haven, Conn.: Yale University Press, 2008); Stargardt, *The German War*, epilogue.

110. Gregor, *Haunted City*, 3.

111. Katharina Von Kellenbach, *The Mark of Cain: Guilt and Denial in the Post-War Lives of Nazi Perpetrators* (Oxford: Oxford University Press, 2013), 26–27.

112. Von Kellenbach, *The Mark of Cain*, 93, 26–27. See also Mary Fulbrook and Ulinka Rublack, "In Relation: The 'Social Self' and Ego-Documents," *German History* 28, no. 3 (2010): 263–72.

113. Von Kellenbach, *The Mark of Cain*, 148.

114. Schwab Collection, 3066.

115. Schwab Collection, 457.

116. Schwab Collection, 2258.

117. Schwab Collection, 1176.

118. Schwab Collection, 2273, 2266, 1305, 1351, 1362, 1126.

119. Schwab Collection, 1031.

120. Schwab Collection, 1085.

121. Schwab Collection, 1399.

122. Schwab Collection, 2779.

123. *Hanauer Anzeiger*, 7 January 1955.

124. Schwab Collection, 1579.

125. Schwab Collection, 1681.

126. Schwab Collection, 1612.

127. Schwab Collection, 3468.

Chapter 4

1. Schwab Collection, 591, 1561.

2. Schwab Collection, 2601.

3. Richard Mendelsohn and Milton Shain, *The Jews in South Africa: An Illustrated History* (Johannesburg and Cape Town: Jonathan Ball, 2008), 99.

4. Steven E. Aschheim, *Brothers and Strangers: The East European Jew in German and German Jewish Consciousness, 1800–1923*, 2nd ed. (Madison: University of Wisconsin Press, 1999).

5. Cited in Stone, *Seeking Asylum*, 114.

6. Stone, *Seeking Asylum*, 73, but see also Jocelyn Hellig, "German Jewish Immigration to South Africa during the 1930s: Revisiting the Charter of the SS Stuttgart," in *Jewish Journeys: From Philo to Hip Hop*, edited by James Jordan, Tony Kushner, and Sarah Pearce (London: Vallentine Mitchell, 2010), 146–62.

7. Edna Bradlow, "South African Policy and Jewish Refugee Immigration in the 1930s," in *False Havens: The British Empire and the Holocaust*, edited by Paul R. Bartrop (Lanham, Md.: University Press of America, 1995), 239–52, here 240. See also Hellig, "German Jewish Immigration."

8. Bradlow, "South African Policy"; Mendelsohn and Shain, *The Jews in South Africa*, 106–11. On antisemitism in South Africa during the 1930s and 1940s, see Milton Shain, *A Perfect Storm: Antisemitism in South Africa, 1930–1948* (Johannesburg and Cape Town: Jonathan Ball, 2015). For a detailed account of Jewish immigration to South Africa, see Sally Peberdy, *Selecting Immigrants: National Identity and South Africa's Immigration Policies 1910–2008* (Johannesburg: Witwatersrand University Press, 2009), 57–83.

9. Patrick J. Furlong, *Between Crown and Swastika: The Impact of the Radical Right on the Afrikaner Nationalist Movement in the Fascist Era* (Middletown, Conn.: Wesleyan University Press, 1991), 16, 20, 61–69, 83, 138–43, 161–62; Gideon Shimoni, *Community and Conscience: The Jews in Apartheid South Africa* (Hanover, N.H.: Brandeis University Press, 2003), 11–16; Christoph Marx, *Oxwagon Sentinel: Radical Afrikaner Nationalism and the History of the Ossewabrandwag* (Pretoria: Unisa Press, 2008); *Report of the Executive Council of the South African Jewish Board of Deputies, August 1947 to May 1949* (Johannesburg: South African Jewish Board of Deputies, 1949), 21; Milton Shain, "South Africa," in *The World Reacts to the Holocaust*, edited by David S. Wyman, 670–89 (Baltimore: Johns Hopkins University Press, 1996), 675–76.

10. Kaplan Centre Archives, University of Cape Town, Hilda Jeidel interview with Eve Horwitz, BC949 #125, 28.

11. Michael Burleigh, *The Third Reich: A New History* (London: Pan Books, 2001), 72; Aschheim, *Brothers and Strangers*.

12. Schwab Collection, 1932, 1951; Bradlow, "South African Policy," 241.

13. Schwab Collection, 582, 612, 589; Coetzee et al., *Seeking Refuge;* Franz Auerbach, "German Jews and Their Baggage," *Jewish Affairs* 60, no. 4 (2005): 16–19; Sichel, *From Refugee to Citizen;* author interview with Madeleine Fane.

14. Author interview with Madeleine Fane.

15. Schwab Collection, 871, 1025, 800, 871.

16. Schwab Collection, 1480.

17. Schwab Collection, 2250, 192, 2143; author interview with Norman Schwab.

18. Schwab Collection, 890.

19. South African Jewish Board of Deputies Rochlin Archives (hereafter SAJBD Archives), Arch 210.13, box entitled "German Immigrants: Applications to Join the South African Defence Force 1940–1944."

20. Schwab Collection, 192, 788, 829, 890.

21. Schwab Collection, 79, 1561, 696, 1831, 958–59, 1232, 865, 2142.

22. Schwab Collection, 917.

23. Schwab Collection, 872, 888.

24. Schwab Collection, 970.

25. Schwab Collection, 802.

26. *Report of the Executive Council of the South African Jewish Board of Deputies, August 1947 to May 1949*, 20–21, 23; *Report of the Executive Council of the South African Jewish*

Board of Deputies, June 1949 to May 1951 (Johannesburg: South African Jewish Board of Deputies, 1951), 13–14.

27. *Report of the Executive Council of the South African Jewish Board of Deputies, June 1951 to May 1953* (Johannesburg: South African Jewish Board of Deputies, 1953), 11.

28. Schwab Collection, 1077.

29. Schwab Collection, 889.

30. Schwab Collection, 1689.

31. Schwab Collection, 2215.

32. Schwab Collection, 3249.

33. Schwab Collection, 1258, 727.

34. Schwab Collection, 710, 712.

35. Schwab Collection, 1105, 1083, 800, 2172, 1961, 2104, 890.

36. Schwab Collection, 1085.

37. Schwab Collection, 3084, 1437, 1411.

38. Schwab Collection, 2913, 2004, 3879.

39. Schwab Collection, 1463, 1480, 1491, 1724, 1850, 1823, 1850, 1852.

40. Schwab Collection, 1232; author interview with Norman Schwab; Laqueuer, *Generation Exodus*, 285.

41. Schwab Collection, 1518, 1445, 1696, 1768, 457, 2111, 2118.

42. Schwab Collection, 1025, 1857, 2054, 1540.

43. Schwab Collection, 2637–38.

44. Schwab Collection, 1540, 1633.

45. Schwab Collection, 1531.

46. Schwab Collection, 1442, 2111.

47. Schwab Collection, 1321.

48. Schwab Collection, 3354, 1543, 1613, 1677.

49. Schwab Collection, 2759.

50. Schwab Collection, 1100, 244.

51. Schwab Collection, 183–84.

52. For an overview of the United Party before 1948, see William Beinart, *Twentieth-Century South Africa* (Oxford: Oxford University Press, 2001), chap. 5.

53. See Beinart, *Twentieth-Century South Africa*, 138.

54. Schwab Collection, 132.

55. SAJBD Archives, Biographical boxes, SCHRE-SEARL; Schwab Collection, 3226, 2913.

56. Schwab Collection, 1021.

57. Schwab Collection, 1076.

58. Franz Auerbach, "Our Responsibility," *Etz Chayim News* 2, no. 6 (September 1960): 33–37, here 34; Franz Auerbach, *No Single Loyalty. Many Strands One Design: A South African Teacher's Life* (Münster: Germany: Waxmann Verlag GmbH, 2002). On the links between apartheid and the Holocaust more generally, see Shirli Gilbert, "Anne

Frank in South Africa: Remembering the Holocaust During and After Apartheid."
Holocaust and Genocide Studies 26, no. 3 (2012): 366–93; Shain, "South Africa," in
Wyman, *The World Reacts to the Holocaust*, 670–89. Auerbach's lifelong opposition to
apartheid, which he frequently linked to Nazism in his many writings and public
addresses, is a subject for another book. See University of the Witwatersrand Historical Papers, Dr. Franz Auerbach collection, 1950–2006 (Collection number A3267).

59. www.sahistory.org.za/people/harry-heinz-schwarz (accessed 14 July 2015).

60. Benjamin Pogrund, *War of Words: Memoir of a South African Journalist* (New York:
Seven Stories Press, 2000), 31; Thomas Karis, Gwendolen Carter, Gail Gerhart, and
Sheridan Johns, eds., *From Protest to Challenge. Vol. 2: Hope and Challenge* (Stanford,
Calif.; Hoover Institution, 1973), 358.

61. Schwab Collection, 1422.

62. Schwab Collection, 2726.

63. Schwab Collection, 2810, 2802, 2803, 1264, 2792.

64. Gideon Shimoni, *Community and Conscience: The Jews in Apartheid South Africa*
(Hanover, N.H.: Brandeis University Press, 2003), 23, 29; Joseph Sherman, "Serving
the Natives: Whiteness as the Price of Hospitality in South African Yiddish Literature," *Journal of Southern African Studies* 26, no. 3 (2000): 505–21, here 511.

65. Schwab Collection, 1712, 1578, 818.

66. Schwab Collection, 916.

67. Schwab Collection, 957–58.

68. Richard Mendelsohn, "The Boer War, The Great War, and the Shaping of South Afri-
can Jewish Loyalties." In *Memories, Realities and Dreams: Aspects of the South African
Jewish Experience*, edited by Milton Shain and Richard Mendelsohn (Johannesburg:
Jonathan Ball, 2000), 50-59.

69. Saul Dubow, "Smuts, the United Nations and the Rhetoric of Race and Rights,"
Journal of Contemporary History 43, no. 1 (2008): 45–74, here 50–54, 64–65. For a review
of recent literature on the complex history of human rights, see Devin O. Pendas,
"Toward a New Politics? On the Recent Historiography of Human Rights," *Contemporary European History* 21, no. 1 (2012): 95–111.

70. Deon van Tonder, "'First Win the War, Then Clear the Slums': The Genesis of the
Western Areas Removal Scheme, 1940–1949," 1990, http://wiredspace.wits.ac.za/
bitstream/handle/10539/8106/HWS-422.pdf?sequence=1 (accessed 11 June 2012).

71. Schwab Collection, 1021.

72. Schwab Collection, 2090, 2173, 3873; Shirli Gilbert, "Jews and the Racial State: Legacies of the Holocaust in Apartheid South Africa, 1945–60," *Jewish Social Studies* 16,
no. 3 (2010): 32–64.

73. Shimoni, *Community and Conscience*, 194.

74. Schwab Collection, 1232, 1083.

75. Schwab Collection, 1578, 2748, 2264.

76. Schwab Collection, 1076, 1049–50, 1305. On the Suppression of Communism Act, see Nancy L. Clark and William H. Worger, *South Africa: The Rise and Fall of Apartheid* (Edinburgh: Pearson, 2011), 58.

77. Schwab Collection, 3029.

78. Schwab Collection, 1049.

79. See, for example, the memoirs of Jewish Labour parliamentarian Morris Kentridge, *I Recall* (Johannesburg: Free Press, 1959). For an honest account of the paradoxes of White liberalism see also Dan Jacobson, "A White Liberal Trapped by his Prejudices," *Commentary* 15, no. 5 (1953): 454–59.

80. Schwab Collection, 768.

81. Shimoni, *Community and Conscience*, 6.

82. Author interviews with David Mandelstam (17 November 2014) and Norman Schwab; Schwab Collection, 1190, 1320, 2712.

83. Schwab Collection, 3078, 1411, 3084, 3093.

Epilogue

1. Schwab Collection, 82–83, 2046; Meise, "Löwenstein, Schwab und Hanau."

2. Schwab Collection, 753.

3. Schwab Collection, 60–61, 746.

4. Schwab Collection, 2549, 2565, 2584.

5. Schwab Collection, 2584.

6. Bamberger and Meise, *Der jüdische Friedhof in Hanau*, 108.

7. Schwab Collection, 52–53; Flämig, *Hanau im Dritten Reich*, vol. 2, 280–87; Pfeifer and Kingreen, *Hanauer Juden*, 84–85; Meise, "Löwenstein, Schwab und Hanau"; Ophir et al., *Pinkas Ha-kehilot*, 427–34.

8. Schwab Collection, 1932.

9. Schwab Collection, 1932.

10. Schwab Collection, 60, 66, 71, 77, 79, 80.

11. Bamberger and Meise, *Der jüdische Friedhof in Hanau*, 149, 121, 129–30.

12. Bamberger and Meise, *Der jüdische Friedhof in Hanau*, 131, 138.

13. "Hanau erinnert an Deportation seiner Juden," *Frankfurter Allgemeine Zeitung*, 31 May 2006.

14. "Bronzetafeln erinnern an Hanaus ermordete Juden," *Frankfurter Allgemeine Zeitung* (*Rhein-Main & Hessen*), 1 June 2010.

15. www.stolpersteine.eu/ (accessed 2 November 2015).

16. *Frankfurter Rundschau*, 31 May 2010, R12.

17. Schwab Collection, 2163.

18. On the significance of name changing after the Holocaust, see Kirsten Fermaglich, "'This Too Is Partly Hitler's Doing': American Jewish Name Changing in the Wake of the Holocaust, 1939–57," in *After the Holocaust: Challenging the Myth of Silence*,

edited by David Cesarani and Eric J. Sundquist (New York: Routledge, 2012), 170–80.

19. Author interview with Daniel Schwab, Jerusalem, 16 September 2011.

20. Schwab Collection, 2585, 2601.

21. Schwab Collection, 3637.

22. Email correspondence with Norman Schwab, 7 October 2013.

23. Schwab Collection, 789, 1391, 1746, 1896, 923, 1342.

24. Daniel Schwab, public lecture in Hanau, 31 May 2010; author interview with Daniel Schwab, Jerusalem, 11 October 2011.

Bibliography

Archives

Israel

Yad Vashem, Jerusalem (Collection of Rudolf Erwin Alexander Schwab)

Germany

Bundesarchiv, Berlin
Deutsche Dienststelle, Berlin
Hessisches Hauptstaatsarchiv, Wiesbaden (HHStAW)
International Tracing Service Archive, Bad Arolsen (ITS)
KZ-Gedenkstätte Dachau Archive
Stadtarchiv Hanau

South Africa

Kaplan Centre Archives, University of Cape Town
South African Jewish Board of Deputies Rochlin Archives, Johannesburg (SAJBD Archives)
University of the Witwatersrand Historical Papers

United States

National Archives and Records Administration (NARA), Washington, DC
USC Shoah Foundation Visual History Archive

Newspapers

Frankfurter Rundschau
Frankfurter Algemeine Zeitung
Hanauer Anzeiger

Published Sources

Alroey, Gur. *Bread to Eat and Clothes to Wear: Letters from Jewish Migrants in the Early Twentieth Century*. Detroit: Wayne State University Press, 2011.

Altman, Avraham, and Irene Eber. "Flight to Shanghai, 1938–1940: The Larger Setting." *Yad Vashem Studies* 28 (2000): 51–86.

Anderson, Mark M., ed. *Hitler's Exiles: Personal Stories of the Flight from Nazi Germany to America*. New York: New Press, 1998.

Appignanesi, Lisa. *Losing the Dead*. London: Chatto & Windus, 1999.

Applebaum, Peter C. *Loyal Sons: Jewish Soldiers in the German Army in the Great War*. Portland, Ore.: Vallentine Mitchell, 2014.

Arendt, Hannah. "We Refugees." In *The Jewish Writings/Hannah Arendt*, edited by Jerome Kohn and Ron H. Feldman, 264–74. New York: Schocken Books, 2007.

Armbrüster, Georg. *Leben im Wartesaal: Exil in Shanghai 1938–1947*. Berlin: Stiftung Stadtmuseum, 1997.

Armbrüster, Georg, Michael Kohlstruck, and Sonja Mühlberger, eds. *Exil Shanghai, 1938–1947: Jüdisches Leben in der Emigration*. 1. Aufl. Schriftenreihe des Aktiven Museums Berlin, Bd. 9. Teetz: Hentrich & Hentrich, 2000.

Arnsberg, Paul. *Die jüdischen Gemeinden in Hessen: Anfang, Untergang, Neubeginn*. Frankfurt am Main: Societäts-Verlag, 1971.

———. *Die jüdischen Gemeinden in Hessen: Bilder, Dokumente*. Darmstadt: Eduard Roether Verlag, 1973.

Aschheim, Steven E. *Beyond the Border: The German-Jewish Legacy Abroad*. Princeton, N.J.: Princeton University Press, 2007.

———. *Brothers and Strangers: The East European Jew in German and German Jewish Consciousness, 1800–1923*. 2nd ed. Madison: University of Wisconsin Press, 1999.

———. *In Times of Crisis: Essays on European Culture, Germans, and Jews*. Madison: University of Wisconsin Press, 2001.

Auerbach, Franz. "German Jews and Their Baggage." *Jewish Affairs* 60, no. 4 (2005): 16–19.

———. *No Single Loyalty. Many Strands One Design: A South African Teacher's Life*. Münster: Waxmann Verlag GmbH, 2002.

———. "Our Responsibility." *Etz Chayim News* 2, no. 6 (September 1960): 33–37.

Auslander, Leora. "Beyond Words." *American Historical Review* 110, no. 4 (2005): 1015–45.

Baader, Benjamin Maria, Sharon Gillerman, and Paul Lerner, eds. *Jewish Masculinities: German Jews, Gender, and History*. Bloomington: Indiana University Press, 2012.

Bacharach, Zwi, ed. *Last Letters from the Shoah*. Jerusalem: Devora, 2004.

Bajohr, Frank. "The 'Folk Community' and the Persecution of the Jews: German Society under National Socialist Dictatorship, 1933–1945." *Holocaust and Genocide Studies* 20, no. 2 (2006): 183–206.

Bajohr, Frank, and Dieter Pohl. *Der Holocaust als offenes Geheimnis: Die Deutschen, die NS-Führung und die Alliierten*. München: Beck, 2006.

Bamberger, Naftali Bar-Giora, and Eckhard Meise, eds. *Der jüdische Friedhof in Hanau*. Hanau: Hanauer Geschichtsverein 1844 e.V, 2005.

Bankier, David. *The Germans and the Final Solution: Public Opinion under Nazism*. Jewish Society and Culture. Oxford: Basil Blackwell, 1992.

————, ed. *Probing the Depths of German Antisemitism: German Society and the Persecution of the Jews, 1933–1941*. New York: Berghahn Books, 2000.

Barlay, Nick. *Scattered Ghosts: One Family's Survival through War, Holocaust and Revolution*. London: I. B. Tauris, 2013.

Bar-On, Dan. *Fear and Hope: Three Generations of the Holocaust*. Cambridge, Mass.: Harvard University Press, 1995.

Barton, David, and Nigel Hall, eds. *Letter Writing as a Social Practice*. Studies in Written Language and Literacy, vol. 9. Amsterdam: John Benjamins, 2000.

Bartov, Omer. "German Soldiers and the Holocaust: Historiography, Research and Implications." In *The Holocaust: Origins, Implementation, and Aftermath*, edited by Omer Bartov, 162–84. New York: Routledge, 2000.

————. *Germany's War and the Holocaust: Disputed Histories*. Ithaca, N.Y.: Cornell University Press, 2003.

————. *Hitler's Army: Soldiers, Nazis, and War in the Third Reich*. New York: Oxford University Press, 1991.

Bartrop, Paul R. *False Havens: The British Empire and the Holocaust*. Lanham, Md.: University Press of America, 1995.

Baum, Steven K. *The Psychology of Genocide*. Cambridge: Cambridge University Press, 2008.

Bazyler, Michael J., and Roger P. Alford, eds. *Holocaust Restitution: Perspectives on the Litigation and Its Legacy*. New York: New York University Press, 2006.

Behnken, Klaus, ed. *Deutschland-Berichte der Sozialdemokratischen Partei Deutschlands (Sopade), 1934–1940*. 7 vols. Salzhausen: Nettelbeck & Zweitausendeins, 1980.

Beinart, William. *Twentieth-Century South Africa*. 2nd ed. Oxford: Oxford University Press, 2001.

Benz, Wolfgang, ed. *Das Exil der kleinen Leute: Alltagserfahrung deutscher Juden in der Emigration*. München: Beck, 1991.

Berghahn, Marion. *Continental Britons: German-Jewish Refugees from Nazi Germany*. Oxford: Berg, 1988.

Biddiscombe, Perry. *The Denazification of Germany 1945–48*. 7th ed. NPI Media Group, 2007.

Boas, Jacob. "The Shrinking World of German Jewry, 1933–1938." *Leo Baeck Institute Year Book* 31 (1986): 241–66.

Bodemann, Y. Michal. *A Jewish Family in Germany Today: At Home in the Geography of Time*. Durham, N.C.: Duke University Press, 2005.

Boehling, Rebecca L., and Uta Larkey. *Life and Loss in the Shadow of the Holocaust: A Jewish Family's Untold Story*. Cambridge: Cambridge University Press, 2011.

Böhner, Jürgen. *Echoes and Memories: The Refugees Speak*. SA Jewish Board of Deputies and Geothe-Institut, Johannesburg, 2005.

Bradlow, Edna. "South African Policy and Jewish Refugee Immigration in the 1930s." In *False Havens: The British Empire and the Holocaust*, edited by Paul R. Bartrop, 239–52. Lanham, Md.: University Press of America, 1995.

Brenner, Michael. *The Renaissance of Jewish Culture in Weimar Germany.* New Haven, Conn: Yale University Press, 1996.

Brenner, Michael, and Derek Penslar, eds. *In Search of Jewish Community: Jewish Identities in Germany and Austria, 1918–1933.* Bloomington: Indiana University Press, 1998.

Browning, Christopher R. *Collected Memories: Holocaust History and Postwar Testimony.* Madison: University of Wisconsin Press, 2003.

———. "Ordinary Germans or Ordinary Men? A Reply to the Critics." In *The Holocaust and History: The Known, the Unknown, the Disputed, the Reexamined*, edited by Michael Berenbaum and Abraham J. Peck. Bloomington: Indiana University Press, 1998.

———. *Ordinary Men: Reserve Police Battalion 101 and the Final Solution in Poland.* New York: HarperCollins, 1992.

Browning, Christopher R., Richard S. Hollander, and Nechama Tec, eds. *Every Day Lasts a Year: A Jewish Family's Correspondence from Poland.* Cambridge: Cambridge University Press, 2007.

Burleigh, Michael. *The Third Reich: A New History.* London: Pan Books, 2001.

Cahnman, Werner J. "Village and Small-Town Jews in Germany: A Typological Study." *Leo Baeck Institute Year Book* 19, no. 1 (1974): 107–30.

Capazorio, Bianca. "Holocaust through the Eyes of a Refugee in SA." *Weekend Argus.* 20 May 2012. http://www.iol.co.za/news/south-africa/western-cape/holocaust-through-the-eyes-of-a-refugee-in-sa-1.1300175#.T9G3u7VuJ3t.

Cesarani, David. *Final Solution: The Fate of the Jews 1933–1949.* London: Macmillan, 2016.

Cesarani, David, and Eric J. Sundquist, eds. *After the Holocaust: Challenging the Myth of Silence.* London: Routledge, 2012.

Clark, Nancy L., and William H. Worger. *South Africa: The Rise and Fall of Apartheid.* 2nd ed. Edinburgh: Pearson, 2011.

Clavin, Patricia. "Defining Transnationalism." *Contemporary European History* 14, no. 4 (2005): 421–39.

Coetzee, Linda, Myra Osrin, and Millie Pimstone, eds. *Seeking Refuge: German Jewish Immigration to the Cape in the 1930s Including Aspects of Germany Confronting Its Past.* Cape Town: Cape Town Holocaust Centre, 2003.

Cohen, Richard. *By the Sword: Gladiators, Musketeers, Samurai Warriors, Swashbucklers, and Olympians.* London: Pan Books, 2003.

Cohen, Roger. "Dreaming of Mandela." *New York Times.* 8 July 2013. http://www.nytimes.com/2013/07/09/opinion/global/roger-cohen-dreaming-of-mandela.html?_r=0.

Creet, Julia. "The Archive as Temporary Abode." In *Memory and Migration: Multidisciplinary Approaches to Memory Studies*, edited by Julia Creet and Andreas Kitzmann, 280–98. Toronto: University of Toronto Press, 2014.

Davidson, Martin. *The Perfect Nazi: Uncovering My SS Grandfather's Secret Past and How Hitler Seduced a Generation.* London: Viking, 2010.

Doerry, Martin. *My Wounded Heart: The Life of Lilli Jahn, 1900–1944.* London: Bloomsbury, 2004.

Doetzer, Oliver. *"Aus Menschen werden Briefe": Die Korrespondenz einer jüdischen Familie zwischen Verfolgung und Emigration 1933–1947*. Selbstzeugnisse der Neuzeit, Bd. 11. Köln: Böhlau, 2002.

Dörner, Bernward. *Die Deutschen und der Holocaust: Was niemand wissen wollte, aber jeder wissen konnte*. Berlin: Propyläen, 2007.

Douglas, R. M. *Orderly and Humane: The Expulsion of the Germans after the Second World War*. New Haven, Conn.: Yale University Press, 2012.

Dubow, Saul. "Smuts, the United Nations and the Rhetoric of Race and Rights." *Journal of Contemporary History* 43, no. 1 (2008): 45–74.

Dwork, Deborah, and R. J. van Pelt. *Flight from the Reich: Refugee Jews, 1933–1946*. 1st ed. New York: W. W. Norton & Company, 2009.

Eaglestone, Robert. "Reading Perpetrator Testimony." In *The Future of Memory*, edited by Richard Crownshaw, Jane Kilby, and Antony Rowland, 123–34. New York: Berghahn Books, 2010.

Earle, Rebecca. *Epistolary Selves: Letters and Letter-Writers, 1600–1945*. Aldershot: Ashgate, 1999.

Eber, Irene, ed. *Voices from Shanghai: Jewish Exiles in Wartime China*. Chicago: University of Chicago Press, 2008.

Elliot, Bruce S., David A. Gerber, and Suzanne M. Sinke. *Letters across Borders: The Epistolary Practices of International Migrants*. Annotated ed. New York: Palgrave Macmillan, 2006.

Elon, Amos. *The Pity of It All: A Portrait of Jews in Germany 1743–1933*. London: Penguin, 2004.

Feiner, Hertha. *Before Deportation: Letters from a Mother to Her Daughters, January 1939–December 1942*. Edited by Karl Heinz Jahnke. Translated by Margot Bettauer Dembo. Jewish Lives. Evanston, Ill.: Northwestern University Press, 1999.

Figes, Orlando. *Just Send Me Word: A True Story of Love and Survival in the Gulag*. London: Allen Lane, 2012.

Fischer, Lars. "A Tale of Two Books. Benedikt Kautsky's Teufel und Verdammte and Gustav Mayer's Erinnerungen," in Regina Fritz, Eva Kovács and Béla Rásky, eds. *Before the Holocaust Had Its Name. Early Confrontations of the Nazi Mass Murder of the Jews*. Vienna: new academic press, 2016, 299–315.

———. "'It Could All Have Been Much Worse': Benedikt Kautsky's Post-War Response to the Shoah." In *The Holocaust in the Twenty-First Century: Contesting/Contested Memories*, edited by David Seymour and Mercedes Camino. Abingdon: Routledge, 2016.

Flämig, Gerhard. *Hanau im Dritten Reich*. 3 vols. Hanau: Magistrat der Stadt, 1983.

Förster, Jürgen. "Complicity or Entanglement? The Wehrmact, the War and the Holocaust." In *The Holocaust and History: The Known, the Unknown, the Disputed and the Reexamined*, edited by Michael Berenbaum and Abraham J. Peck, 266–83. Bloomington: Indiana University Press, 1998.

Fraenkel, Peter. *No Fixed Abode: A Jewish Odyssey to Africa*. London: I. B. Tauris, 2005.

Franz, Margit, and Heimo Halbrainer. *Going East—Going South*. Graz: Clio, 2014.

Frei, Norbert. *Adenauer's Germany and the Nazi Past: The Politics of Amnesty and Integration*. New York: Columbia University Press, 2002.

Friedländer, Saul. *Nazi Germany and the Jews, 1933–1945*. London: Phoenix, 2014.

Friedman, Jonathan C. *The Lion and the Star: Gentile-Jewish Relations in Three Hessian Communities, 1919–1945*. Lexington: University Press of Kentucky, 1998.

Fulbrook, Mary. *A Small Town near Auschwitz: Ordinary Nazis and the Holocaust*. Oxford: Oxford University Press, 2012.

Fulbrook, Mary, and Ulinka Rublack. "In Relation: The "Social Self" and Ego-Documents." *German History* 28, no. 3 (2010): 263–72.

Furlong, Patrick J. *Between Crown and Swastika: The Impact of the Radical Right on the Afrikaner Nationalist Movement in the Fascist Era*. Middletown, Conn.: Wesleyan University Press, 1991.

Gay, Peter. *My German Question: Growing up in Nazi Berlin*. New Haven, Conn.: Yale University Press, 1998.

Geehr, Richard S., ed. *Letters from the Doomed: Concentration Camp Correspondence 1940–1945*. Lanham, Md.: University Press of America, 1991.

Geldermann, Barbara. "'Jewish Refugees Should Be Welcomed and Assisted Here!': Shanghai: Exile and Return." *Leo Baeck Institute Year Book* 44 (1999): 227–43.

Gilbert, Martin. *The Dent Atlas of the Holocaust*. 2nd ed. London: J. M. Dent, 1993.

———. *Kristallnacht: Prelude to Destruction*. New York: HarperCollins, 2006.

Gilbert, Shirli. "Anne Frank in South Africa: Remembering the Holocaust during and after Apartheid." *Holocaust and Genocide Studies* 26, no. 3 (2012): 366–93.

———. "Jews and the Racial State: Legacies of the Holocaust in Apartheid South Africa, 1945–60." *Jewish Social Studies* 16, no. 3 (2010): 32–64.

Goebel, Eckart, and Sigrid Weigel, eds. *"Escape to Life": German Intellectuals in New York: A Compendium on Exile after 1933*. Berlin: De Gruyter, 2012.

Goldfinger, Arnon. *The Flat*. IFC Independent Film, 2013.

Grady, Tim. "Fighting a Lost Battle: The Reichsbund jüdischer Frontsoldaten and the Rise of National Socialism." *German History* 28, no. 1 (2010): 1–20.

———. *The German-Jewish Soldiers of the First World War in History and Memory*. Liverpool: Liverpool University Press, 2012.

Gregor, Neil. *Haunted City: Nuremberg and the Nazi Past*. New Haven, Conn.: Yale University Press, 2008.

Grossmann, Atina. "Family Files: Emotions and Stories of (Non-)Restitution." *German Historical Institute Bulletin* 34, no. 1 (2012): 59–78.

———. "German Jews as Provincial Cosmopolitans: Reflections from the Upper West Side." *Leo Baeck Institute Yearbook* 53, no. 1 (2008): 157–68.

———. "Remapping Relief and Rescue: Flight, Displacement, and International Aid for Jewish Refugees during World War II." *New German Critique* 39, no. 3 (2012): 61–79.

———. "Versions of Home: German Jewish Refugee Papers out of the Closet and into the Archives." *New German Critique* 90 (2003).

Grossmann, Kurt Richard. *Emigration. Geschichte der Hitler-Flüchtlinge 1933–1945.* Frankfurt am Main: Europäische Verlagsanstalt, 1969.

Haffner, Sebastian. *Defying Hitler: A Memoir.* London: Weidenfeld & Nicolson, 2002.

Halberstam, Adele. *"Geliebte Kinder -": Briefe aus dem Amsterdamer Exil in die Neue Welt 1939–1943.* Edited by Wilhelm Halberstam, Irmtraud Wojak, and Lore Hepner. Schriften der Bibliothek für Zeitgeschichte, n. F., Bd. 3. Essen: Klartext, 1995.

Hamburger Institut für Sozialforschung, ed. *The German Army and Genocide: Crimes against War Prisoners, Jews and Other Civilians in the East, 1939–1944.* Translated by Scott Abbott. New York: New Press, 1999.

Haskew, Michael E. *The Wehrmacht, 1935–1945: The Essential Facts and Figures for Hitler's Germany.* London: Amber, 2011.

Hedgepeth, Sonia M., and Rochelle G. Saidel, eds. *Sexual Violence against Jewish Women during the Holocaust.* Waltham, Mass.: Brandeis University Press, 2010.

Heer, Hannes, and Klaus Naumann, eds. *War of Extermination: The German Military in World War II.* New York: Berghahn Books, 2000.

Hellig, Jocelyn. "German Jewish Immigration to South Africa during the 1930s: Revisiting the Charter of the SS Stuttgart." In *Jewish Journeys: From Philo to Hip Hop*, edited by James Jordan, Tony Kushner, and Sarah Pearce, 146–62. London: Vallentine Mitchell, 2010.

Hellig, Jocelyn, Myra Osrin, and Millie Pimstone, eds. *Seeking Refuge: German Jewish Immigration to Johannesburg in the 1930s Including Aspects of Germany Confronting Its Past.* Johannesburg: South African Jewish Board of Deputies, 2005.

Heppner, Ernest G. *Shanghai Refuge: A Memoir of the World War II Jewish Ghetto.* Lincoln: University of Nebraska Press, 1993.

Heuberger, Georg, and Anton Merk, eds. *Moritz Daniel Oppenheim: Die Entdeckung des jüdischen Selbstbewusstseins in der Kunst.* Frankfurt am Main: Wienand Verlag, 1999.

Hobbs, Catherine. "Personal Archives: The Character of Personal Archives: Reflections on the Value of Records of Individuals." *Archivaria* 52 (2001): 126–35.

Horwitz, G. J. *In the Shadow of Death: Living outside the Gates of Mauthausen.* New York: Free Press, 1990.

Hoskins, Janet. *Biographical Objects: How Things Tell Stories of People's Lives.* New York: Routledge, 1998.

Imhoff, Roland, Michał Bilewicz, and Hans-Peter Erb. "Collective Regret Versus Collective Guilt: Different Emotional Reactions to Historical Atrocities." *European Journal of Social Psychology* 42, no. 6 (2012): 729–42.

Jacobson, Dan. "A White Liberal Trapped by His Prejudices." *Commentary* 15, no. 5 (1953): 454–59.

Janowitz, Morris. "German Reactions to Nazi Atrocities." *American Journal of Sociology* 52, no. 2 (1946): 141–46.

Jarausch, Konrad H., ed. *Reluctant Accomplice: A Wehrmacht Soldier's Letters from the Eastern Front*. Princeton, N.J.: Princeton University Press, 2011.

Jenkins, Jennifer. "Transnationalism and German History." *H-German*, 23 January 2006. http://h-net.msu.edu/cgi-bin/logbrowse.pl?trx=vx&list=H-german&month=0601& week=d&msg=jdQ5FjF3i2OWwWSkGlTt/w&user=&pw=.

Jensen, Olaf, and Claus-Christian W. Szejnmann, eds. *Ordinary People as Mass Murderers: Perpetrators in Comparative Perspectives*. Basingstoke: Palgrave Macmillan, 2008.

Jilovsky, Esther. "Grandpa's Letters: Encountering Tangible Memories of the Holocaust." In *In the Shadows of Memory: The Holocaust and the Third Generation*, edited by Esther Jilovsky, Jordana Silverstein, and David Slucki, 135–48. Portland, Ore.: Vallentine Mitchell, 2015.

Jolly, Margaretta. "Myths of Unity: Remembering the Second World War through Letters and Their Editing." In *Arms and the Self*, edited by Alex Vernon, 144–70. Kent, Oh.: Kent State University Press, 2005.

Jolly, Margaretta, and Liz Stanley. "Letters As/not a Genre." *Life Writing* 2, no. 2 (2005): 91–118.

Joseph, Anne, ed. *From the Edge of the World: The Jewish Refugee Experience through Letters and Stories*. London: Vallentine Mitchell, 2003.

Jung, Carl G. "After the Catastrophe." In *Essays on Contemporary Events: The Psychology of Nazism*, translated by R.F.C. Hull. Princeton, N.J.: Princeton University Press, 1989.

Kaczynski, William, and Charmian Brinson. *Fleeing from the Fuhrer: A Postal History of Refugees from Nazi Germany*. Stroud: History Press, 2011.

Kaplan, Marion A. *Dominican Haven: The Jewish Refugee Settlement in Sosúa, 1940–1945*. New York: Museum of Jewish Heritage, 2008.

———. "'A Very Modest Experiment'—The Jewish Refugee Settlement in Sosúa, 1940–1945." *Leo Baeck Institute Yearbook* 53, no. 1 (2008): 127–55.

———. *Between Dignity and Despair: Jewish Life in Nazi Germany*. New York: Oxford University Press, 1998.

———, ed. *Jewish Daily Life in Germany, 1618–1945*. Oxford: Oxford University Press, 2005.

———. *The Making of the Jewish Middle Class: Women, Family, and Identity in Imperial Germany*. Studies in Jewish History. New York: Oxford University Press, 1991.

Kaplinski, Solly. *Lost and Found: A Second Generation Response to the Holocaust*. Cape Town: Creda Press, 1992.

Karis, Thomas, Gwendolen Carter, Gail Gerhart, and Sheridan Johns, eds. *From Protest to Challenge*. Stanford, Calif.: Hoover Institution, 1972.

Katz, Jacob. *Out of the Ghetto: The Social Background of Jewish Emancipation, 1770–1870*. Cambridge, Mass: Harvard University Press, 1973.

Kaufman, Menahem. "The Daily Life of the Village and Country Jews in Hessen from Hitler's Ascent to Power to November 1938." *Yad Vashem Studies* 22 (1992): 147–98.

Kentridge, Morris. *I Recall: Memoirs of Morris Kentridge*. Johannesburg: Free Press, 1959.

Kessler, Edmund. *The Wartime Diary of Edmund Kessler.* Edited by Renata Kessler. Brighton, Mass.: Academic Studies Press, 2010.

Kirshenblatt-Gimblett, Barbara. "Objects of Memory: Material Culture as Life Review." In *Folk Groups and Folklore Genres: A Reader,* edited by Elliott Oring. Logan: Utah State University Press, 1989.

Klee, Ernst, Willi Dressen, and Volker Riess. *"Those Were the Days": The Holocaust through the Eyes of the Perpetrators and Bystanders.* London: Hamish Hamilton, 1991.

Klemperer, Victor. *The Diaries of Victor Klemperer 1933–1945: I Shall Bear Witness to the Bitter End.* Translated by Martin Chalmers. London: Phoenix, 2000.

Klier, Freya. *Promised New Zealand: Fleeing Nazi Persecution.* Translated by Jenny Rawlings. Dunedin, N.Z.: Otago University Press, 2009.

Kolmar, Gertrud. *My Gaze Is Turned Inward: Letters 1934–1943.* Evanston, Ill.: Northwestern University Press, 2004.

Kranzler, David. *Japanese, Nazis & Jews: The Jewish Refugee Community of Shanghai, 1938–1945.* Hoboken, N.J.: KTAV, 1976.

Krause-Vilmar, Dietfrid. *Das Konzentrationslager Breitenau: Ein staatliches Schutzhaftlager 1933/34.* Marburg: Schüren Presseverlag, 1998.

Krohn, Claus-Dieter, Patrik von zur Mühlen, Gerhard Paul, and Lutz Winckler, eds. *Handbuch der deutschsprachigen Emigration 1933–1945.* Darmstadt: Wissenschaftliche Buchgesellschaft, 1998.

Krondorfer, Björn, Norbert Reck, and Katharina von Kellenbach. *Mit Blick auf die Täter: Fragen an die deutsche Theologie nach 1945.* Gütersloher: Gütersloher Verlagshaus, 2006.

Kühne, Thomas. *Belonging and Genocide: Hitler's Community, 1918–1945.* New Haven, Conn.: Yale University Press, 2010.

———. *Kameradschaft: Die Soldaten des nationalsozialistischen Krieges und das 20. Jahrhundert.* Göttingen: Vandenhoeck & Ruprecht, 2006.

Kulka, Otto Dov, and Eberhard Jäckel, eds. *The Jews in the Secret Nazi Reports on Popular Opinion in Germany, 1933–1945.* Translated by William Templer. New Haven, Conn.: Yale University Press, 2010.

Kurzweil, Edith, ed. *Nazi Laws and Jewish Lives: Letters from Vienna.* New Brunswick, N.J.: Transaction, 2004.

Kushner, Tony. *Remembering Refugees: Then and Now.* Manchester: Manchester University Press, 2006.

Kushner, Tony, and Katharine Knox. *Refugees in an Age of Genocide: Global, National, and Local Perspectives during the Twentieth Century.* London: Frank Cass, 1999.

Kwiet, Konrad. "Without Neighbors: Daily Living in Judenhäuser." In *Jewish Life in Nazi Germany: Dilemmas and Responses,* edited by Francis R. Nicosia and David Scrase, 117–48. New York: Berghahn Books, 2010.

Laqueur, Walter. *Generation Exodus: The Fate of Young Jewish Refugees from Nazi Germany.* London: I. B. Tauris, 2004.

———, ed. *The Holocaust Encyclopedia.* New Haven, Conn.: Yale University Press, 2001.

Levsen, Sonja. "Constructing Elite Identities: University Students, Military Masculinity and the Consequences of the Great War in Britain and Germany." *Past & Present* 198 (2008): 147–83.

Lorenz, Ina Susanne. *Verfolgung und Gottvertrauen: Briefe einer Hamburger jüdisch-orthodoxen Familie im "Dritten Reich."* Studien zur jüdischen Geschichte, Bd.5. Hamburg: Dölling und Galitz, 1998.

Lowenstein, Steven M. "Decline and Survival of Rural Jewish Communities." In *In Search of Jewish Community: Jewish Identities in Germany and Austria, 1918–1933,* edited by Michael Brenner and Derek Penslar, 223–42. Bloomington: Indiana University Press, 1998.

Ludi, Regula. *Reparations for Nazi Victims in Postwar Europe.* Cambridge: Cambridge University Press, 2012.

———. "The Vectors of Postwar Victim Reparations: Relief, Redress and Memory Politics." *Journal of Contemporary History* 41, no. 3 (2006): 421–50.

Marcus, Audrey Friedman, and Rena Krasno. *Survival in Shanghai: The Journals of Fred Marcus 1939–49.* Berkeley, Calif.: Pacific View Press, 2008.

Marrus, Michael Robert. *The Unwanted: European Refugees from the First World War through the Cold War.* Politics, History, and Social Change. Philadelphia: Temple University Press, 2002.

Marx, Christoph. *Oxwagon Sentinel. Radical Afrikaner Nationalism and the History of the Ossewabrandwag.* Pretoria: Unisa Press, 2008.

Matthäus, Jürgen. "Historiography and the Perpetrators of the Holocaust." In *The Historiography of the Holocaust,* edited by Dan Stone, 197–215. Basingstoke: Palgrave Macmillan 2004.

McCarthy, Angela. "Personal Letters, Oral Testimony and Scottish Migration to New Zealand in the 1950s: The Case of Lorna Carter." *Immigrants & Minorities* 23, no. 1 (2005): 59–79.

Meise, Eckhard. "Leopold Löwenstein, Max Schwab und Hanau." *Neues Magazin für Hanauische Geschichte* (2005): 78–95.

Mendelsohn, Richard. "The Boer War, The Great War, and the Shaping of South African Jewish Loyalties." In *Memories, Realities and Dreams: Aspects of the South African Jewish Experience,* edited by Milton Shain and Richard Mendelsohn, 50–59. Johannesburg: Jonathan Ball, 2000.

Mendelsohn, Richard, and Milton Shain. *The Jews in South Africa: An Illustrated History.* Johannesburg and Cape Town: Jonathan Ball, 2008.

Mendes-Flohr, Paul. "Rosenzweig and the Kameraden: A Non-Zionist Alliance." *Journal of Contemporary History* 26, no. 3/4 (1991): 385–402.

Mendes-Flohr, Paul R. *German Jews: A Dual Identity.* New Haven, Conn.: Yale University Press, 1999.

Meyer, Michael A., and Michael Brenner, eds. *German-Jewish History in Modern Times.* New York: Columbia University Press, 1996.

Militärgeschichtliches Forschungsamt, ed. *Germany and the Second World War*. Oxford: Clarendon Press, 1990.

Morsch, Günter, and Astrid Ley, eds. *Das Konzentrationslager Sachsenhausen 1936–1945: Ereignisse und Entwicklungen*. Berlin: Metropol, 2008.

Mosse, George L. *German Jews beyond Judaism*. The Modern Jewish Experience. Bloomington: Indiana University Press; Cincinnati: Hebrew Union College Press, 1985.

Natt, Bernard. "Growing Up in Nazi Germany: Experiences and Memories." *Leo Baeck Institute Yearbook* 51, no. 1 (2006): 267–85.

Neitzel, Sönke, and Harald Welzer. *Soldaten: Protokolle vom Kämpfen, Töten und Sterben*. Frankfurt am Main: Fischer, 2011.

Nicosia, Francis R. "The End of Emancipation and the Illusion of Preferential Treatment: German Zionism, 1933–1938." *Leo Baeck Institute Year Book* 36 (1991): 243–65.

Nicosia, Francis R., and David Scrase, eds. *Jewish Life in Nazi Germany: Dilemmas and Responses*. New York: Berghahn Books, 2012.

Nye, Robert A. "Fencing, the Duel and Republican Manhood in the Third Republic." *Journal of Contemporary History* 25, no. 2/3 (1990): 365–77.

O'Donnell, Krista, Renate Bridenthal, and Nancy Reagin, eds. *The Heimat Abroad: The Boundaries of Germanness*. Ann Arbor: University of Michigan Press, 2005.

Olick, Jeffrey K. "The Guilt of Nations?" *Ethics and International Affairs* 17, no. 2 (2003): 109–17.

Ophir, Baruch Z., Chasia Turtel-Aberzhanska, Shlomo Schmiedt, Joseph Walk, and Bracha Freundlich, eds. *Pinḳas Ha-ḳehilot. Entsiḳlopedyah Shel Ha-Yishuvim Ha-Yehudiyim Le-Min Hiyasdam Ve-'ad Le-Aḥar Sho'at Milḥemet Ha-'olam Ha-Sheniyah: Germania*. Vol. 3. Jerusalem: Yad Vashem, 1972.

Passerini, Luisa. *Europe in Love, Love in Europe: Imagination and Politics in Britain between the Wars*. London: I. B. Tauris, 1999.

Paucker, Arnold. "Researching German-Jewish Responses and German-Jewish Resistance to National Socialism: Sources and Directions for the Future." *Leo Baeck Institute Yearbook* 51, no. 1 (2006): 193–208.

———. "Responses of German Jewry to Nazi Persecution 1933–1943." In *The German-Jewish Dilemma: From the Enlightenment to the Shoah*, edited by Edward Timms and Andrea Hammel, 211–27. Lewiston, N.Y: Edwin Mellen Press, 1999.

Paul, Gerhard, ed. *Die Täter der Shoah: Fanatische Nationalsozialisten oder ganz normale Deutsche?* Göttingen: Wallstein, 2003.

Peberdy, Sally. *Selecting Immigrants: National Identity and South Africa's Immigration Policies 1910–2008*. Johannesburg: Witwatersrand University Press, 2009.

Peck, Abraham J., ed. *The German-Jewish Legacy in America, 1938–1988: From Bildung to the Bill of Rights*. Detroit: Wayne State University Press, 1989.

Pendas, Devin O. "Toward a New Politics? On the Recent Historiography of Human Rights." *Contemporary European History* 21, no. 1 (2012): 95–111.

Penslar, Derek. "The German-Jewish Soldier: From Participant to Victim." *German History* 29, no. 3 (2011): 423–44.

———. *Jews and the Military: A History*. Princeton, N.J.: Princeton University Press, 2015.

Pfeifer, Monika Ilona, and Monica Kingreen. *Hanauer Juden 1933–1945: Entrechtung, Verfolgung, Deportation*. Hanau: CoCon, 1998.

Pierson, Ruth. "Embattled Veterans: The Reichsbund jüdischer Frontsoldaten." *Leo Baeck Institute Year Book* 19 (1974): 139–54.

Pilgrim, Volker Elis, Doris Liffman, and Herbert Liffman, eds. *Fremde Freiheit. Jüdische Emigration nach Australien: Briefe, 1938–1940*. 1. Aufl. Reinbek bei Hamburg: Rowohlt, 1992.

Pogrund, Benjamin. *War of Words: Memoir of a South African Journalist*. New York: Seven Stories Press, 2000.

Polt, Renata, ed. *A Thousand Kisses: A Grandmother's Holocaust Letters*. Tuscaloosa: University of Alabama Press, 1999.

Report of the Executive Council of the South African Jewish Board of Deputies, August 1947 to May 1949. Johannesburg: South African Jewish Board of Deputies, 1949.

Report of the Executive Council of the South African Jewish Board of Deputies, June 1949 to May 1951. Johannesburg: South African Jewish Board of Deputies, 1951.

Report of the Executive Council of the South African Jewish Board of Deputies, June 1951 to May 1953. Johannesburg: South African Jewish Board of Deputies, 1953.

Richarz, Monika, ed. *Jewish Life in Germany: Memoirs from Three Centuries*. Translated by Stella P. Rosenfeld and Sidney Rosenfeld. The Modern Jewish Experience. Bloomington: Indiana University Press, 1991.

Richarz, Monika, and Reinhard Rürup, eds. *Jüdisches Leben auf dem Lande: Studien zur deutsch-jüdischen Geschichte*. Schriftenreihe wissenschaftlicher Abhandlungen des Leo Baeck Instituts 56. Tübingen: Mohr Siebeck, 1997.

Richter, Gunnar, ed. *Breitenau: Zur Geschichte eines nationalsozialistischen Konzentrations- und Arbeitserziehungslagers*. Kassel: Verlag Jenior & Pressler, 1993.

———. *Das Arbeitserziehungslager Breitenau (1940–1945): Ein Beitrag zum nationalsozialistischen Lagersystem*. Kassel: Verlag Winfried Jenior, 2009.

Ristaino, Marcia R. *Port of Last Resort: The Diaspora Communities of Shanghai*. Stanford, Calif.: Stanford University Press, 2001.

Robins, Steven. *Letters of Stone: From Nazi Germany to South Africa*. Cape Town: Penguin Books, 2016.

———. "Silence in My Father's House: Memory, Nationalism, and Narratives of the Body." In *Negotiating the Past: The Making of Memory in South Africa*, edited by Sarah Nuttall and Carli Coetzee, 120–40. Oxford: Oxford University Press, 1998.

Rockman, Chaim. *None of Them Were Heroes: Letters between the Lines, 1938–1942*. New York: Devora, 2003.

Roemer, Nils H. "Between the Provinces and the City: Mapping German-Jewish Memories." *Leo Baeck Institute Yearbook* 51, no. 1 (2006): 61–77.

———. *German City, Jewish Memory: The Story of Worms*. 1st ed. Tauber Institute Series for the Study of European Jewry. Waltham, Mass.: Brandeis University Press; Hanover, N.H.: University Press of New England, 2010.

Roseman, Mark. "'Der Dank des Vaterlandes': Memories and Chronicles of German Jewry in the 1930s." Paper delivered at the Lessons and Legacies Conference, Florida Atlantic University, 2010.

———. "Holocaust Perpetrators in Victims' Eyes." In *Years of Persecution, Years of Extermination : Saul Friedlander and the Future of Holocaust Studies*, edited by Christian Wiese and Paul Betts. London: Continuum, 2010.

———. *The Past in Hiding*. London: Allen Lane, 2000.

Rosenberg, V. "The Power of a Family Archive." *Archival Science* 11, no. 1–2 (2011): 77–93.

Rosner, Bernat, and Frederic C. Tubach. *An Uncommon Friendship: From Opposite Sides of the Holocaust*. Berkeley: University of California Press, 2001.

Ross, James R. *Escape to Shanghai: A Jewish Community in China*. New York: Free Press, 1994.

Roth, Milena. *Lifesaving Letters: A Child's Flight from the Holocaust*. Seattle: University of Washington Press, 2004.

Rubin, Evelyn Pike. *Ghetto Shanghai*. New York: Shengold, 1993.

Rubin, Susan Goldman, in association with the Museum of Tolerance (Simon Wiesenthal Center). *Searching for Anne Frank: Letters from Amsterdam to Iowa*. New York: Harry N. Abrams, 2003.

Schenderlein, Anne Clara. "Making German History in Postwar Los Angeles: German Jewish Refugees, Rabbi Max Nussbaum, and West German Diplomats." Paper delivered at the Jewish History Seminar, Institute for Historical Research, London, 4 January 2016.

Schlör, Joachim. "Ausgrenzung, Heimatverlust, Neubeginn: Jüdische Auswanderung und die NS-Volksgemeinschaft." In *Nationalsozialistisches Migrationsregime und Volksgemeinschaft*, edited by Jochen Oltmer. Paderborn: Ferdinand Schöningh, 2011.

———. *Endlich im gelobten Land? Deutsche Juden unterwegs in eine neue Heimat*. Berlin: Aufbau, 2003.

———. "Irgendwo auf der Welt: German-Jewish Emigration as a Transnational Experience." In *Three-Way Street: Jews, Germans and the Transnational*, edited by Jay Geller and Leslie Morris. Ann Arbor: University of Michigan Press, 2016.

———. "'Take Down Mezuzahs, Remove Name-Plates': The Emigration of Objects from Germany to Palestine." In *Jewish Cultural Studies, Vol. 1: Jewishness: Expression, Identity and Representation*, edited by Simon J. Bronner, 133–50. Oxford: Littman Library of Jewish Civilization, 2008.

Schorsch, Emil. "The Rural Jew: Observations on the Paper of Werner J. Cahnman." *Leo Baeck Institute Year Book* 19, no. 1 (1974): 131–33.

Schrire, Gwynne, ed. *In Sacred Memory: Recollections of the Holocaust by Survivors Living in Cape Town*. Cape Town: Cape Town Holocaust Memorial Council, n.d.

Schwab, Hermann. *Jewish Rural Communities in Germany*. London: Cooper Book Company, 1956.

Schwab, Max. "Die Freiheitskriege von 1813/15 und die kurhessischen Juden (I)." *Hanauisches Magazin* 4 (1930): 27–32.

———. "Die Freiheitskriege von 1813/15 und Die kurhessischen Juden (II)." *Hanauisches Magazin* 5 (1930): 33–37.

Secher, H. Pierre. *Left Behind in Nazi Vienna: Letters of a Jewish Family Caught in the Holocaust, 1939–1941*. Jefferson, N.C.: McFarland, 2004.

Shain, Milton. *A Perfect Storm: Antisemitism in South Africa, 1930–1948*. Johannesburg and Cape Town: Jonathan Ball, 2015.

———. "South Africa." In *The World Reacts to the Holocaust*, edited by David S. Wyman, 670–89. Baltimore: Johns Hopkins University Press, 1996.

Shain, Milton, and Richard Mendelsohn, eds. *Memories, Realities and Dreams: Aspects of the South African Jewish Experience*. Johannesburg: Jonathan Ball, 2000.

Shepherd, Ben. "The Clean Wehrmacht, the War of Extermination, and Beyond." *Historical Journal* 52, no. 2 (2009): 455–73.

Sherman, Joseph. "Serving the Natives: Whiteness as the Price of Hospitality in South African Yiddish Literature." *Journal of Southern African Studies* 26, no. 3 (2000): 505–21.

Shils, Edward A., and Morris Janowitz. "Cohesion and Disintegration in the Wehrmacht in World War II." *Public Opinion Quarterly* 12, no. 2 (1948): 280–315.

Shimoni, Gideon. *Community and Conscience: The Jews in Apartheid South Africa*. Hanover, N.H.: Brandeis University Press, 2003.

Sichel, Frieda H. *Challenge of the Past*. Johannesburg: Pacific Press, 1975.

———. *From Refugee to Citizen: A Sociological Study of the Immigrants from Hitler-Europe Who Settled in Southern Africa*. Cape Town and Amsterdam: A. A. Balkema, 1966.

Solzhenitsyn, Aleksandr. *The Gulag Archipelago 1918–56: An Experiment in Literary Investigation*. Translated by Thomas P. Whitney and Harry Willets. London: Harvill Press, 2003.

Spector, Shmuel, and Geoffrey Wigoder, eds. *The Encyclopedia of Jewish Life before and during the Holocaust*. New York: New York University Press, 2001.

Spitzer, Leo. *Hotel Bolivia: The Culture of Memory in a Refuge from Nazism*. New York: Hill and Wang, 1998.

Stanley, Liz. "The Epistolarium: On Theorizing Letters and Correspondence." *Autobiography* 12, no. 3 (2004).

Stargardt, Nicholas. *The German War: A Nation under Arms, 1939–1945*. London: Bodley Head, 2015.

———. "The Troubled Patriot: German Innerlichkeit in World War II." *German History* 28, no. 3 (2010): 326–42.

Steber, Martina, and Bernhard Gotto, eds. *Visions of Community in Nazi Germany: Social Engineering and Private Lives*. Oxford: Oxford University Press, 2014.

Steege, Paul. *Black Market, Cold War: Everyday Life in Berlin, 1946–1949.* New York: Cambridge University Press, 2007.

Steinweis, Alan E. *Kristallnacht 1938.* Cambridge, Mass.: Belknap, 2009.

Stephan, Alexander, ed. *Exile and Otherness. New Approaches to the Experience of the Nazi Refugees.* Bern: Peter Lang, 2005.

Stone, Lotta M. "Seeking Asylum: German Jewish Refugees in South Africa, 1933–1948." Ph.D. dissertation, Clark University, 2010.

Strauss, Herbert A. "Jews in German History: Persecution, Emigration, Acculturation." In *International Biographical Dictionary of Central European Emigres 1933–1945*, edited by Herbert A. Strauss and Werner Roeder, xi–xxvi. New York: K. G. Saur, 1983.

Streit, Christian. *Keine Kameraden: Die Wehrmacht und die sowjetischen Kriegsgefangenen 1941–1945.* Bonn: Verlag J.H.W. Dietz Nachf, 1991.

———. "Soviet Prisoners of War in the Hands of the Wehrmacht." In *War of Extermination: The German Military in World War II*, edited by Hannes Heer and Klaus Naumann, 80–91. New York: Berghahn Books, 2000.

Taylor, Fred. *Exorcising Hitler: The Occupation and Denazification of Germany.* 1st U.S. ed. New York: Bloomsbury Press, 2011.

Tessin, Georg. *Verbände und Truppen der deutschen Wehrmacht und Waffen-SS im Zweiten Weltkrieg 1939–1945.* 17 vols. Osnabrück: Biblio Verlag, 1978–2002.

Twiss, Sumner B. "Can a Perpetrator Write a Testimonio? Moral Lessons from the Dark Side." *Journal of Religious Ethics* 38, no. 1 (2010): 5–42.

Ungerson, Clare. *Four Thousand Lives: The Rescue of German Jewish Men to Britain, 1939.* Stroud: History Press, 2014.

Vaizey, Hester. *Surviving Hitler's War: Family Life in Germany, 1939–48.* Genders and Sexualities in History. Basingstoke: Palgrave Macmillan, 2010.

van Tijn, Gertrude. "Werkdorp Nieuwesluis." *Leo Baeck Institute Yearbook* 14, no. 1 (1969): 182–99.

van Tonder, Deon. "'First Win the War, Then Clear the Slums': The Genesis of the Western Areas Removal Scheme, 1940–1949." 1990. http://wiredspace.wits.ac.za/bitstream/handle/10539/8106/HWS-422.pdf?sequence=1.

Volkov, Shulamit. *Germans, Jews, and Antisemites: Trials in Emancipation.* Cambridge: Cambridge University Press, 2006.

von Kellenbach, Katharina. *The Mark of Cain: Guilt and Denial in the Post-War Lives of Nazi Perpetrators.* Oxford: Oxford University Press, 2013.

———. "Vanishing Acts: Perpetrators in Postwar Germany." *Holocaust and Genocide Studies* 17, no. 2 (2003): 305–29.

Wachsmann, Nikolaus. *KL: A History of the Nazi Concentration Camps.* Boston: Little, Brown, 2015.

Waller, James E. *Becoming Evil: How Ordinary People Commit Genocide and Mass Murder.* 2nd ed. New York: Oxford University Press, 2007.

Welzer, Harald, Sabine Moller, and Karoline Tschuggnall. *Opa war kein Nazi: National-sozialismus und Holocaust im Familiengedächtnis*. 3. Aufl.. Frankfurt am Main: Fischer Taschenbuch, 2002.

Wette, Wolfram. *The Wehrmacht: History, Myth, Reality*. Cambridge, Mass.: Harvard University Press, 2006.

Whiteman, Dorit Bader. *The Uprooted: A Hitler Legacy: Voices of Those Who Escaped before the "Final Solution."* New York: Insight Books, 1993.

Wildt, Michael. *Hitler's Volksgemeinschaft and the Dynamics of Racial Exclusion: Violence Against Jews in Provincial Germany, 1919–1939*. Translated by Bernard W. Heise. New York: Berghahn Books, 2012.

Wituska, Krystyna. *Inside a Gestapo Prison: The Letters of Krystyna Wituska, 1942–1944*. Translated by Irene Tomaszewski. Detroit: Wayne State University Press, 2006.

Index